# Daniel Webster and the Trial of American Nationalism 1843-1852

*Danl Webster*

# *Daniel Webster* and the
# Trial of American Nationalism
## 1843–1852

Robert F. Dalzell, Jr.

Houghton Mifflin Company Boston   1973

FIRST PRINTING  **W**

ISBN: 0-395-13998-8
LIBRARY OF CONGRESS CATALOG CARD NUMBER: 72-2284
PRINTED IN THE UNITED STATES OF AMERICA

2-16-73

For L.B.D.
and A.

# Acknowledgments

Aᴛ ᴛʜᴇ ʀɪsᴋ of burdening them with the responsibility for errors of fact or interpretation that can only be my own I should like to thank some of the many people who have helped with this book. To the late David M. Potter of Stanford University I am indebted for first proposing Webster as a topic of study. To Professor William Goetzmann of the University of Texas whose many stimulating suggestions helped focus my thinking about Webster's nationalism, to Professor John M. Blum of Yale University who with unfailing interest, patience, and good will served as my adviser in preparing the first five chapters of the book as a dissertation, and to Professor Michael F. Holt, also of Yale, who read the entire manuscript, making countless invaluable suggestions, I owe a special debt. I also wish to thank Professors C. Vann Woodward and Sidney Ahlstrom of Yale and Phillip Cantelon of Williams College. At various times each of them has read all or part of what I have written about Webster and offered much-appreciated criticism and encouragement.

The staffs of Sterling Library, Yale University; the Library of Congress; the Dartmouth College Library; Houghton Library, Harvard University; the Buffalo Historical Society; the New Hampshire Historical Society; and the Williams College Library have all been most kind and helpful. To Mr. Stephen T. Riley and Mr. Malcolm Freyburg of the Massachusetts Historical Society I am particularly grateful. On my many visits to the Society they went out of their way to aid my research.

The final typing of the manuscript was made possible by a grant from the Class of 1900 Fund of Williams College. The task itself was performed with commendable efficiency by Miss Bessie Wright.

Finally, I should like to express my share of the gratitude that every scholar owes the long-suffering souls who share his roof. To four children who grew up learning to tiptoe in certain parts of the house at certain hours, to a wife who taught them how, produced hot lunches on request — all the while living her own life — and still sat down at the end of the day to read, edit, reread, sympathize, and encourage, what can one say, except thank you? Whatever may be worthwhile in this book is yours too.

# Preface

THERE IS SOMETHING very grand — and to a midtwentieth-century-consciousness ultimately unfathomable — about a man who could draw a hundred thousands souls to the down side of a hill on a hot summer afternoon simply to hear him speak, without benefit of artificial amplification, for an hour or so. When one adds to the picture the knowledge that the man was not infrequently and with a fair degree of accuracy described as the paid agent of some of the nation's leading business interests, that his ambition was virtually limitless, that he lived in a style which verged on being ducal by the standards of his time, and that even his closest associates often found him cold and aloof, the wonder grows. Yet such a man was Daniel Webster.

The book that follows is not, strictly speaking, a biography of Webster. It is also not the book I intended to write when I began. That book was to have been a study of the figure at the center of those great ritualistic celebrations at places like Plymouth and Bunker Hill, of the man who rose in the Senate time and again at the end of his life to point the way to peace in an increasingly divided nation, and more particularly of what he said on such occasions. What I proposed was a detailed analysis of the rhetoric of Daniel Webster's nationalism.

I chose Webster's nationalism because it stands as his most significant contribution to American political and intellectual life. Of all that he did or said it was his nationalism on which he lavished the greatest amount of attention; it was also what his contemporaries came to know him best for. An attempt to understand the nature and dimensions of that contribution seemed a useful way into an understanding not only of the man himself but of his era.

To this point the basic design proved sound. Implicit in it, however, was the assumption that Webster's rhetoric could be treated separately from the rest of his career, and on that score I was mistaken, both as to the possibility of the thing and as to the wisdom of doing it that way even if it had been possible. Supposing at the outset that I would find the day-to-day details of Webster's political career fully recorded in any one of several existing biographies, I discovered that the earlier studies — a number of which are admirable in many respects — were inadequate for my purposes. This meant returning to the sources to do my own job of reconstruction, and the further I progressed the more I became convinced that Webster's nationalism could be understood only within the context of his political activities, that the two were inextricably bound up with one another. The Second Bunker Hill Address and the Seventh of March Speech were not articles in the *North American Review* written by some anonymous "Publius," and treating them as such promised to yield little of value.

On the other hand, as the scope of the inquiry grew, the problem of how to limit it became more acute. To concentrate on the early development of Webster's nationalism, relating it to his rise in national politics, was an obvious solution, but not the one that seemed most interesting to me. Rather I have chosen that period when nationalism, however defined, faced its severest challenge in America — the years of the growing controversy between the North and the South, or roughly the last decade of Webster's life. Whatever lay behind his own nationalism, this was when the pressures on him to confirm, modify, or abandon it altogether were greatest. Confused and ambiguous at first, his response to those pressures poses an intriguing study of a man fighting simultaneously to save his political career and to defend something in which he believed most deeply.

I stress the duality of Webster's concern here because a sizable number of his contemporaries and most historians since have argued that his actions during those years could be explained more simply. Thus his great effort of the period, the Seventh of March Speech, becomes either "a bid for the Presidency," as Theodore Parker first called it, or a rare example of disinterested statesmanship. My own conclusion is that both interpretations are wrong. Webster was ambitious and he was a nationalist, and if he was a nationalist at least in part because he was ambitious, over most of his career there had been no necessary conflict between the two. He chose the course he did in 1850 because to a greater extent than any of the others open to him it satisfied the requirements of both politics and ideology.

Still, for all the splendid "interested" statesmanship of the Seventh of March Speech, the conscience of New England got left out of the balance. That, of course, was the true burden of the case Parker and those who agreed with him drew against Webster. For the man who galvanized his state and party to oppose the annexation of Texas, even more for the author of the Plymouth Address of 1820 with its ringing denunciation of the South's peculiar institution, to have bowed at the last to Southern arrogance and turned slave chaser seemed a crime no amount of human charity could forgive. The only possible explanation, it seemed, was that Webster's character was flawed — flawed beyond even his all-consuming ambition; that lacking the ability to perceive the moral issue involved, he was alike incapable of seeing how others felt about it. The trouble was

Webster had "animal powers, but no morals," wrote Ralph
Waldo Emerson. "All the drops of his blood have eyes that look
downward."

Law and conservatism versus conscience, religion, and liberty
— two apparently separate sets of values between which ran
an unbridgeable gulf. That was the choice Parker and Emerson
saw in 1850, and precisely because the issues of the period presented themselves with such force it has seemed reasonable to
suppose other men saw and chose in similar terms. But did
they? Did Webster? Even if he had joined, as Emerson charged,
"the attorneys of great and gross interests," it is worth noting
that lawyers have ever been adept at maneuvering out of such
tight corners. And in fact Webster spent a lifetime doing just
that, as a lawyer, as a politician — and above all as a nationalist.

Believing that a viable balance of sections, interests, and
rights was at once the very essence of the American nation and
its finest achievement, he devoted himself to articulating the
principles of that balance and defining what maintained it.
Since none of the components of the system could be required
to sacrifice any of their fundamental identity or vigor for the
sake of the whole, and since the usual agencies for maintaining
balance — a ruling family, a class of hereditary aristocrats, a
state church, a standing army — had all been banished from
the American scene, the task was at best a difficult one. Nor did
the list of difficulties end there, for Webster's formulation, once
he arrived at it, had to function on so many different levels.
One could explain how attachment to a particular town or state
was an expression of national patriotism and do so in relatively
simple terms, perhaps. The problem became more complex
if at the same time it had to be made clear that a tariff on im-
ported cotton cloth benefited all Americans, producers, and
consumers alike, and further that the man who made such a
point was not just a spokesman for regional economic interests,
but a great national statesman, uniquely qualified for election
to the highest office in the land.

As intimately involved as he was with the day-to-day realities of American politics and the requirements they imposed, Webster might have erected a system of them and stopped there. His great rival Henry Clay owed his singular success as a national politician to just such an accommodation. But Webster's way was different. He chose to go further and, before he had finished, managed to transmute the national experience into a kind of grand, romantic vision that — ironically — resembled Emerson's own transcendentalism far more thoroughly than it did Henry Clay's American System.

The resemblance stemmed from the fact that, in terms of political philosophy, Webster and Emerson were embarked on similar missions and found similar answers to the overriding question that preoccupied them both. From Benjamin Franklin to Alexis de Tocqueville a dozen thoughtful observers of the American experiment had voiced the same query: how in a situation of fundamental equality did one insure order without sacrificing individual liberty. For Webster the national balance itself stood as the expression and embodiment of liberty. Less sure that true liberty could be taken for granted in America, Emerson focused on the process of liberation. But both men avoided what was static in favor of essentially dynamic conceptions and both centered their hopes finally on the same elusive entity. If the conflict between liberty and order was to be resolved, the key to its resolution would be an exaltation of the national character. "That which all things tend to educe," wrote Emerson in his essay "Politics," "which freedom, cultivation, intercourse, revolutions, go to form and deliver, is character."

Character, that "continent, persisting, immovable" quality that ever "believing in a vast future, — sure of more to come than is yet seen, — postpones the present hour of the whole life." To Emerson the ultimate embodiment of such "sublime prudence" was "the wiseman." Inclined to work with materials that came more readily to hand, Webster preferred George Washington as a model and saw the world of practical affairs, rather than

Emerson's generalized "Nature," as the premier school of character. But however shaped, character was attainable by all men and it performed for the nation as a whole the same function it did in the lives of individuals. "The fly wheel of the mill," it distributed motion "equably over all the wheels," protecting the system from "destructive shocks." What in other cultures was accomplished — if at all — through traditional centers of power and authority in America would flow naturally from the enlightened consciousness of the people themselves. The conjunction of liberty and order would be the work of ordinary citizens, somehow rendered extraordinary in the crucible of everyday experience. Skeptics might doubt, the wise man might seem a long time in coming, or the average American something less than Washingtonian in character; to the end of their lives Webster and Emerson continued to hope.

Yet such faith, while it could survive the apparent contradiction of events, still left events to be dealt with on one level or another. And right there a difficulty arose, for the faith itself was sufficiently loose to permit any number of responses — which was what happened increasingly after 1843. In the growing crisis Emerson and Webster defined the proper exercise of character differently. The one saw a clear choice between mutually exclusive alternatives, the other a question of priorities and emphasis.

The tragedy was that neither definition met the realities of the situation. Emerson's moral imperatives were hardly those of the rest of the country, and Webster's nationalism, despite the breadth of its vision, contained no lasting solution to the sectional crisis. Within little more than a decade after the Seventh of March Speech, Emerson would find himself torn between a willingness to let the South go in peace and the conviction that a trial by fire might well bring the final purification of the American character. The trial by fire turned out to be a war that lasted four years and left better than half a million Americans dead.

In Webster's case, the proof of his miscalculation came more quickly. Not only did the slavery issue continue to dominate national politics during the remaining two years of his life, but 1852 found him no nearer the presidency than he had ever been. In spite of everything the old objections to his candidacy still held. He was too closely identified with Northern interests; he was not popular with the average voter. To these could have been added the fact that he had no real talent for political organization. In his view it was tedious business to be left to friends — friends, who, in 1852, as they had all too often in the past, served him badly.

But if Webster was badly served by his friends, and if the American people seemed disinclined to reward him with the one thing he wanted above all else, he for his part had failed to convince them. Somehow the great vision had become too abstract, too divorced from the mundane stuff of daily life. And this was the real heart of the tragedy, for it was precisely with such material he had begun, only to find in the end that the mold which fused the two — the ideal and reality — had shattered on the paired reefs of sectionalism and democratic politics.
Sweden, Maine
August 1972

ROBERT F. DALZELL, JR.

# Contents

# Daniel Webster and the Trial of American Nationalism 1843-1852

"There was the Monument,
and here was Webster."

— RALPH WALDO EMERSON

# One
# Charlestown, June 17, 1843

IT WAS SIXTY-EIGHT YEARS to the day since an untrained and
wretchedly supplied band of citizen troops had met and narrowly missed defeating an army of British regulars. Almost two
decades had passed since the cornerstone was laid. Now the
Bunker Hill Monument was finished, and like some solemn, ancient Panathenaea set down amidst the complexities of the nineteenth century, the procession that was to dedicate it wound,
three miles long, past the Statehouse in Boston, down Beacon
Hill to the river, across to Charlestown, and up the heights beyond. The streets were narrow and a gap in the ranks developed
at one point that widened steadily to a distance of almost a third
of a mile, but for most people the day and the weather were
enough to make up for anything. A fresh breeze lifted the flags
suspended everywhere along the way, and the sun flashed from
the regalia of the more than fifty volunteer militia units — National Lancers and Augusta Rifle Grays, Polaski Guards and
Salem Mechanic Light Infantry — that marched eight abreast at
the head of the procession.[1]

Behind the military, in an open barouche drawn by six fine
horses, rode John Tyler, President of the United States, his republican dignity carefully shielded from the sun by a Negro
slave with a long-handled umbrella. After Tyler there followed
a seemingly endless line of carriages and men on foot: greater

and lesser government officials and no fewer than 107 Revolutionary War veterans; foreign consuls and clergymen; the entire student body of Harvard College, its president and all its officers; the members of King Solomon's Lodge and its Auxiliaries and representatives of the New England Society of New York; the Benevolent German Tailors and at least five different Irish charitable and reform societies; the Independent Order of Odd Fellows and the ancient and honorable Society of the Cincinnati; the Massachusetts Charitable Mechanic Association and St. Mary's Mutual Benevolent Catholic Total Abstinence Society. On and on they came, kept in order somehow by the fifty-five marshals whose task it was to do so.

Even with the rain the day before that had spoiled the President's reception, the dust would have posed a problem for the spectators. Yet at every point along the way they were gathered, standing and sitting, people of all ages. There was an especially large number of women, for women did not march in processions then, and the rousing "cheers for the ladies" of the Harvard students were met time and again with ripples of waving handkerchiefs and bobbing parasols. Once the procession had passed, the spectators fell in behind it on foot, or in still other carriages that clogged the roads, adding to the confusion in Charlestown, where all the carriages had to be left for the final walk up the hill.

The day had begun with the firing of a "grand salute" at sunrise. By eight o'clock the militia units were already forming on the Common. It took two hours for the procession to assemble and one hour and twenty minutes for it to pass a given point. Not until the middle of the afternoon was everybody gathered on the other side of the Charles River, ready for the ceremonies to begin.

With all the excitement it must have been a tiring day, and for at least one person in the procession it proved to be a good deal more than that. The cheering when the Revolutionary

War veterans passed was invariably louder than at any other point, and old as they were the veterans seemed to enjoy the spectacle immensely, waving and cheering with the crowd. Unfortunately, however, one of their weary number died that evening. That this particular veteran should have been one of the few remaining survivors of the Battle of Bunker Hill made his death appear all the more poignant, and ironic, though this was not an age that looked for irony in such things.

## II

Until he rose to speak, the orator of the day was — as much as Daniel Webster ever could be — simply another figure in the procession. But from that moment, standing erect and alone, with only the 221-foot obelisk of Quincy granite that was the Bunker Hill Monument rising above him, he dominated the scene completely. Of the tens of thousands of people spread out before him many had come for no other reason than to hear him speak, and he looked fully as august as that fact and the occasion required. Within a decade the somber pall of black broadcloth would envelop public men everywhere, but in 1843 Webster was still free to wear what he chose. His choice, at times like these, was invariably the same: white breeches, buff waistcoat, and a blue coat with brass buttons. Already by 1843 the fashion for such dress had passed. It was the property of an earlier generation; still, the impression created was far from inappropriate. At a distance Webster might almost have been wearing a Revolutionary parade uniform. Yet even then the magnificent head with its massive brow and smoldering dark eyes would have stamped the image indelibly as his. Age had blurred none of the outlines; at sixty-one Webster was as marvelous to behold as ever.

The crowd applauded. Whatever ran through his mind during that brief interval before he spoke, it was by no means a simple task he faced. The heart of any ritual is what it celebrates, but here at Bunker Hill there were a dozen possibilities. Above all it would be his duty to select one, to take the tableau around him with its jumble of disparate, potentially conflicting elements and give it meaning. Nor did that duty carry with it, by half, the measure of freedom it seemed to.

In a scene so thoroughly dominated by Webster's presence it would have been surprising if many men in the crowd had bothered to consider how much of what he said then, or on other, similar occasions, was prescribed before he began. Yet to a very substantial extent it was prescribed; prescribed by custom and tradition, by the nature of the occasion and the expectations of his audience. The Monument, the history of the battle, a tribute to those who had fought in it and particularly those who had died, the Revolution, independence, freedom, the nation, its glorious past and brilliant future — those were the things people had come to hear about. They were the given and a great deal of Webster's rhetoric was always the given, was not, strictly speaking, original. In the end he was free only to arrange and give emphasis.

Within the narrow range open to him, however, Webster had managed over the years to create a rhetorical formulation that was uniquely his own. Essentially it was a definition of the nation, as a nation, and of what it meant to be an American. He never deluded himself that those were simple things to define, but he did have the wisdom to speak of them simply, with a minimum of flourish, so people might more easily understand and accept what he said. The nation was still less than seventy years away from its founding and endlessly diverse as the crowd before him attested. The forces that tended to divide it — class and sectional interests, local customs and local pride — were powerful. All of that Webster knew, yet he was prepared to continue the process of definition. The crucial question was how accurately he gauged the strength of what he opposed.

## III

No man can do something twice and avoid the risk of comparison. It was Webster's misfortune that day to have spoken eighteen years earlier at Bunker Hill when the cornerstone of the Monument was laid and to have given one of the finest speeches of his career. The inevitable comparisons have not been kind to the Second Bunker Hill Address, and justly so.[2] It lacked the unity of focus, and hence the force, of its predecessor. Yet to say only this ignores both the nature of what Webster was trying to do in 1843 and the relative difficulty of the task. In 1825 he was concerned primarily with defining the nation's mission in the world and the conditions necessary for the fulfillment of that mission.[3] The subject was a discrete one; its outlines were clear and it lent itself to a unified treatment without undue effort. Webster's other great speech of the period was the Second Reply to Hayne, and the same is true of its subject, the legal and constitutional bases of nationhood.[4] By any standard the Second Bunker Hill Address was a more ambitious undertaking. In it Webster defined as precisely as he ever did what made the nation a nation. If the result lacked unity, there was, after all, no readily available unifying theme or proposition that might have remedied the defect. Moreover, absolute unity was very far from being anything that Webster felt either was, or ought to be, a national characteristic.

He began simply, drawing his listeners' attention to the Monument — a device he used throughout the speech whenever he wished to make a transition.[5] Each time the Monument took on a different meaning, new associations. Here they were the obvious ones.

A duty has been performed. A work of gratitude and patriotism is completed. This structure, having its foundations in soil which drank deep of early Revolutionary blood, has at length reached its destined height, and lifts its summit to the skies.

There followed a history of the building of the Monument and the groups and individuals connected with it. Then Webster mentioned the others present who had a special reason for being there: the veterans of the battle and their descendants. To the veterans they all owed an incalculable debt and he greeted them by name, drawing around them as he did so the proud cloak of an honored old age.

They have long outlived the trouble and dangers of the Revolution; they have outlived the evils arising from the want of united and efficient government; they have outlived the menace of imminent dangers to the public liberty; they have outlived nearly all their contemporaries; but they have not outlived, they cannot outlive, the affectionate gratitude of their country.

Immediately after this salutation the first major break in the speech occurred. Thus far Webster's references had been purely personal and local. Now he returned to the Monument and, broadening the field tremendously with a few rapid strokes, made it the orator of the day — one that spoke alike to all Americans everywhere.

The powerful speaker stands motionless before us. It is a plain shaft. It bears no inscriptions, fronting to the rising sun, from which the future antiquary shall wipe the dust. Nor does the rising sun cause the tones of music to issue from its summit. But at the setting of the sun; in the blaze of noonday; and beneath the milder effulgence of lunar light; it looks, it speaks, it acts, to the full comprehension of every American mind, and the awakening of glowing enthusiasm in every American heart.

In the space of a paragraph Webster had anchored the Monument and the day securely within a national context. It was a singular achievement and nonetheless so because all that had gone before — all the purely private and local — remained, transformed perhaps, but there still. This movement from the nonnational to the national, ending in a combination of the two that somehow preserved the essence of each, ran, like a leitmotif, through the entire Second Bunker Hill Address. Again and again Webster returned to it, but nowhere were its implications clearer than here and in the next section of the speech where he first retraced for emphasis, and then summarized, the steps that had brought him to this point.

The section began as a welcome to the "thousands of natives of New England now residents in other states" who had come for the dedication. For everything they brought with them — "family associations and the recollections of the past . . . local attachment and private affection" — Webster was grateful, and to each in a nicely turned phrase he gave its due. Here the national context had been left behind, but he quickly moved back to it again, declaring that commendable as such emotions were, the day had a character quite apart from them. "This occasion is respectable, nay it is grand, it is sublime, by the nationality of its sentiment." In the next moment the point became a warning.

> Woe betide the man who brings to this day's worship feelings less than wholly American! Woe betide the man who can stand here with the fires of local resentments burning, or the purpose of fomenting local jealousies and the strifes of local interests festering and rankling in his heart.

Hearing this one might well have wondered precisely what distinguished "local attachment" from "the fires of local resentments" and "the strifes of local interests." The one, clearly, was desirable; the others were not. The one came as an honored guest to the celebration; the others could only disrupt its deepest purposes. Yet the difference between them was hardly great. Ultimately it came to a matter of balance, and in the concept of balance lay the heart of Webster's nationalism.

The purpose and finally the essential quality of the nation was balance. Everything Webster said began and ended there. If the nation was composed of elements that gravitated irresistibly toward it and yet in the process lost none of their identity, and if even the best of those elements contained a darker, destructive potential, the force at the center had to equilibrate or chaos would result. Stated thus the doctrine might have seemed rather negative and the nation it envisioned little more than a product of grim necessity, but there were other possibilities.

One of the most striking aspects of Webster's conception was the breadth of its accommodation. As long as the fundamental balance was maintained there was room for everything, and any sacrifice of individual uniqueness or vigor that did prove necessary was always more than compensated for by the good obtained in return. That good, a vital corollary of the first principles of the system, amounted to the assertion that whatever the nation drew into the balance it also protected, and by protecting, preserved. The effect was to make the nation not only the logical counterpoise of national diversity, but its principal guarantor as well. Here, on the most elementary level, were the Liberty and Union of the unforgettable conclusion to the Second Reply to Hayne, "now and forever, one and inseparable."

All of which was eminently practical and realistic. Elsewhere — indeed throughout human history — nationhood might have been equated with the interests and ambitions of a particular class or family, or with some ancient faith or body of doctrine, but not here. Webster postulated no vain, quixotic search for a unity unobtainable in America in 1840. The most he called for was union — a union that had nothing to do with leveling or attempts to abolish the endless and cherished variety of the country and its people. To a very considerable extent his formulation left Americans free to follow their separate ways and interests and still think of themselves as good Americans. It even offered the nation as a haven for variety and separateness. Nothing could have been more appropriate or better adapted to the nation as it was in 1840. Yet at this point in the Second Bunker Hill Address the structure remained only half complete.

Webster had defined the nation as balance, but what maintained the balance was still at issue. In fact the question had not even been posed.

Too practiced a logician to ignore such an obvious question and too well aware of its difficulty to meet it head-on, Webster moved by indirection. With the Monument still lying in figurative pieces around him, destroyed in a deftly conjured image by the clash of unbalanced local interests and local jealousies, he turned to the Battle of Bunker Hill. Briefly he outlined its history, and then, taking again the familiar route from the nonnational to the national, he asked what the battle's consequences had been and answered that they "were just of the same importance as the Revolution itself."

> If there was nothing of value in the principles of the American Revolution, then there is nothing valuable in the battle of Bunker Hill and its consequences. But if the Revolution was an era in the history of man favorable to human happiness, if it was an event which marked the progress of man all over the world from despotism to liberty, then this Monument is not raised without cause.

What, then, was "the true and peculiar principle of the American Revolution, and of the system of government which it has confirmed and established"? The question followed logically enough, but asking it Webster appeared to have wandered rather far from the subject of balance. Normally the essence of revolution is violent change, suggesting nothing if not imbalance. The way around the difficulty, of course, was to make the American Revolution a different kind of occurrence — in fact not a revolution at all — which is precisely what Webster now undertook to do.

> The truth is, that the American Revolution was not caused by the instantaneous discovery of principles of government before unheard of, or the practical adoption of political ideas such as had

never before entered into the minds of men. It was but the full development of principles of government, forms of society, and political sentiments, the origin of all of which lay back two centuries in English and American history.

In Webster's mind there were three things that maintained the fundamental national balance. The Revolution was important because it insured the continued existence of two of them and added a third. The two that formed a balance of their own were a common culture, derived from England, and a uniquely American set of political institutions. The third was character — the sort of character the militiamen had shown at Bunker Hill, and of which Webster found an even better example before he was through. The shared culture, free political institutions, and character — without those the whole system would fly apart. Nor could any two of them alone prevent such a catastrophe. Each played a necessary role.

Basically it was a simple line of reasoning, and being simple might have lacked drama, but Webster had on hand that day a more than adequate supply of lights and shadows, villains and heroes. Eighteen years before, when the cornerstone of the Monument was laid, his subject had been the mission of America in the world and nowhere then had the hopes he expressed seemed to enjoy a better promise of fulfillment than in the newly liberated nations of the Southern Hemisphere. There, "at the mighty bidding of the voice of political liberty," Webster had seen "the waters of darkness retire." But such visions had long since proved illusory and the steady tide he thought he saw, nothing more than a weak and erratic current. Faced with the error of his predictions Webster might have ignored the subject in 1843, yet he chose not to and for good reason. If nothing else, the dreary sequel to the south offered, when compared with developments at home, a splendid lesson in national balance and what maintained it. That comparison he carried through the entire second half of the Address, beginning with the section on the Revolution, and ringing change after change on it until each of his major points was developed. By the time he had finished no one would have complained of a lack of drama.

The details of the comparison in the present were all too familiar, but they bore repeating. Even the forces of nature were made to conspire in the image of chronic imbalance — or balance preserved by force, an equally undesirable condition — which Webster now fastened on the Southern republics.

Suppose an assembly, in one of the valleys or on the side of one of the mountains of the southern half of the hemisphere, to be held, this day, in the neighborhood of a large city; — what would be the scene presented? Yonder is a volcano, flaming and smoking, but shedding no light, moral or intellectual. At its foot is the mine sometimes yielding, perhaps, large gains to capital, but in which labor is destined to eternal and unrequited toil, and followed by penury and beggary. The city is filled with armed men; not a free people, armed and coming forth voluntarily to rejoice in a public festivity, but hireling troops, supported by forced loans, excessive impositions on commerce, or taxes wrung from a half-fed and a half-clothed population. For the great there are palaces covered with gold; for the poor there are hovels of the meanest sort. There is an ecclesiastical hierarchy, enjoying the wealth of princes; but there are no means of education for the people. Do public improvements favor intercourse between place and place? So far from this, the traveller cannot pass from town to town without danger, every mile, of robbery and assassination.

Then the contrast. Webster had only to point to the spectacle around him and Boston, clearly visible across the river.

Look at that fair City, the abode of so much diffused wealth, so much general happiness and comfort, so much personal independence, and so much general knowledge, and not undistinguished, I may be permitted to add, for hospitality and social refinement. She fears no forced contributions, no siege or sacking from military leaders or rival factions. The hundred temples in which her citizens worship God are in no danger of sacrilege. The regular administration of the laws encounters no obstacle. The long procession of children and youth which you see this day, issuing by thousands from her free schools, prove the care and anxiety with which a popular government provides for the education and morals of the people. Everywhere there is order; everywhere there is security.

In a word balance, and a balance inherent in the society, not forced upon it from above or without.

Like the principles of the Revolution — for they were largely the same — the factors that produced this striking contrast lay in the beginnings of the colonial experience. Balance in the present was a direct outgrowth of balance in the past. The British colonies in North America achieved it early and in a unique fashion. "The distinctive characteristic of their settlement is the introduction of the civilization of Europe into a wilderness, without bringing with it the political institutions of Europe." In British America people had been free to frame institutions "anew, such as should be adapted to the state of things." Elsewhere in the New World matters were handled differently. The institutions of the mother country were simply recreated across the ocean.

> The monarchy of Spain was not transferred to this hemisphere, but it acted in it, as it acted at home through its ordinary means, and its true representative, military force. The robbery and destruction of the native race was the achievement of standing armies, in the right of the King, and by his authority; fighting in his name, for the aggrandizement of his power and the extension of his prerogatives; with military ideas under arbitrary maxims, a portion of that dreadful instrumentality by which a perfect despotism governs a people.

With such tutors what could a people be expected to learn of liberty and free institutions, and without that knowledge how was any balance, other than a purely arbitrary one imposed by fiat, possible? The answer was obvious.

Yet to concentrate too heavily on the institutional problem sacrifices the force of Webster's argument, for ultimately, he believed, "the European civilization" that the North American colonists simply transplanted was every bit as important in securing the happiness of their posterity as the institutions they created afresh. The fact that it was not just European, but British civilization, too, made a tremendous difference; that and the matter of timing. The Spanish began settling the New World in the sixteenth century. The English were forced to wait until the seventeenth. By then the spirit of economic adventure and independence, the rise of a powerful new middle class, and the development of the theory of individual liberty stemming both from those causes and from the religious controversies of the period had already gone far toward transforming English society. Webster dealt with each of these factors in turn and then with the part they had played together in shaping the British colonial enterprise.

> The colonists of English America were of the people, and a people already free. They were of the middle, industrious, and already prosperous class, the inhabitants of commercial and manufacturing cities, among whom liberty first revived and respired, after a sleep of a thousand years in the bosom of the Dark Ages.

Coming as they did from the vanguard of the new order in England, the colonists naturally brought with them what was best and most progressive in English life and left behind or quickly abandoned in the wilderness all that was antiquated, feudal.

> The arts, sciences, and literature of England came over with the settlers. That great portion of the common law which regulates the social and personal relations and conduct of men came also. The jury came; the habeas corpus came; the testamentary power came; and the law of inheritance and descent came also, except that part of it which recognizes the rights of primogeniture, which either did not come at all, or soon gave way to the rule of equal partition of estates among children.

In a similar manner the monarchy, the aristocracy, and the church "as an estate of the realm," too, were disposed of.

On this level the corollary for the Spanish colonies reduced

itself to a simple rhetorical question: "As there was no liberty in Spain, how could liberty be transmitted to Spanish colonies?" And as for the nations those colonies became, was it any wonder that hitherto they seemed to have "discovered quite too much of the spirit of that monarchy from which they separated themselves," with their military dictatorships, their "mock elections supported by the sword," their lack of even a semblance of self-sustaining national balance? None at all, Webster argued.

Balance was organic. Its roots lay in the past. It grew and developed over time; continuity was its vital force. Thus read the broader conclusions of Webster's comparison between America and its unfortunate neighbors to the south. In terms of specifics the comparison had dealt with the cultural and institutional factors that operated to maintain — or prevent — balance. A long heritage of English culture and free, republican institutions growing logically from the conditions of the new environment had made possible a remarkable degree of balance in British America, even during the colonial period. The Revolution had insured the continuation of that happy arrangement, and the years since had only improved it. Such a state of affairs was unique in the new world, however. Beyond America's borders a repressive, medieval culture and institutions appeared to have doomed men to live forever in the midst of chaotic imbalance, or a balance that was lifeless, inorganic — the product of dictatorial military force.

It was not an encouraging picture and it raised at once a difficult question. In 1825 at Bunker Hill Webster had implied that culture and institutions could be transplanted. Indeed many of the Latin American nations had studiously tried to copy the glorious example to the north. After twenty years the growth should have been hardier, even by the standards Webster outlined in 1843. What had gone wrong? What was missing?

The answer was character, which Webster now offered as America's greatest gift to the world, and which became by implication the third in the triarchy of elements that maintained the fundamental national balance. Significantly the character he chose was Washington's — Washington the man above faction and local interests, the man who sacrificed himself freely for his country and then refused the dictatorial power he might have had in return.

> To him who denies or doubts whether our fervid liberty can be combined with law, with order, with the security of property, with the pursuits and advancement of happiness; to him who denies that our forms of government are capable of producing exaltation of soul and the passion of true glory, to him who denies that we have contributed anything to the stock of great lessons and great examples; — to all these I reply by pointing to Washington.

Liberty, union, mission, and balance — the figure of Washington stood as the apotheosis of these. To argue that Latin American republics had failed because Simón Bolívar was a lesser man than George Washington would have been a gross oversimplification of Webster's point, but not a total misrepresentation of it. The hope was that those nations, guided by the experience of America, would produce their own Washingtons in time, their own examples of high and noble character. Upon that their salvation — the achievement of a viable national balance — depended.

The eulogium of Washington brought Webster to the conclusion of the Address. In his brief peroration he turned from the character of one man to the character of the nation as a whole. The standard, and the lesson, remained the same, however.

> Let us hold fast to the great truth, that communities are responsible, as well as individuals; that no government is respectable which is not just; that without unspotted purity of public faith, without sacred public principle, fidelity and honor, no mere forms of government, no machinery of laws, can give dignity to political society.

To follow, as a people, the example of Washington: that was the ultimate national duty.

At the very end Webster returned to the Monument and in the last of many transformations it became a symbol of the future and the continuing process of national affirmation.

> And then, when honored and decrepit age shall lean against the base of this monument, and troops of ingenious youth shall be gathered round it, and when the one shall speak to the other of its objects, the purposes of its construction, and the great and glorious events with which it is connected, there shall rise from every youthful breast the ejaculation, "Thank God, I — I also — AM AN AMERICAN!"

## IV

The ritual had ended. Webster's definition was complete. For a moment longer the crowd remained silent, and then the applause broke, wave upon wave of it, rising upward to the platform where he stood.

As always he had spoken with a lawyer's respect for the issue at hand, arguing every point closely and moving logically from point to point. For the period his allusions were restrained. His language was simple and direct; he had an obvious preference for words of Anglo-Saxon origin. In every way possible he had tried to make his case a clear one.

To a substantial extent he succeeded. In that moment of silence which followed the speech he probably sensed this. If he did, however, he knew too from long experience that success here had definite limitations. He could provide a foundation, a beginning, but that was all. The first ringing cheer brought the world into the circle of rhetoric, and with the world came the question of its comprehension. That one question, moreover, carried a host of others in its train.

Of those questions, the most crucial by far was the matter of context. The process of interpretation could move in any one of a number of directions. The direction taken depended on the context chosen — or assumed — at the outset. For Webster's contemporaries the initial context, always, was the ritual itself. This was logical, indeed inevitable.

The ritual was not, however, a particularly fruitful place to turn. Everything about its marshaled processions, its stately gestures, its studied solemnity operated to set it apart from the normal concerns of life. In the midst of that carefully wrought design Webster's rhetoric — the supreme act of consecration — moved as the pivotal element. Yet what made it pivotal was the fact that it could not be worked in a vacuum; it required an object to exalt, and the object in this case was a complex of precisely those ordinary, tangible, everyday aspects of national life that the tableau seemed at first glance contrived to mask. The intention should have been obvious. One climbs a hill for a better view of the world, not the hill, but here — perhaps because the hill was of such majestic proportions — it sometimes hid the scene it was meant to reveal. Even Emerson, who usually saw so much, could assert in all seriousness of Webster's role at the dedication that "the whole occasion was answered by his presence," and the ease with which he "walked through his part"; that "it was a place for behavior more than speech"; that "a little more or less of rhetoric signified nothing" at Bunker Hill.[6]

Where interpretation stopped with the ritual, rhetoric became a sort of aimless shadow play. So ran one explanation of Webster's achievement, but it narrowed the context to virtually nothing, and the average person, less accustomed than Emerson to reading first principles in the shape of a leaf, needed more room. As confining as such abstractions were, on the other hand, few people were prepared to abandon the abstract entirely. It was a question of finding some middle ground — a broader field, yet one where the boundaries were still clearly marked.

In that search art often seemed the ideal solution. At a time when the speeches of famous men were printed, bound, and sold in editions numbering in the tens of thousands, and in a place where the more ordinary productions of high culture were seldom found and little encouraged, oratory quite naturally assumed the status of an art form. It was essential to the proper functioning of democratic institutions; there was an abundance of it and an obvious lack of alternatives. Seventy-five years later George Santayana would call public eloquence the "republican art" and argue that nothing in the entire range of American belles lettres had more deeply plumbed the meaning of "the great national experiment." [7]

Webster's rhetoric was art. The attempt to erect a high culture using resources available in an environment fundamentally hostile to culture sometimes led Americans astray, but here was no mistake — at least as far as the fitness of the designation was concerned. Its usefulness was another matter. Art has a life of its own, apart from the life of the man who created it. Its meaning may have nothing to do with his intentions; its merits and value, too, are judged independently of his. In Webster's case there were men who had little enough use for him, yet few of them failed to admit the consummate mastery of his oratory. John Quincy Adams detested Webster and considered an address by him at Bunker Hill on the anniversary of the battle a stupid "burlesque upon them both," but the speech itself he thought "brilliant." [8]

The tenacity with which Webster's contemporaries held to the distinction between the man and his art perhaps explains why the passage of time has done so little to blur it. For those who admire Webster, the brilliance of his rhetoric continues to justify much in his life that is difficult to excuse otherwise. For those who do not, or have not, his genius as an orator becomes a rare gift, senselessly thrown away in the pursuit of false gods — a standard against which to measure what might have been. Both lines of reasoning have points in their favor, but they leave the major issue unsettled; neither answers the question of meaning. Nor can they. Whatever Webster's rhetoric meant, it was a part and product of the rest of his life. The two cannot be separated.

In 1812, at the age of thirty, Webster ran for and was elected to the Thirteenth Congress. From then until the end of his life he was a politician, and the thorny imperatives of politics shaped everything he did and said. In his own mind the literary merit of his speeches mattered less than their political utility. If rhetoric and politics carried with them different imperatives, an adjustment might be made, but politics would always take precedence in determining the substance and tone of the adjustment. In a sense the problem reduced itself to finding that point in the circle transcribed by politics where rhetoric intersected or could be made to intersect. For Webster the point turned out to be nationalism, and a nationalism indelibly marked with the sign of the conjunction that produced it. At every turn the Second Bunker Hill Address fairly bristled with political reality. The balance it contemplated was pre-eminently one of concrete entities — classes, sections, and interests — the raw material of politics always. Moreover, bringing those elements into a state of equilibrium was in fact the overriding task of American politicians and politics during the period. Without a balance of some sort, given the diversity of the country and the peculiar nature of its institutions, concerted action at any point would have been impossible.

Whether in the long run politics itself — even when filtered through the triple media of institutions, culture, and character — could insure the balance that politics required was at least debatable, but not as far as Webster was concerned. That he simply assumed. A half a century before, weighing the potential stability of republican government in *Federalist* 10, James Madison had dared to voice the same hope.

## V

When Webster began his political career, he was not a nationalist. He was elected to Congress from Portsmouth, New Hampshire, as a Federalist, and the interests of that party, his city, and state made opposition to the power of the national government an obligation that no one, and certainly not a neophyte in the business of politics, could afford to ignore. In conjunction with the opposition thus required of him the vigorously articulated nationalism of his later career would have seemed incongruous to say the least. A studious cultivation of national balance may have been a necessary prerequisite for national action, but in 1812 the voters of Portsmouth most earnestly desired the government at Washington to stop acting. Webster was elected to express that desire, and nothing more.

Yet the same man who entered politics on such restrictive terms had also, by the time he reached thirty, traveled a long way from even less promising beginnings.

When Webster was born in Salisbury, New Hampshire, the town was still scarcely a generation removed from the frontier. His father, Ebenezer — a Revolutionary War veteran and later justice of the peace — was a person of some consequence in the vicinity, but the family was a large one and always poor. Only the fact that Webster himself was the youngest child and far from robust excused him from the usual farm chores. Given the opportunity he made good use of it, however. Much alone, he read a great deal, and whenever school was in session in the neighborhood he attended, showing such promise that his father finally decided to make the extraordinary sacrifices necessary to send him to Exeter Academy and later Dartmouth College. Though he was awarded none of the laurels that went in those days to the outstanding scholars at such schools his record was a creditable one and he had already, by graduation, gained a reputation as an orator at local Fourth of July celebrations. Still more to the point, as meager as the standard academic fare of the time was, the entire experience had expanded his horizons considerably.

After Dartmouth Webster read law in Salisbury for a year, taught school in Maine for another to help pay an older brother's way through Dartmouth, returned to Salisbury briefly, and then went to Boston to finish his legal studies. Despite the fact that he was there for only a short while, the time in Boston was crucial to his development. Law may have been one of the learned professions, but as practiced in many small New England towns in the early nineteenth century it was hardly calculated to broaden the imagination. In Boston, by contrast, legal questions were becoming increasingly complex and varied, just as life itself was. From Webster's standpoint, too, it helped enormously that his introduction to life and law in Boston should have been supervised by Christopher Gore, in whose office he became a clerk. An accomplished lawyer and the owner of a countryseat sufficiently grand to be called a "palace," Gore was a man of wide interests as well as ability and a Federalist of the old school. Having recently returned from two years abroad as a commissioner under the terms of the Jay treaty, he was later elected governor of the state and served a term as a United States senator. The influence such a commanding personality must have had on an impressionable young clerk from the provinces would be hard to overestimate.

Under Gore's sponsorship Webster was admitted to the Massachusetts Bar in 1805. Returning to New Hampshire he set up an office in Boscawen near his family's home and then following his father's death in 1807 moved to Portsmouth where his practice grew rapidly. Within a short time he was recognized as one of the leading lawyers in the state. There followed his entry into politics, a field in which he seemed destined from the beginning to accomplish great things. Observers had long since begun commenting on his distinguished presence and skill as a public speaker. If they noted as well a certain aloofness the fact would probably not have bothered him. Whether out of instinct or a deliberate attempt to emulate his older associates at the bar, Webster had already adopted the rather formal manners of what was fast becoming a bygone era, and like many very ambitious men he formed few close personal relationships.

Even more indicative than points of style and bearing was his decision to align himself with the conservative cause in the hurly-burly of New Hampshire politics. Though at the time of his election to Congress the Federalists had been for several years the beneficiaries of widespread opposition to the national government's foreign policy, that situation was a temporary one. The party of Washington and Adams had early on succumbed to the state's better organized and more imaginatively led Jeffersonians and would do so again. On the other hand, many of the men Webster most admired, including his father, were Federalists, and his own attitudes and opinions clearly placed him within the same fold. For the rest of his life, through all the changes that were to affect parties, their structure and ideology, he would remain on the conservative side in American politics.

But conservatism could mean many things — even in 1812. The group of young Federalist leaders who engineered the party's revival in New Hampshire differed from their elders in more than just age. In 1800 the rallying cry everywhere had been legitimacy. The whole force of such feeble electioneering efforts as the Federalists undertook was aimed at making their opponents seem a dangerous and improper faction. Party spirit, party rhetoric, and above all party organization were anathema. When it became clear that the long harangue had failed, not a few of the older Federalists, who doubtless believed their own predictions of doom and in any case had no desire to continue under a different set of ground rules, simply retired from politics. In so doing they left the field to a new generation

of conservatives, one determined to avoid the errors of its prede-
cessors. Among other things, the young Federalists frankly accepted the two-party system and worked within the framework it
imposed. At the time the adjustment might have appeared as
much a matter of necessity as anything else, but it had far-
reaching implications. In acknowledging the legitimacy of parties they accepted the principle of choice in politics, and choice
in turn implied change — not as a cataclysmic transformation
but as part of the normal course of events.[9]

If a conservatism that embraced change seemed strange most
of the young Federalists, including Webster, managed to live
with the anomaly comfortably enough. For the time being it
spelled success. A good many of its adherents, too, had every
reason to accept — even applaud — the idea of change. Certainly Webster did. The son of a penniless backcountry farmer
he had become, by the age of thirty, a prosperous lawyer and
United States congressman. The system that made such things
possible was open and flexible. Change in fact was its lifeblood,
and Webster, for all his conservatism, never — then or afterward — equated that persuasion with what was merely static or
opposed to change.

For the rest, equally important in shaping his later thinking
was something in his New England background less specific than
either the political battles he fought or the details of his personal success. To someone who had not shared the experience,
daily life in Salisbury, Boston, or Portsmouth might have
seemed confining, and in many ways it was. But Webster was
not alone in finding in it an abundance of the sort of stuff of
which philosophies are made. At no other point in time and
space, perhaps, have the elements of existence been better arranged to produce a sense of optimism about man's ability to
combine in a single system such difficult entities as liberty,
order, and change.

Having just passed through a violent revolution and so made

good their claim of independence from a vastly older and more powerful nation, Americans everywhere, during the period, were busy consolidating the gains of their momentous achievement. Yet nowhere did the pace of adjustment and change beat faster than in New England. Its commerce ruined by the Revolution, the region had, by 1800, made a complete recovery in economic terms. Hard won on the oceans of a world at war, that recovery was a source of pride to most New Englanders, but the prosperity it brought altered old ways and institutions, inevitably leading to quarrels among people, just as other changes occurring at the same time in religion and politics and society did. Still, with the exception of a few sharp clashes in the decade immediately following the Revolution, a deep and abiding stability seemed to underlie all the energetic striving and agitation. In a thousand towns from the coast of Connecticut to northern Maine, voters met annually to elect officials who — whatever the differences dividing them — managed to conduct governments that were models of progressive efficiency by the standards of any age. Budgets were small, but there was no standing army, or even in most places a local police force to support, nor was there any need for either. If not always happily, men obeyed the laws their representatives enacted, confident that if the burden became too oppressive the institutions themselves afforded adequate means of remedy.

In the end even the abrasive enthusiasms of Jeffersonian politics could not disrupt the underlying calm. Separated for the first time into two distinct political parties the electorate was treated to a fair amount of impassioned rhetoric, and when the government at Washington — with the Embargo and later a full-scale war — struck at the very heart of New England's prosperity the system seemed for a time on the brink of collapse. But the moment passed. The Hartford Convention met and, much to the relief of moderates like Webster, passed its surprisingly mild resolutions and disbanded — a revolution that never materialized.

Here in short was a society at once open and orderly, progressive and stable. What it lacked in glory it more than made up for in the number of human values it affirmed and went far toward fulfilling. A skeptic might have pointed out, of course, that the marvel of accommodation Webster witnessed in New England in the early years of the nineteenth century was the result of causes largely beyond human control; that it was America's abundance not American institutions that insured both progress and order; that the striking homogeneity of the population had more to do with guaranteeing liberty than anything as vague as character. But Webster was not a skeptic, at least in this sense. He was ambitious and could be ruthless in the pursuit of his own interests; even those who knew him well found him cold — an impression that all too often grew stronger the further one found oneself from the source, to the point where, for many of his countrymen, it would amount to a settled conviction that after all the magnificent head held little but an elegantly furnished legal mind. They were wrong, however. In an age that romanticized everything from childhood to macroeconomics Webster was by no means immune. Surveying the scene around him as a young man he found it good and was prepared to believe not only that men had made it so, but that with the proper measure of good will and intelligence they could keep it that way. Translated from the local to the national level it was that kind of faith which underlay his nationalism.

With the War of 1812 over, and Federalism waning, the translation itself took place fairly rapidly. The next decade, like the preceding three, was full of change, and out of the matrix of those years Webster emerged a nationalist. There were many factors compelling him in this direction: his move to Boston, the shifting economic interests of New England, his election to the Senate, and the legal cases he argued, especially before the Supreme Court, involving as they more and more often did an uncompromising adherence to the doctrine of national supremacy.

In politics he marked the change dramatically in 1828 by supporting the tariff of that year. Until then his opposition to the protective system had been steady and energetic. In law the change came even earlier. It was clear in the Dartmouth College case of 1818. Finally, these were the years of Webster's first great addresses, and they too brilliantly reflected the sense of his developing nationalism. From a legal and political position to its rhetorical equivalent is a short step.

By 1830 the process of transformation was everywhere complete, its result an established fact, and if it seemed that having traveled so far in a relatively short period Webster might at any moment turn and move again in the opposite direction, events soon dispelled that fear, or hope — as the case may have been — and gave him in the bargain an excellent reason for staying precisely where he was. In January of 1830 he made two speeches in the Senate, each of them a reply to earlier speeches by Robert Y. Hayne of South Carolina. Ostensibly the subject of the Webster-Hayne debates was a resolution to limit the sale of Western lands. In fact they dealt with much else besides, and ultimately with the burning issue of state and national sovereignty. By the time Webster had finished there could be no doubt of the strength of his commitment to the principle of nationalism — in law, in politics, or in rhetoric.

The debates had a second effect. They added tremendously to Webster's reputation. Virtually overnight he became to his generation that larger-than-life figure he remained to the end. Searching for a way to express this expansion in scale the following year, George Ticknor compared him to Antaeus, "the fabulous giant of antiquity who gathered his strength from the very earth that produced him." [10] It was an apt image. It evoked, as Ticknor intended, both a sense of magnitude and the deep-rooted Americanness — the "generous nationality" — of Webster's principles and beliefs, and it did something further. To Ticknor and many men like him it was of the greatest significance that Webster had reached such impressive heights from singularly humble beginnings and after a formal training no better than ordinary common schools and a rural college could provide. Here was reassuring proof, which Ticknor especially was prone to need, of the potential inherent in American democratic institutions. This too the earthborn demigod Antaeus symbolized.

The praise of men like Ticknor must have pleased Webster, but chiefly as part of a more general phenomenon. Ticknor was an old friend and had little to offer but kind words. The fact that his admiration seemed to be shared by so many people, on the other hand — and people who lived beyond the narrow confines of Boston or New England — was enormously important. No doubt the thought that he might one day be President had occurred to Webster years before the debates with Hayne, but now for the first time he was widely mentioned as a possible candidate. This was heady wine, which he drank to its depths. For the next twenty-two years there was never a period when Daniel Webster was not, in one form or another, a candidate for the presidency.

No man can aspire to the presidency without its affecting his life and actions profoundly. There were innumerable differences that Webster's status as a candidate made, but one of the most important was the added stimulus it gave to his nationalism. Prior to 1830 his reputation had rested almost entirely on the skill and flexibility with which he defended the interests of his state and section. Even in the replies to Hayne a significant proportion of what he said could be interpreted merely as an attempt to rescue New England from Southern and Western charges of selfishness and injustice. The people of New England, of course, were delighted with all this advocacy, but from the standpoint of Webster's ambition it was hardly an asset. Only two of the seven Presidents from Washington to Jackson — and the only two not to be reelected to a second term — had been New Englanders. By 1840 the section's strength in the electoral college had fallen to 50 out of 294 votes, or a bare one sixth of the total. The inference was clear. Politically New England was weak and growing weaker all the time. If Webster were to be elected President he would have to associate himself with something larger than regional interests. Nationalism was an obvious solution, so obvious that if he had not already become a nationalist, his addition to the list of presidential hopefuls might well have made him one. Fortunately for his sake the issue was settled and there was even much in his particular variety of nationalism that admirably suited it to be a candidate's platform. To characterize the nation as the chief protector of local differences and local interests, for example, allowed him to maintain his position as a nationalist and still give New England the better part, if not all, of her due, which in turn was an invaluable piece of accommodation. New England was weak; by herself she could never have made Webster President, yet without her support that objective was equally unobtainable.

From the moment Webster thought of himself as a serious contender for the presidency, his nationalism and the rhetoric that expressed it became something calculated in the infinitely complex and often frustrating realm of presidential politics. If what he said admitted of varying interpretations, a part of its meaning, always, lay there. His definition of the ritual at Bunker Hill that June day in 1843 was a nationalist's definition, but it was also a candidate's appeal.

In the years since 1830 Webster's fame had grown steadily, but his larger ambition remained unrealized. For all the brilliance of his rhetoric and the sweeping vistas of his nationalism, his political following in the country as a whole was small. In 1836 the Massachusetts Whigs had nominated him for the presidency, but he received no electoral votes outside New England.[11] Four years later when that history threatened to repeat itself, he threw his support behind William Henry Harrison. At the time this seemed a good way to insure a nomination in 1844, but events proved otherwise. Indeed by 1843 Webster's stock as a presidential candidate had fallen to zero. He was out of power and out of favor in Whig circles everywhere, even in Massachusetts. And if that situation seemed disheartening, the factors that produced it were just beginning their operation in 1843; the decade ahead held no respite — though few men, and certainly not Webster, saw this then.

# Two
# Washington, 1841–1843

ON THE DAY — a little more than three years before the Second
Bunker Hill Address — when William Henry Harrison was in-
augurated, only a born pessimist would have questioned Webster's confidence. The nation was in safe hands and though
technically no decision had been made as to who would lead the
Whig party during the next four years or carry its standard in
1844, it was at least well understood the President himself would
not, which left Webster, as Secretary of State, the logical choice
in both cases. Within a month, however, Harrison was dead and
the entire situation had changed. Having given the impression
that he might accept Webster's primacy under Tippecanoe,
Henry Clay began at once to press his own claims as party
leader. For years the rivalry between Clay and Webster had operated like a polestar in anti-Jacksonian politics, a fixed point
around which everything else moved. Now Clay was issuing a
new challenge. From Webster's standpoint it was not a pleasant
prospect, and it became still less so when one added the figure of
Harrison's successor, who seemed bent on ruining them all,
himself included. John Tyler was a good Whig, but several
basic differences separated him from the majority of his party,
and he was both too honest and too poor a politician to skirt
those differences. He also gave every indication of harboring
ambitions of his own for 1844, which simply multiplied the developing confusion.

In Webster's mind what all this threatened — quite apart from his personal interest in the matter — was nothing less than the continued existence of the Whig party. A good many Whigs agreed with him. At any other time being wooed simultaneously from three different directions might have been a gratifying experience, but not now, especially when the suitors were of such different opinions as to what ought to be done once the match was consummated. On the other hand as severely threatened as they were by the situation, the Whigs — and Webster with them — could scarcely disavow all blame for its creation. Granted the times were difficult and fate had dealt an unexpected blow in Harrison's death, the ensuing struggle over party policy and leadership was still an internal affair, part and parcel of the organization itself, and clearly the responsibility of the men who comprised it.

## II

The Whig party had come into being during the administration of Andrew Jackson as an opposition party. At its birth it included a wide variety of different and potentially conflicting elements — former National Republicans, Anti-Masons, and disaffected Democrats of all sorts. In time those elements should have fused, but there is always a temptation to argue that they did not, that the Whig party remained to the end little more than a loosely formed opposition coalition. Its penchant for choosing popular military figures as candidates and then avoiding the niceties of party platforms, its relatively brief period of existence, and most of all the fact that on each occasion when, after the only two presidential candidates it ever elected had the misfortune to die in office, the inauguration of a successor brought a marked change in policy — all of these seem to argue a continuing and chronic instability.

In fact, however, such an indictment of the Whigs is unfair. The Democrats during those years displayed an all but equal fondness for candidates of military renown, and their platforms, while there may have been more of them, were often marvels of evasion. Moreover, considering that the Democratic party came into being in 1828 and by 1860 had broken down hopelessly along sectional lines, its existence as a national party in the pre-Civil War period was of only slightly longer duration than that of the Whigs. As for the changes in policy that followed the deaths of Harrison and Zachary Taylor, had Jackson died in 1830 the break in Democratic continuity would certainly have been as sharp.

In short, the Whig party was no more or less unstable than its rival. Granting, furthermore, its composite character and the definite disagreements that did exist between some of its adherents on crucial issues, it is still not difficult to outline a general body of Whig doctrine. To begin with, the Whigs demanded a strong national government, acting decisively to channel and develop the resources of the country. Specifically this meant Clay's American System: a protective tariff, a national bank, and internal improvements financed by the national government. In addition to these three positions, there were other, less important items: an effective general bankruptcy law, for example, and a commitment to a limited use of the veto power by the President. The vast majority of Whigs in 1840 were agreed as to the wisdom of such a program. Of the three leading contenders for the party's presidential nomination that year, two, Clay and Webster, were its chief formulators and Harrison, by his silence, gave it tacit approval. Amidst the general agreement only one group raised any substantial objection, and that was the group from which the party's vice-presidential candidate was drawn.

Today much in the Whig program seems progressive, even liberal. And it was, but only through the eyes of the twentieth century. The party's leaders considered themselves conservative and were proud to bear the title. It was the opposing philosophy of government, which advocated leaving the development of the nation's resources to the random, untrammeled energies of the people, that stood as the liberal doctrine of the period. Moreover, the party's program was clearly aimed at appealing to the "haves," as opposed to the "have-nots," in American society at the time. The tariff would most immediately benefit Northern manufacturers and large-scale producers of staple crops like hemp and sugar in the South. A national bank would be of greatest service to Eastern bankers, men who had an obvious interest in the maintenance of a sound currency. And internal improvements could vitally concern only those producers, of whatever, who produced more than they could use themselves or sell locally — a relatively small group in America even as late as 1860. Indeed, recognizing the avowed conservatism of the Whig party and given its frank appeal to the most powerful economic elements in the society, it was something of a wonder that its leaders entertained any hopes at all of securing the favor of electoral majorities. They did, however, and thanks to what, for want of a better phrase, might be called the theory of natural harmonies — a body of belief that underlies, surrounds, and penetrates the whole of American Whiggery like a kind of life-sustaining amniotic fluid.

According to the theory of natural harmonies all social classes, all economic interest, and all geographical sections of the country existed in a state of fundamental concord. Thus, any apparent conflict within the system was an affair of the moment, in no way related to the true interests of the individuals involved. Thus too, it was possible to give aid to a particular class, or interest, or section directly and at the same time benefit every other class, interest, or section. A protective tariff on textile manufactures, for example, became not just a favor granted a privileged group of mill owners, but a tangible boon to every American. Endlessly elaborated in campaign oratory, it was this sort of reasoning that enabled the Whigs to take their program with all its special appeals and benefits before the country and hope for a favorable hearing.

Successful as the theory of natural harmonies was at times in making the Whig program palatable, however, it had several severe limitations as a political philosophy. First it presupposed a highly intelligent and rather imaginative electorate. For a subsistence farmer in Arkansas to appreciate that a tariff raising the price of cotton cloth ultimately benefited him as much as it did a New England textile manufacturer was no mean feat of perception. Many Americans simply could not, or would not, attempt it. That difficulty, in turn, might have been more easily overcome had not the theory of natural harmonies also been in constant danger of denying the very essence of the political process: of denying the kind of bargaining and trading on specific issues that makes it possible for different groups to unite and act together in accomplishing ends desired by them all. Precisely to the extent that the natural harmonies of the Whig theory were "natural," to that extent was this sort of activity unnecessary — an attitude that may help explain why Whig politicians were generally less successful than their Democratic rivals, who had fewer misgivings about using the rhetoric of conflict.

The greatest shortcoming of the theory of natural harmonies, however, was not the short shrift it gave normal political processes. All too many of the stars in its heaven were fixed forever in their orbits, and if they did revolve around a central axis, the system as a whole moved slowly and nothing entered it and nothing departed. In an obvious sense this had to be. With everything so delicately poised, any violent motion, any addition or subtraction of mass, was bound to bring disaster. This was unfortunate, for it appeared to commit the Whigs to a constant defense of the status quo at a time when much in the country was in a state of flux and not a few Americans expected to benefit directly from that situation. Most of the time the party managed one way or another to reconcile the implications of its doctrine with the fact of change, as for example when it side-stepped the entire matter of social mobility in 1840 simply by discovering that in the United States social classes did not exist. But such efforts were difficult, and there always remained areas where no reconciliation was possible. The most crucial of those, as it turned out, was the question of territorial expansion.

With few exceptions the Whigs were steadfastly opposed to any acquisition of new territory. Within the existing boundaries of the nation harmony was an established fact. To extend those boundaries would only invite chaos. "With how much of mutual intelligence and how much of a spirit of conciliation and harmony," Webster asked in 1844, could "those who live on the St. Lawrence and the St. John . . . be expected ordinarily to unite in the choice of a President with the inhabitants on the banks of the Rio Grande del Norte and the Colorado?" The answer in his own mind was obvious. "You have a Sparta," he advised, "embellish it!" [1] That remark could well stand as a summation of the entire body of Whig doctrine.

Time would make the limitations of Whiggery painfully apparent to the party's leaders, but in 1840 the signs were still too dim to read. Indeed, in that year the Whig point of view, for all its limitations, admirably suited the emotional needs of the nation. A dozen years of conflict and change had brought the economy to the verge of ruin. It was time for a rest and an end, for the present, to innovations and experiments, especially those involving the currency. What the country needed was a stable government based on sound, tested principles. All of this, amid the tumult and excitement of the log cabin campaign, the Whigs promised, and for good measure they chose as a candidate a general who had received his first commission from George Washington. In a mood to accept the promise and the man who stood for it, Harrison's countrymen had given him the electoral votes of nineteen out of twenty-six states and a total of 53 per cent of the vote cast. No other Whig presidential candidate ever did as well.

The scope of the victory was as impressive as its size. In 1828 the party's most immediate predecessor, the National Republicans, had won no electoral votes west of New York or south of Maryland. By contrast, the Whigs carried a majority of the states in every section of the country in 1840. Only along the westernmost tier of states, where they lost Arkansas, Missouri, and Indiana together, was the showing notably poor. To complement the presidential victory the party also returned safe majorities to both houses of Congress. All told, it was a striking achievement and a tribute as much to the Whigs' organization as to their program and its convenient adaptation to the mood of the times. A decade of ceaseless labor had produced across the nation a host of ward, town, county, and state committees capable of functioning with remarkable effectiveness, while the lines of communication and command that tied the whole system together were strong and efficient.

No less than the essential features of the Whig program was that organization threatened by Harrison's unfortunate death.

For Webster's part, any misfortune that befell the Whigs was bound to affect him deeply. His stake in the party was tremendous. More than any other single individual, except Clay, he was responsible for its program and its organization. Its leaders were his friends; its doctrine nicely complemented his own rhetorical nationalism. Everything, in short, combined to make the association a close one. As close as it was, however, any political association in the end mattered to Webster chiefly as it led to, or away from, one goal. If it developed that the Whigs would not or could not make him President, if the party gave clear indications of preferring Henry Clay's lead to his own, or if it so bogged down in chaos and failure that victory under its standard seemed impossible, then it would become necessary to consider the value of other associations.

## III

In the growing confusion of the first few months of Tyler's presidency, Webster labored mightily to keep the peace, but it was a hopeless task. He watched the assembling of the special session of Congress that Clay had urged Harrison to call, knew that the first objective on the agenda of its Whig members was the establishment of a national bank, and knew, too, that right there trouble was bound to come. Tyler was unalterably opposed on states-rights constitutionalist grounds to the kind of bank that the majority of the Whigs — Clay and Webster included — favored. Though neither side in the dispute was likely to change its views, Webster repeatedly advised conciliation and compromise. "There is but one remedy for the urgent necessities of the country, but one hope for the salvation of the Whig Party," he argued, "it is *union,* immediate UNION. Let us try such a bank as we can agree upon and establish." [2] As often as the Secretary of State counseled union, however, and as strenuously as he worked to accomplish it, the rift in the party continued to grow. By September 9 the Whigs in Congress, under Clay's leadership, had passed two bank bills and Tyler had vetoed them both.[3] From such a crisis nothing could emerge unchanged.

On September 11, barely two days after the veto message had gone to Congress, five of the six members of the Cabinet resigned. The sixth — the only man who did not resign — was Webster. Given his aspirations and the turn events had taken, he had no alternative.

The night before the resignations Webster had met with the entire Massachusetts delegation in Congress to tell them what was about to happen and to ask their advice. At one point during the course of the meeting he referred to the pending resignations as a "Clay movement." [4] The label was accurate. From the beginning it had been Clay's strategy to use the bank issue first to check, and then to isolate, Tyler — and with him Webster — thereby making good his own claim to the succession. The breakup of the Cabinet was designed to complete the process. Four of the five members involved were committed Clay men. For Webster to have resigned, under the circumstances, would have signified nothing less than a complete desertion of the field to Clay in their long and bitter struggle over the prize of party leadership.

That by itself was a sufficient reason for staying, but there were others. Webster's decision left him in an excellent position to appeal to the Whigs in the role of party-unifier, which Clay could no longer do. Moreover, there was always a possibility that — everything else failing — some new combination cutting across existing party lines might develop to take Webster's lead. All of which, perhaps, Tyler himself meant to imply when, if the story is true, he greeted Webster's decision not to resign and thanked him for it, saying: "Give me your hand on that and now I will say to you that Henry Clay is a doomed man." [5]

No doubt Tyler considered it a foregone conclusion that Webster would be persuaded by such assurances. What induced the President to offer assurances, however, or to keep Webster on in the first place, was less readily apparent. Certainly he had an alternative. At their interview on the day of the resignations Webster offered to go with the rest if Tyler wished it. Far from accepting this proposal, Tyler had brushed it aside and instead welcomed his Secretary of State virtually with open arms. Considering that some of his closest political associates were advising him to dispense with Webster's services as quickly as possible and that Webster, along with the other members of the Cabinet, had been under heavy attack in the Tyler press, the President's decision must have seemed surprising. [6]

Why did he accept with such alacrity Webster's offer to remain in the Cabinet? Not, surely, because he found, or expected to find, in Webster an ally on the issue that had split the party, and if he did entertain any hopes on this score, they must have been dispelled quickly enough. On September 14 a letter, written by Webster to the paper's editors, appeared in the *National Intelligencer* explaining his reasons for not resigning. The second paragraph of the letter read: "I am perfectly persuaded of the absolute necessity of an institution under the authority of Congress, to aid revenue and financial operations, and to give the country the blessings of a good currency and cheap exchanges." [7] In spite of everything, on the bank question Webster felt as he had always felt. Nor did this probably surprise Tyler, or even greatly concern him. Time and the peculiarities of the situation were creating a new set of political imperatives that had little or nothing to do with the bank.

In the first place Tyler was quite unwilling to sacrifice all association with the Whig party. Whatever Whig support he could get he needed, and Webster, whose following in the party was large, represented one of the few remaining avenues to that support. But there was a second, even more pressing consideration involved. At odds as he was with his party on matters of domestic policy, the field on which Tyler could act with some hope of accomplishment had narrowed considerably. In fact the only area left to him was diplomacy and there, above all, he would need a good Secretary of State. By the close of 1841 the crisis in Anglo-American relations over the northeast boundary had come and gone, but a plan for final negotiations was just beginning to take shape. Tyler knew that Webster's services in those would be invaluable.

As long as it confined itself to party politics and the northeastern boundary there was nothing in Tyler's reasoning to give Webster cause for concern. He was as anxious as the President to effect a rapprochement between England and the United States.[8] Unfortunately, however, Tyler's diplomatic imagination did not stop with the mere settlement of a sixty-year-old dispute over a few thousand acres of virgin timberland. He had other, far grander plans in mind — plans that did pose a substantial difficulty for Webster.

A month to the day after the five Cabinet resignations reached Tyler's desk he wrote Webster a letter that even then must have startled the Secretary of State. For the most part the letter dealt with the new Cabinet, Tyler congratulating Webster "in an especial manner upon having such co-workers." There was also a warm assurance of presidential good will: "I shall truly rejoice in all that shall advance your fame." Welcome as such a remark may have been, what followed it most assuredly was not. "I gave you a hint as to the possibility of acquiring Texas by treaty —" Tyler wrote. "I verily believe it could be done — Could the North be reconciled to it would anything throw so bright a lustre around us?" [9] Texas! Apparently Tyler had broached the subject earlier, or "hinted" at it, so at least his mention of it here was not a complete surprise. On that initial occasion, however, Webster would have made his views quite clear and to find the matter still under consideration — given those views — was surely neither pleasant nor encouraging.

To any and all attempts to acquire Texas, Webster was bound to stand opposed, however much Tyler might seek thereby to cover them both with glory. The reasons were not difficult to understand. A half a decade before when annexation was first suggested, Webster had argued publicly against it.[10] To reverse that position would be embarrassing to say the least. There was, too, the long-standing Whig opposition to territorial expansion. And finally, even if a way around those objections could have been found, there remained the simple matter of political expediency.

Regardless of what may have occurred to him at odd moments, or of how he felt later, Webster still saw his future essentially in Whig terms. His position in the party, on the other hand, was becoming increasingly difficult. Shortly after the Cabinet resignations a group of some fifty ultra-Whig congressmen had issued an address reading Tyler, in effect, out of the party. Where this left Webster — the leader of Tyler's administration — was a perplexing question. For the time being his hold on Massachusetts was secure. On September 24 the Whig State Central Committee had met and evidenced, as Albert Fearing, one of its members, wrote Webster later, "a strong determination to support you in your present position." [11] Under the command of William Seward and Thurlow Weed the New York organization also remained loyal, thanks to the appointment of John Spencer as Secretary of War — a move especially urged on Webster by Seward. [12] And apart from Massachusetts and New York there were other pockets of support throughout the country on which Webster, personally, could count. [13] In every one of those places, including Massachusetts and New York, however, he was open to attack, and attacks there were, beginning late in 1841 and rising to a kind of crescendo in the early months of 1842. [14] In the midst of all this, one point was clear. Nothing would win the day for Webster's opponents more quickly, especially in the North and East, than the slightest suspicion he was laboring with Tyler to acquire Texas.

As convenient as it was for Webster and Tyler to continue their official relationship, then, they were from the beginning operating at cross-purposes. In the long run this was bound to prove troublesome for them both; whether it would over a shorter period remained to be seen. It helped that they knew where they stood with one another. Webster could suggest, and as long as the suggestions were reasonable Tyler's convenience would incline him to agree. The only danger was that Webster might exhaust his supply of reasonable suggestions and thus leave the President free to act on his own initiative. At that point Texas would become inescapable. The Texas government did little to help the situation from Webster's standpoint. Officially withdrawn in 1836, its offer of annexation was twice renewed in 1842.

Meanwhile, keeping Tyler away from Texas was only one of Webster's goals as Secretary of State after 1841. There were two others: to settle the northeastern boundary dispute and to find some less conspicuous, but still important, place within the administration to which he might "retire." As the months passed and the volume of criticism leveled at Tyler grew, this last became increasingly important. At the same time Webster also began to consider the possibility of developing a new political combination with himself and Tyler as its leaders. He well knew, however, that both objectives were doomed the moment Tyler made the least move toward Texas.

## IV

The simplest way to keep Tyler's mind off Texas was to distract it, ideally with some other, safer program of territorial expansion. As much as Webster opposed the whole idea of expansion, anything, almost, was preferable to Texas. Where to find a workable substitute for the object of Tyler's desires, on the other hand, was puzzling. Not until April 1842 did the first solution to that problem present itself. The source of the solution was Waddy Thompson.

Earlier in the year Thompson, himself an expansionist and advocate of annexation, had been sent to Mexico as United States minister. Once there he lost no time in exploring the possibilities for his favorite project. He also acquired a new one. In his first dispatch, dated April 29, he outlined a plan whereby Mexico might be induced to cede not only Texas, but California as well, in return for a settlement of the outstanding claims of American citizens against the Mexican government. Of the two territories, furthermore, Thompson considered California by far the more desirable. It was, in his opinion, "the richest, the most beautiful and the healthiest country in the world." [15]

Whatever Webster thought of the wonders of California, it did provide a convenient device for drawing Tyler's attention away from Texas. With typical caution the Secretary of State wrote Thompson and instructed him to proceed "to sound the Mexican Government upon the subject of a cession of the Territory upon the Pacific in satisfaction of these claims or some of them." At no point in the letter was there any mention of acquiring Texas, which Thompson in his dispatch had linked with the California project.[16]

After the initial instructions to Thompson and a tentative attempt at sounding out the British government, the negotiations over California were allowed to drift, at least for the next few months. Even if Webster had wished to push them to an early conclusion, he lacked the opportunity to do so. Already by the end of June, he was in the midst of the negotiations with Lord Ashburton over the Maine boundary.

Men at the time as well as historians since have questioned Webster's finesse in the Webster-Ashburton negotiations, but to the end of his life he remained proud of what he had accomplished in them and in the treaty that grew from them. Left unsettled in 1783 and constantly disputed since that time, the northeastern boundary was the principal subject of the negotiations, but there were others. The hoary issue of impressment, international extradition, arrangements for suppressing the African slave trade, the *Caroline* incident, the McLeod case, and the *Creole* affair had all contributed to the steadily worsening state of Anglo-American relations in recent years. In the end the treaty and its accompanying correspondence covered every major point at issue between the two countries — with one exception.[17] That exception, however, was a matter of some importance. Still jointly occupied under the Convention of 1818,

Oregon had begun to fill with settlers. The time when its future could be determined peaceably was passing.

On October 1, Edward Everett, whose conspicuous talents and loyalty to Webster amid the vagaries of Massachusetts politics had netted him the post of United States minister to the Court of St. James's, wrote his chief describing a conversation with Lord Aberdeen, the British Foreign Minister, about the recently completed treaty. In the course of the conversation Aberdeen brought up the subject of Oregon and remarked that he was at a loss to know why the treaty made no attempt at resolving the issue. Lord Ashburton had gone to America fully instructed with respect to it.[18] Two weeks later, when ratifications of the treaty were officially exchanged, Aberdeen reiterated his point.[19] In the meantime, Everett — anxious for a diplomatic success of his own — had suggested to Webster as early as the end of August that the time was ripe for an Oregon settlement and offered to take up the negotiations himself. Even without Aberdeen's remarks it was clear the British government wished the issue dispensed with as quickly as possible. No less a person than Sir Robert Peel had first suggested it to Everett, noting that if something were not done soon, "the settlement of the country" was bound to render it "still more embarrassing." [20] Through all of this Webster, with a single exception, maintained an absolute silence with regard to Oregon. Not until November 28 did he finally outline for Everett what he considered an acceptable basis for settlement, and even then he did not, nor did he ever, explain why nothing had been accomplished in the negotiations with Ashburton.

Since Ashburton had in fact come prepared to deal with the Oregon question, it may have been that no agreement was reached because his instructions made one impossible. Even so, it would have been necessary to discuss the matter at some length to determine that fact, and it was difficult to understand why Webster refrained from saying anything at all about such discussions to Everett. Either he did not care about Oregon, or he had other ends to serve with the issue.

Of the alternatives, the second was undoubtedly the correct one. Oregon represented an ideal solution to both the problems Webster faced during this period — finding substitutes for Texas to preoccupy Tyler and finding for himself a less vulnerable position within the administration than the one he held. The uses to be made of Oregon in the first case were obvious. As for the second, Webster gave a clear enough picture of what he had in mind the one time, prior to late November, he did mention Oregon to Everett. That was in a letter dated August 25, a good part of which was devoted to a singularly subtle and roundabout attempt to discover whether Everett would consider exchanging his post for Paris, thereby making room in London for Webster. "There are two or three subjects remaining for negotiation with England," he remarked in passing and then mentioned specifically: "1) Some formal stipulation for such cases as that of the Creole. 2) The Oregon Boundary. 3) A new arrangement about the W.I. trade." [21]

A mission to England with an Oregon settlement as its objective would have removed Webster from the center of the political stage and yet still left him with a role to play, a role that might well have resulted in a substantial measure of popular acclaim. Throughout the vicissitudes of the next eight months he held fast to the idea, though as time passed and the aspect of affairs changed, the details of the plan as well as what he hoped to accomplish by it underwent a number of significant modifications.

When the initial effort was made to sound Everett out on the possibility of relinquishing his post, the aspect of politics generally, and of Webster's situation in particular, was discouraging. With the end of the Maine negotiations the pressures on him to leave the administration had trebled. At the same time a Clay movement was gathering momentum everywhere. In several states — including Massachusetts — Whig conventions had even gone to the extent of placing the Great Compromiser's name formally in nomination. Tyler, on the other hand, appeared to be almost totally without support. To Webster this meant one thing: as he wrote Everett, "the President must hereafter look for support principally to that party which did not bring him to power"; and for such an arrangement Webster himself had little taste. "I do not expect to stay long where I am," he predicted. "I can bring the President no support, nor can I act with those on whom he is most likely hereafter to rely." [22] In this context a foreign mission became little more than a face-saving strategic retreat.

Two months later the situation had changed considerably. The fall elections resulted in a severe defeat for the Whigs, particularly in those areas where the Clay banner had been run up during the summer. Here was a scene that Webster could survey with confidence. "The result so far, is as disastrous to the Whig cause as was foreseen by all persons of any sagacity," he wrote Everett. "Blights and mildews afford the same auspices for good hope, as Mr. Clay's name does for political comfort and success." As for the future, a complete reorganization of the party was imminent, Webster believed. "The name may remain, but without entirely new leaders, the members of the party can never again be rallied." Clearly Webster saw himself, with Tyler, as one of those "new leaders," and if the pending reorganization were to involve him with certain elements of the Democratic party, he now apparently found little to object to in such a prospect. "A vast portion of the moderate and disinterested will join in support of the President; and there is reason to think some portion of the other party, composed of persons of like character will take a similar course." [23] The time had come to consider the value of new associations.

Bright as the aspect of affairs had become, it in no way altered

Webster's desire to go to England. An attempt at so difficult and complex a party realignment might fail, in which case to have been some place other than in the thick of the negotiations would definitely be an advantage. On the other hand, the problem of getting to England had become rather more difficult, chiefly as a result of Everett's reluctance to give up his post. He had hinted at his feelings in this respect in a letter to Webster dated September 16.[24] He also communicated with Caleb Cushing on the subject and in terms a good deal plainer than those he used to his chief. "Had it been proposed that after I have been here a reasonable and usual term I should give way in order to be succeeded by Mr. W.," he wrote, "I should have consented readily. But to be displaced before I am warm in my seat is a different affair. It cannot, I think, be reasonably expected that I should become a party to any arrangement for that purpose." This information Cushing was free to give the President, but Everett went on to "charge you by our ancient friendship to let it go no further." [25] The erratic congressman from Salem, however, had become one of Webster's closest allies so that sooner or later Everett's letter probably came before the very eyes he least wished to see it.

Everett's unwillingness to leave England was an inconvenient, but scarcely insurmountable, obstacle to Webster's goal. One relatively simple way around it was a special mission, of the sort Lord Ashburton's had been, from the United States to Britain. In proposing the idea to Everett, Webster was careful to state, of course, that it had been conceived not "from any want of confidence in your skill and ability, but as a return of the respect showed to us by Lord Ashburton's mission" [26] — an assurance that may or may not have satisfied Everett's conception of what was due him.

Ordinarily the special mission would have been an apt solution to Webster's problem, but while the details of the plan were being worked out the shape of affairs in general underwent a marked change. From the beginning it had been his intention to use Oregon and California to draw Tyler's attention away from Texas. Their value in that connection, however, depended on whether or not there was a reasonable chance of acquiring them, and a series of incidents now occurred that rendered the issue a good deal less promising in both cases.

The first incident involved California. It was an *opéra bouffe* affair, of little long-range importance, but at the time it embarrassed Webster and the United States government exceedingly. On October 19 Commander Thomas A. C. Jones of the Pacific Fleet, acting under the impression — received, apparently, from reading an incorrect newspaper account — that the United States and Mexico were at war, sailed into the harbor of Monterey and demanded its surrender. Finding himself both outmanned and outgunned, the Mexican officer of the port complied with Jones's demand promptly. The following day Jones discovered his error and just as quickly apologized and left. Though word of what had happened did not reach Washington until early in January, by the end of the month Jones was removed from command, the appropriate notes had all been exchanged, and Mexican-American relations were restored to normal.[27] Still, the whole passage did little to aid the negotiations over California.

In the meantime Oregon too was becoming a problem, and if anything an even greater one than California. In this case the source of the difficulty was Senator Louis Linn of Missouri. For several years Linn had been attempting to make an issue of Oregon in Congress, though with little effect. In August 1841 and again in January the following year he had proposed resolutions requesting the President to give the British notice that the United States wished to terminate the joint occupation agreement. On both occasions the matter was referred to the Committee of Foreign Relations and no further action was taken. Having lost the point Linn changed his approach. In December 1842 he offered two new resolutions, and this time met with a good deal more success.

The first of the resolutions called for extending United States commercial law to Oregon, the establishment of a chain of forts along the route to the territory, and finally the actual sale of land within Oregon to settlers by the federal government. Neither of the first two proposals was especially unusual, but the third was, and so was the resolution's preamble that described the United States title to Oregon as "certain" and stated flatly that it would "not be abandoned." [28] Had the resolution passed with its third provision and the preamble unchanged, any hope of an Oregon settlement would have been at an end. Moreover Linn's second resolution was equally troublesome. It requested the President to inform the Senate why no agreement with respect to Oregon had been reached during the Webster-Ashburton negotiations, and further to explain the nature and extent of any exploratory talks that might have taken place on the subject. [29]

Ultimately, neither of Linn's resolutions did the damage they might have. The first — with a reworded preamble — passed the Senate but was reported out of committee unfavorably in the House, [30] and Tyler simply refused to comply with the request of the second, deeming it not at that time "consistent with the public interest to make any communication on the subject." [31] As surely as Webster had escaped what could have been a catastrophe of major proportions, however, Linn's resolutions cost him something. First, by bringing up the Oregon question in the manner they did, the resolutions rendered the negotiations with England perforce more difficult, and second, they served to reinforce in the minds of a number of Americans a belief in the validity of a United States claim to all of the Oregon territory, thereby increasing the potential opposition to a compromise settlement — the only kind of arrangement Webster ever envisioned.

*

In view of the growing number of complications attaching to the California and Oregon questions, it now seemed wise to settle them both as quickly as possible and even, if practicable, to combine them. The suggestions for doing the latter may have come from Tyler during the Ashburton negotiations.[32] Lord Aberdeen mentioned it to Everett in October in one of their conversations about Oregon. As Everett described Aberdeen's plan the United States was to accept the Columbia River as its boundary to the north and northwest "in consideration of some extension to the South, to be obtained from Mexico, so as to give us another port in that direction." Aberdeen did not say so, but Everett assumed the extension south was "to be procured for us by Great Britain," since if the United States were to obtain it directly from Mexico it could be, he pointed out, "no consideration for a concession, on our part, to Great Britain." [33]

Aberdeen apparently failed to renew his suggestion after October, and Webster took no immediate notice of it. At the end of January, however, he instructed Everett to explore the possibilities of a settlement almost identical to the one outlined in the British proposal. He prefaced his remarks by noting that Oregon was "exciting a good deal of interest in Congress" and later asserted that as to "Oregon alone" he hardly knew what instructions to give Everett since he could no longer tell "what sort of treaty two thirds of the Senate would be sure to agree to." Specifically what he had in mind was a tripartite agreement involving Mexico, the United States, and Britain in which Mexico would cede upper California to the United States, the Oregon question would be settled on a compromise basis, and Mexico would be paid an undetermined amount of money to be used in meeting the claims of British and American citizens against its government. Toward such an agreement both the Senate and the British government, he believed, would be favorably inclined. Waddy Thompson was attempting to determine Mexico's interest in the plan, and the Mexican minister in Washington would also be sounded out.[34]

In confiding all this to Everett, Webster neglected to tell him only one thing, and that was how difficult it must have been to get Tyler to accept precisely this form of the plan. The President's passion for diplomatic accomplishment had diminished not a whit, and as the possibility of acquiring either California or Oregon lessened he had begun to hedge his bets.

The idea of combining the California and Oregon questions in a single negotiation was perfectly acceptable to Tyler. Where he differed with Webster was over whether those two issues alone ought to be combined in this manner. His own inclination was to throw Texas into the diplomatic hopper along with California and Oregon. He made this clear in a note written to Webster sometime during January in which he expressed his agreement with the tripartite plan, but argued in addition for putting "into the same treaty" some provision for the "joint recognition of Texas." He was aware that "Texas might not stand alone," but neither possibly, "would the line proposed for Oregon." This being the case a combination of all three issues seemed the wisest course. "Texas would reconcile all to that line [for Oregon], while California would reconcile or pacify all to Oregon." [35]

Tyler had proposed only a joint recognition of Texas by the three powers, but recognition of Texas by Mexico was a logical preface to annexation. It would have eliminated what had been from the beginning one of the strongest objections to the move: the danger of war with Mexico. Webster knew this, and if he managed to convince Tyler that Texas should be kept out of the California and Oregon negotiations — as apparently he did — he must have known too that it was more in the nature of a conditional truce than an absolute victory. The President had agreed to wait a little longer, but that was all.

## V

Thus far Webster had been able to control events or at least deal with them in such a way that his ultimate objectives still admitted some hope of accomplishment. By the end of January 1843 that was ceasing to be the case. Tyler's renewed interest in Texas was one aspect of the change. An equally unnerving development was the opposition of the British government to the idea of a special mission. At Webster's request Everett had taken the matter up with both Aberdeen and Ashburton, who both felt that such a step was too extreme under the circumstances.[36] When outlining the proposed tripartite agreement to Everett, Webster noted the objection, but said unless the British government were absolutely opposed a mission would be sent regardless. At the same time he took the precaution of inquiring whether Everett would accept a mission to China should one be undertaken.[37]

The British attitude toward a special mission was troublesome, not simply for its own sake, but because it deprived Webster and Tyler of one of their strongest arguing points before Congress in raising the necessary funds for the project. As it was they could hardly claim England would welcome such a mission, and the required amendment to the civil and diplomatic appropriations bill lost in the House Foreign Affairs Committee by a vote of three to six.[38] The vote, too, was indicative of yet another of the difficulties Webster now faced.

Every one of the six men against the amendment was a Whig. It had been proposed by John Quincy Adams, who undoubtedly pointed out in so doing that Tyler was quite eager to send a mission and wished the means made available as quickly as possible. This information he had on good authority from Cushing, and both men voted for the measure.[39] As for the six Whigs who did not, what their action suggested — and most emphatically — was how wide the gulf between the President and his party remained for all that might have narrowed it.

After the congressional elections of 1842 Webster had looked forward confidently to a sweeping political reorganization. It was always his belief, however, that the disastrous outcome of the elections would force a substantial number of Whigs to rally around the President so that the resulting organization — which he and Tyler together would lead — would be a combination of elements from both parties. Webster was quite unprepared to rely solely on the Democrats. Tyler, on the other hand, had fewer qualms about such an arrangement, and the longer the predicted Whig rally delayed, the readier he seemed to switch his allegiance completely. The moment he did so Webster's presence in the administration was bound to become a nuisance. Already by the end of February there were rumors: reports that Tyler would be "relieved" if Webster decided to step aside. "I could not come to any other conclusion than that your position kept him from receiving the . . . support of the opposition," one informant wrote after an interview with the President.[40]

With the California and Oregon negotiations virtually at a standstill, with all hope of a special mission gone, and with Tyler turning irrevocably toward Texas and the Democratic party, there was little Webster could offer the President and even less to be gained, from his own standpoint, by remaining in the Cabinet. Still he was slow to reach a decision. Even before the vote on the appropriations amendment he had confided to Robert C. Winthrop, the Whig Representative from Boston, that he was to be, as Winthrop put it, "a private citizen ere long,"[41] but that prediction he doubtless made more with an eye to maintaining the little standing he had left in the Massachusetts Whig organization than anything else. For a month longer at least, he vacillated and later, with his mind substantially made up, he continued to explore other possibilities. In April he was still pressing the Mexican minister about California,[42] and in the meantime he had made one final attempt to get to England.

His approach on this occasion was to make Everett a definite offer of the China mission. In the absence of any reply to his earlier offers he even had the appointment confirmed by the Senate. Both Tyler and Adams wrote Everett urging him to take the post. Adams, however, was chiefly interested in getting the best man for what he considered a vitally important undertaking. He had nothing but scorn for the other aspects of the situation. "It is," he confided to his diary, "the back door by which Webster skillfully secures to himself a safe retreat from the Tyler Cabinet."[43] No doubt the same thought occurred to Everett. But here Webster himself took pains to allay it, protesting that there was "not one chance in a thousand" he would go to England — whatever happened.[44] If Everett remained unconvinced, Webster's statement at least gave him a convenient basis for turning the post down, which he did in a letter to the President dated April 18.[45]

By the time Everett wrote Tyler, Webster had already decided to leave the Cabinet. He would probably still have gone to England had the opportunity presented itself, but Everett's letter insured that it would not. The letter arrived in Washington on May 7, and the following day Webster formally resigned as Secretary of State. Writing Everett a week later, he found little to approve in the scene he was leaving behind. "There is danger that the present Administration will accomplish little more of good," he said and noted in particular the way Tyler "throws himself on the loco-foco party." For the future Webster would return to his law practice and, he added, "I am building a room for a Library at Marshfield, shall there collect my books, and regard that place as home." He said nothing of his disappointment but hinted at it, perhaps, when speaking of Everett's original appointment to England and Washington Irving's as minister to Spain. "Yourself and Irving," he wrote, "are the principal monuments of my Administration of the Department. It is well the appointments were made when they were. We were then all 'going' as the phrase is, for honor and renown." [46] He may also have been telling Everett in a roundabout way that he bore him no grudge for refusing to give up his post, as apparently he did not.

## VI

Webster loved Marshfield and had from the moment he first saw it twenty years before. More than once in that time he had gone there to find consolation in its sea breezes and gently rolling landscape, and now especially he needed those things.

Four years earlier, in 1839, when he withdrew as a candidate for the Whig presidential nomination in favor of Harrison, it was with the expectation that in the normal course of events he would be the old general's successor. But then the course of events had turned out to be anything but normal. In the ensuing crisis Webster sided with Tyler largely out of necessity, but also because his only remaining hope of success lay there. As futile as that hope proved, it might not have had it not been for two things: Tyler's ambition to be a candidate in 1844 and his desire to annex Texas.

Nor had it been a question of the President's ambition alone would Webster necessarily have failed as he did. He might have gone further with Tyler in courting the Democrats, and as long as his own claim four years later went unchallenged he could have let the President have his way in 1844. The loss in this case would not have been great, and party loyalty always mattered less to Webster than securing the object of his ambitions. In the end it was not Tyler's desire to succeed himself so much as Texas, the device he chose to make this possible, that determined Webster's situation. Moreover, even if Webster was wrong about Tyler's candidacy — as he may have been[47] — the President's interest in Texas would still have been a problem of major proportions.

In a long and varied career in politics Webster hardly proved himself to be the least flexible of men. In fact so flexible was he that his categorical refusal to associate himself with Tyler's Texas plans almost seems surprising, considering how much was at stake. There were good reasons for not doing so surely, but they might have been circumvented — and perhaps would have been — except for a single issue that lay behind every one of them.

That issue was slavery. The Whig party explicitly opposed all territorial expansion, yet Webster could move to acquire both Oregon and a substantial piece of California. The difference was that there was little likelihood slavery would ever exist in either place, while in Texas it was not only established but flourishing. Tyler himself understood full well the source of Webster's opposition to annexation. "Slavery," he wrote at one point. "I know that is the objection." [48]

Webster's contest with Tyler over Texas was not his first encounter with the issue of slavery in politics, but it did mark a significant change in the way the issue presented itself. For the first time it had become the principal point around which he had to chart his course. Given his success it was perhaps fortunate — at least for the sake of his own comfort and peace of mind — that he saw no further into the future than men ever have.

In the years before 1840 Webster had formulated a position on slavery that up to that time met admirably both the imperatives of politics and the imperatives of his own nationalism. In essence it was no different from the stated views of most Northern politicians. It involved three basic points: that slavery was, as he put it, "a great moral, social and political evil"; that nothing under any circumstances should be done to favor or encourage its further extension; and finally, that the Constitution having found slavery already in existence in some places, recognized it, and given it a number of "solemn guarantees," Congress was powerless to do anything about it in those places and it was incumbent on every good citizen to fulfill the specified guarantees.[49]

If there was a certain degree of moral turpitude involved in maintaining that slavery was wrong and at the same time refusing to interfere with it where it existed, that attitude — adhered to by Northerners — had the virtue of making national political organization possible, and only within the context of such organization, Webster believed, could any permanent solution to the slavery problem be found. If, too, there was little to distinguish Webster's views from those of almost every other successful Northern politician of the period, on one point he did go substantially beyond the majority of his colleagues. That was in recognizing the depth of feeling on the subject in the North. As early as 1837 he had pointed out that slavery was no longer merely "a question of politics"; that it had "struck a far deeper-toned chord." "It has arrested the religious feeling of the country," he argued. "It has taken strong hold on the consciences of men." Nothing could be more foolish, or dangerous, he felt, than failing to take this development seriously. "He is a rash man, indeed, and little conversant with human nature, and especially has he a very erroneous estimate of the character of the people of this country, who supposes that a feeling of this kind is to be trifled with or despised."[50]

It could, however, "be reasoned with." That Webster had to assume or his entire case lapsed into irrelevance. Fortunately the assumption was not a difficult one for him to make. Balance presupposed the operation of reason throughout the system. A clear-sighted reasonableness, which saw in a concern with the protection of others' interests the best protection for one's own, was the basis of character. A reasonable mind, too, would perceive that for all the differences dividing the slaveholding South and the free North, there remained a solid bedrock of common culture uniting them. And finally, when it came to translating those insights into practical policy, would it not be through the medium of institutions that were themselves a triumph in the reasonable adjustment of political ends and means? The reasonable solution reasonably arrived at: that was the quintessence of balance and of Webster's position on slavery.

In 1837 slavery was not a major issue in national politics. Six years later it was becoming one and had already made a substantial difference in Webster's life. Had he been more percipient, he might have wondered if one could go on indefinitely assuming the fundamental reasonableness of Northern antislavery sentiment, or asked, perhaps, what the consequences of having guessed wrong would be. What if so "religious" a feeling were coaxed or driven beyond the bounds of intelligent moderation? What then would the imperatives of politics and rhetoric dictate, and that would become of national balance? As it happened the Texas question provided an apt field for speculation on all of those points, but almost certainly the relevant questions went unasked, at least in May of 1843.

There was too much else to think of. During the months of his association with Tyler, Webster's standing in the Whig party — in Massachusetts as well as in the country at large — had fallen to virtually nothing. A major job of rebuilding lay before him, and logically the place to begin was at home. By the time he had finished, however, Webster would find it necessary to ask some of the questions he had failed to ask earlier.

# *Three*
# Massachusetts, 1838–1845

THE MASSACHUSETTS WHIG PARTY to which Webster returned in 1843 resembled a private club far more closely than it did a modern political organization. Linked by a sturdy network of family, social, and financial ties, the men who controlled it were close personal friends. They took shares in the same business ventures, they supported the same worthy causes, their children married one another. In State Street offices and Beacon Hill drawing rooms they met daily, and out of quiet conversations in such places party policy and party strategy grew almost by accident.

Thus organized the party ought to have been weak, but it was not, at least in terms of achievement. Founded in 1834 on the twin issues of the tariff and opposition to King Andrew, it had a virtually unbroken record of success at the polls. Only once in the period prior to 1840 was the Whig candidate not chosen in the annual statewide gubernatorial elections, and the showing on other levels was equally impressive. In canvass after canvass the people of Massachusetts returned Whig legislatures, Whig congressmen, and Whig presidential electors. Nationally the party never overcame its minority position. In Massachusetts it not only began as the majority party, but managed to preserve that standing over a considerable length of time.

Because the party was so successful its members were content to let it run on unchanged. Elsewhere in the country the forms of political organization were undergoing radical transformation in the years before 1840. Power was being more broadly distributed, and at the same time political activities were becoming more routinized. To the Massachusetts Whigs, however, innovations seemed unnecessary, and the few that were tried made little practical difference. Even the substitution of the nominating convention for the old caucus system failed to alter the basic pattern. Power remained the property of a relatively small group of men who exercised it informally and in private, secure in the knowledge that under the right circumstances matters could be settled just as smoothly — and effectively — before a convention as they could be before a caucus.

The right circumstances in this case amounted to a state of fundamental agreement among the men themselves, which in the beginning could be taken for granted. As time passed, however, agreement became increasingly difficult to achieve in certain areas. The trouble began in 1837 as a difference of opinion between two of the party's leading figures. By 1842 the entire organization was involved and the affair had had national repercussions. The speed with which a single breach in the inner circle became a full-scale factional war surprised many people, but it was hardly beyond understanding. With little more than personal relationships to give it structure and direction the party had always been in a precarious position, despite its success. If anything, success merely increased the danger by removing those pressures from without that ordinarily operate to enforce cohesion and organizational unity.

For all its clublike intimacy — and its success — then, the party Webster found on his return was divided. Whatever course he might follow to improve his standing with the Massachusetts Whigs would have to take account of that fact. Nor was it the only item to be weighed in the balance. The growing strength of antislavery sentiment in the state was another, and one which ultimately would dwarf everything else in importance. But in May 1843, the slavery issue was still barely a ripple on the surface of Bay State politics; the split in the Whig party remained the major problem. From Webster's standpoint, too, it had a special urgency. He was involved as all Whigs were, but on an even more fundamental level he was involved because the quarrel that produced the split had been his originally and was his still, six years later. If he needed an explanation for his current difficulties with the party it lay there. There and in the character and ambitions of the man who had first taken issue against him — Abbott Lawrence.

## II

Like Webster, Abbott Lawrence was a person of singular ability, but his ability manifested itself in a totally different direction. He was above all an organizer. Adept at managing men in institutional situations and making both conform to his own particular vision of economic and political reality, he did so by dint of logic, patience, and careful attention to detail. His methods were ever those of the successful businessman he was. He had none of Webster's genius for moving men's hearts with words. Beyond the realm of practical affairs his knowledge was slight; his political philosophy never amounted to more than a few, very simple propositions that two headings — the protective tariff and the Whig party — would have summarized nicely. In the end, apart from the general matter of ability, Lawrence resembled Webster in one way, and one way only. Both men devoted their lives to the pursuit of power.[1]

When Lawrence first came to Boston in 1808, his brother Amos recalled later, he had three dollars in his pocket. Forty-seven years later when he died he may well have been, as Robert

Winthrop said he was, "the most important person" in the community.[2] He was certainly one of the richest. His fellow Bostonians, moreover, had cause to be grateful for his success since Lawrence had arranged for them to benefit substantially from it — a fact that no doubt explained a good deal of the importance he had acquired in the minds of men like Winthrop, who were hardly prone to applaud success for its own sake. In his will Lawrence left $10,000 to the Boston Public Library, $50,000 for the construction of model lodging houses for the poor in Boston, and a like amount to the Lawrence Scientific School. His benefactions during his lifetime had been equally grand: another $50,000 to the Scientific School and the payment, from 1847 on, of the full salary of one of its faculty members, plus innumerable other thousands of dollars given away in smaller amounts for other purposes.

What made it all possible was the business of textile manufacturing, which Lawrence himself entered rather late. He came to Boston originally to work for his older brother Amos, an importer who dealt chiefly in English goods. The association, and the business, proved profitable. Within five years the brothers had formed a partnership under the name A. & A. Lawrence with a capital of $50,000. At the time it was the largest house of its kind in the city.

For a number of years, A. & A. Lawrence did quite well, but then the tariff, and the rising domestic textile industry began to cut into its profits. By the early 1820s the brothers were shifting their activities to the marketing of domestic textiles, which they did so successfully that by the end of the decade they provided the principal outlet for the mills at Lowell. From selling textiles to manufacturing them was a short step. In 1830 Lawrence purchased an interest in the Lowell mills, and from there he went on to involve himself heavily in the development and promotion of land and waterpower facilities elsewhere along the Merrimack. The area of his chief interest in this connection was the town that eventually bore his name. With the development of Lawrence several new concerns were established, one of them, in 1849, the Atlantic Cotton Mills, of which Lawrence became principal stockholder and president. Long before then, however, he had added another interest to textile manufacturing and philanthropy.

Like most other Boston merchants of the period Lawrence was at first strongly opposed to the idea of a protective tariff. Yet as his involvement in the domestic textile industry grew, his opinions changed just as Webster's had. Where Webster marked his conversion in the Senate, however, Lawrence did so by becoming a delegate to the 1827 Harrisburg convention on the promotion of domestic manufactures. His presence there was a major victory for the cause of protection, but it may have been even more significant in other ways.

When the convention opened there were delegates from thirteen of the twenty-four states, a large group of influential politicians, editors, and manufacturers. The sessions lasted five days, and by the end of that time the delegates had agreed to cooperate in obtaining higher duties on a wide variety of manufactures, including textiles of all sorts. Such a gathering, working so harmoniously toward such a desirable end, must have appealed to Lawrence. No doubt too it was stimulating to meet and talk with men from different parts of the country and to find oneself so carefully listened to, so obviously respected. For all the opportunities it offered, Boston at times was rather restrained, and restraining. There had always been that in Lawrence's nature which rendered the bold venture — the broad field of action — fascinating, and this part of his make-up, apparently, neither his adopted city nor business ever satisfied completely. During the War of 1812 he had applied for a commission in the army. Unfortunately it failed to arrive until after the war was over.

The Harrisburg convention may or may not have been the

wellspring of Lawrence's political ambitions, but within a very few years thereafter he was standing for election to Congress from the Boston district. Altogether between 1834 and 1840 he served one full term and part of another in the House. For a man in his position there was nothing unusual about this kind of political activity. Only a few years before he took his seat, his good friend Nathan Appleton had served for a brief period. Boston businessmen representing Boston interests: it was a thoroughly practical arrangement and for some almost an obligation. The men who felt so obliged, however, rarely did more than serve a term or two in the House; certainly Appleton never did. But Lawrence's case was more complicated. Writing in his diary early in 1842 Amos A. Lawrence, Abbott's nephew, observed of his uncle: "He still grasps at money though he has more than a million and is the richest man of his age here. He loves power too and office. He does not grow better nor happier as he gets older." [3]

In the beginning Lawrence's political ambitions posed little difficulty for Webster. The two were old friends. Lawrence entered politics, in fact, as one of Webster's chief lieutenants when the Whig party was just drawing a first tentative breath. His particular responsibility was the Massachusetts organization, which he worked tirelessly to develop. He was also more than willing in 1836 to make every effort possible to secure the Whig presidential nomination for the Bay State's proudest adopted son. "This should be your destiny," he wrote Webster the year before the election, "and your friends ought in justice to do for you all that may be required.[4] Three years later John Quincy Adams noted that Lawrence had been "for many years devoted to Mr. Webster, and the main pillar of his support, both pecuniary and political.[5]

By the time Adams made this observation, however, the rift

between Lawrence and Webster had already begun to develop, for as happy as he had been to support Webster in 1836, Lawrence was making no secret of the fact that he felt differently about 1840. The trouble was that even if Webster could get a nomination, the results of 1836 seemed to indicate he would never be elected. With three other Whig candidates in the field, he had received no electoral votes outside of Massachusetts.

For Webster's supporters the election had indeed been a disaster, and many of them would have agreed with Lawrence about the future. Robert Winthrop, for example, was convinced the chances were hopeless. Yet he also believed that keeping "the great man" as he put it, "in good heart and in firm co-operation with the party here and elsewhere" was worth whatever supporting his ambitions cost, and to this end he felt it essential "not to disgust or alienate" Webster "by an appearance of disaffection or abandonment among his natural defenders." [6] Winthrop's line of reasoning was plausible, but for someone in Lawrence's position it by-passed the essential point. If Webster's chances were hopeless, then it was foolish to throw away the bargaining power of the Massachusetts Whig organization by continuing to sponsor him, especially when that power could be used to further other aims and other careers. The only intelligent course was to make oneself as useful as possible, as early as possible, to some candidate with a reasonable hope of success. Politics being what they were, one was sure to benefit in the long run.

By 1838 Lawrence had definitely decided to support Clay for the nomination. This decision he communicated to Webster in an interview that took place in May. Later Lawrence told Edward Everett what had happened, and Everett in turn passed the information on to Winthrop. Everett himself agreed with Winthrop that Webster should not be abandoned, but he also felt that "hammering upon a nail that will not go" was "the poorest sport" he knew. As for Lawrence, he had told "the party most interested," and in no uncertain terms according to Everett, "that the nail could not and would not go, and ought no longer to be driven." [7]

When the contest between Webster and Lawrence over the 1840 nomination began, its result was by no means a foregone conclusion. At the same time he noted how close the relations between Webster and Lawrence had been in the past, Adams remarked on their difference over the nomination and observed in passing that Lawrence was "perhaps, the most leading man of Whig politics in Boston." [8] There could be no mistake about Lawrence's power. The loss of his support presented a major difficulty. Moreover, his was not the only support Webster would have to do without. For years John Davis with all his integrity and rustic dignity had served the state loyally — in the House, as governor, and finally, from 1835 on, in the Senate. If he sometimes felt such service deserved a better reward than it was likely to get as long as Webster dominated the scene, this was only natural. Then, too, it must have been galling to find oneself so often "the other Senator" from Massachusetts. Whatever his reasons, Davis did become Lawrence's ally at this point. Harrison Gray Otis was also a Clay man and in this case the two corresponded frequently. Clay's letters to Otis — full of statements about the hopelessness of Webster's cause and suggestions that his name be withdrawn at once by the Massachusetts Whigs — mention Lawrence and Davis as people to whom these views could safely be communicated. [9]

Both members in good standing of the party's inner circle, Otis and Davis were an impressive addition to Lawrence's ranks, but the array of strength Webster could field was even more formidable. Of his close associates Rufus Choate, Caleb Cushing, Winthrop, and Everett all remained loyal and the last two were particularly well placed to be of service. Winthrop at the time was speaker of the Massachusetts House of Representatives and chairman of the Whig State Central Committee, while Everett was governor of the state. On the lower levels of the party organization Webster's position was equally strong. No one could command a greater measure of support from the rank and file, and certainly not Lawrence, whose influence outside of Boston was still slight.

As powerful as Lawrence's forces were, then, Webster still enjoyed an advantage over them. That advantage was hardly substantial enough to inspire unlimited confidence, however, and there were definite reservations attached to it. Everett's point about driving a nail that would not go was a warning. If Webster continued to press his case he would have to pay a price in lost support — Everett's and probably others'. But happily for Webster this never came to pass, for he himself was under no illusion as to how matters stood. Outside of Massachusetts and western New York, support for his nomination fell off markedly. Lawrence's plain talk may have helped bring the point home, but more than likely Webster had already read the direction of the wind and set his course accordingly.[10] With his own chances as poor as they were and Clay the only other alternative, everything pointed to Harrison.

As the contest developed, the principal objective of Webster's allies became to maintain the Massachusetts party's commitment to him while Harrison's cause gathered momentum around the country. When the proper time came — once a few of the other large state organizations had declared for Tippecanoe — then the necessary shift could be made. It was important not to move too quickly, however, for there was always a danger that, lacking a sufficient show of strength from Harrison, the Massachusetts Whigs might be stampeded into Clay's camp the moment Webster released them. As early as June 1838 Webster had informed Everett of his decision to withdraw from the race, saying, as Everett put it in a letter to Winthrop, "that his only anxiety was that Mass. should keep herself in a position to support Gen'l H." [11] By September Winthrop himself could report to his good friend and fellow Central Committee member John Clifford: "I find the idea that Harrison is to be the man, whether with or without our aid, is gaining ground rapidly," to which he added, "I rejoice we hold on to Webster as we did last winter and there we must hold until we are ready for a harmonious rally upon somebody else." [12]

In the meantime Clay had begun to suspect that Webster's friends were working for Harrison's nomination. The first indication that such a coalition existed, he wrote Otis, was an unusually bitter attack on himself in the pages of the Boston *Atlas* "after that same Atlas had enjoined forebearance in the discussion of the pretentions of Presidential Candidates." The next step was the nomination of Harrison and Webster for President and Vice President respectively by the Anti-Masonic convention in Philadelphia. "I learn that Mr. W. was apprized beforehand and approved of the nomination," he remarked. From there Clay went on to argue that these actions on the part of "the friends of Messers. H. & W." plainly absolved his own associates "from all obligation to practice further silence and forebearance," and lest Otis miss the point he added: "I need not say to you that scarcely anywhere would action favorable to me tell with more effect than in your legislature. But all these matters I leave to the descreation [sic] of yourself and other friends." [13] It was just prior to this that Adams had noted of Lawrence, "He now thinks Webster has coalesced with Harrison against Clay upon the Presidential competition, and is himself for Clay." [14]

With Everett and Winthrop holding the Massachusetts Whigs firmly in line, the amount of political pressure Lawrence could bring to bear on Webster was limited. There were other kinds of pressure, however. The panic of 1837 and the subsequent depression had strained Webster's personal finances almost to breaking. Long accustomed to relying on the generosity of Boston businessmen to help meet expenses, he was more than ever in need of their aid. Of the group of regular contributors, Lawrence had always been one of the most generous; now his name was absent from the list of donors to a $2500 fund collected for Webster in December of 1838,[15] and several months later, when asked to solicit money in Webster's behalf by Thomas W. Ward, Lawrence begged to be excused, though he did send Ward the names of various men who might be approached for contributions.[16]

Had Lawrence been Webster's only source of supply his strategy might have worked, but fifty other pockets were opened as generously as ever. Webster got the money he needed,[17] Clay's suggestions came to nothing, and Harrison's candidacy grew stronger all the time. By the spring of 1839 the way was clear for Webster to withdraw publicly as a candidate. He did so in a letter of June 12 to the people of Massachusetts.[18] The letter nowhere mentioned Harrison, but there was no need to. Whig editors were quick to see the intention behind Webster's move and lost little time in passing the information on to their readers.[19] In due course the party's national convention assembled and Harrison was nominated with the full support of the Massachusetts delegation.

The disagreement between Webster and Lawrence over the 1840 nomination was the opening skirmish in what proved to be a long campaign. Neither side scored a complete victory, though Webster had come off substantially ahead of his rival. If he lost the nomination, his chances for it never had been good, and he did manage, through the entire passage, to keep a firm hand on the local party organization, which was where Lawrence's challenge pressed hardest.

Webster was in England when the Whig convention met. His absence at such a juncture was a tribute to the strength of his command. He even seemed willing to risk the appearance of magnanimity. His letters from abroad sometimes mentioned Lawrence and in more or less friendly terms.[20] The way Lawrence spoke of him may have been a different matter, but by the time of the election the two were once again working together.

There was nothing permanent about this arrangement. Motivated by a specific set of circumstances, it lapsed as soon as the circumstances changed. In the election of 1839, for the first time in the party's history, the Massachusetts Whigs had lost the state.[21] Even if the presidency had not been at stake in 1840, the occasion would have called for the best efforts of a united party; Webster and Lawrence had little choice but to join hands against the common enemy. When the tremendous tide of votes brought out by the log-cabin campaign swept away the specter of a victorious Massachusetts Democracy, however, it carried their uneasy truce with it. Affairs returned to their preelection state, and the two opposing sides stood where they had before.

Hostilities were resumed almost at once. Webster in power was no more inclined to excuse disloyalty, or forgive the disloyal, than politicians have ever been. During the campaign Lawrence had given freely of his time and money in the Whig cause. It soon developed, however, that the ordinary forms of reward would not be forthcoming in his case. Webster did invite him to Washington the week before the inauguration to advise in the organization of the new administration, but his purpose in extending the invitation was simply to get Lawrence's backing for his own projects — the appointment of Edward Curtis as collector of the port of New York, for example.[22]

Far more to the point was the fact that Lawrence's patronage recommendations were not always heeded, and in one very important matter touching his personal situation, where a word from Webster might have made all the difference, that word remained unspoken. Webster's elevation to the Cabinet had left vacant the Senate seat that traditionally fell to Boston and the eastern portion of the state. In the inner circles of the local party organization it was generally understood that Lawrence was most anxious, as John Clifford put it in a letter to Winthrop, "to try the effect of the climate of Washington for the next four years." On the other hand, the chances that this desire would some to anything were slight. Nothing could be done, Clifford felt, "unless new and very powerful influences which are not now apparent are brought into operation." [23] In the end those influences — and this undoubtedly referred to Webster's support — never were placed at Lawrence's disposal. Instead the senatorship went to Rufus Choate, one of Webster's closest and most loyal associates.

At the time of Choate's election there was little Lawrence could do. Clearly Webster meant to check him at every turn and would have to be stopped, but the administration was popular. As its leading figure and heir apparent Webster was secure against every kind of attack. Tyler's veto of the second bank bill, however, changed all that, as it changed so much else.

Personally Lawrence, like Nathan Appleton and a good part of the rest of the Boston business community, had scant use for Clay's banks; he felt that the country was better off *"without* than *with* a Bank unless we can have one of the good old fashioned Alexander Hamilton character" and doubted whether stock in either of the institutions proposed would sell.[24] Yet the bank was still a major part of the Whig program; therefore Webster's decision to stay in the Cabinet when the rest of his colleagues resigned over the issue could, without great effort, be made to seem an act of high apostasy. By November Lawrence was stating openly that he had "lost all confidence" in Webster.[25] Such utterances fell on fertile ground. Inevitably the distribution of federal patronage in Massachusetts had given rise to disappointments, and often the blame was laid at Webster's door.[26] Every disgruntled office seeker became a potential ally for Lawrence.

Having opened his campaign against Webster, Lawrence spent the next few months working behind the scenes. Among other things he took steps to cement his understanding with

John Davis who, in the crisis of 1840, had been called home to save the state by running for governor again. Late in the spring of 1842 Davis appointed Lawrence one of the state's commissioners for the Maine boundary negotiations. Webster himself may have urged the appointment as a sort of peace-keeping gesture, but if so his strategy failed. The commissionership was a poor second to a United States Senate seat. Beyond this, the longer Webster continued his association with Tyler, the more difficult relations between the Massachusetts Whigs and the national party became, a circumstance definitely not to Lawrence's taste. Unlike Webster, he had no personal following in the country at large. A firm bond with the national organization was essential to the realization of his ambitions.

Lawrence's duties as a commissioner kept him in Washington until the end of July 1842. He must have seen Webster often during his stay, though relations between them can hardly have been close. Before leaving he wrote Webster, urging him to resign as soon as the treaty was signed. The letter was cordial but emphatic. "You have achieved all that was expected of you by the country — and your real friends, I think, will unanimously agree with me that *now* is the *accepted* time to quit, with honor, your present *responsible* but *disagreeable* position." [27] Since Lawrence undoubtedly knew Webster had no intention of leaving the Cabinet, this advice might have seemed a waste of energy, but it was not. Upon his return to Massachusetts he could claim to his fellow party members that he had done everything possible to bring their wayward friend back into the fold, and failed. Webster was still a person of considerable influence; he could not be thrust aside lightly.

In the meantime, as difficult as Lawrence's task would have been under normal circumstances, it grew simpler with each passing week. The coup de grâce was Tyler's position on the tariff. Widely unpopular in Massachusetts, this, together with everything else — the bank debacle, disappointments over fed-

eral patronage, the understandable desire of many Massachusetts Whigs to "get right" with the national organization, and
the everywhere-burgeoning Clay movement — had weakened
Webster's position just enough to make a decisive move against
him possible.[28]

Returning to Boston early in August 1842, Lawrence began
to organize his forces immediately. His objective was the Whig
state convention, at that point barely five weeks away. With so
little time to see and convince the necessary people, to shore up
alliances and make the expected promises, the risk he ran was
considerable. Nevertheless, by mid-September everything was
ready. When the convention assembled Lawrence was chosen to
preside over it. Under the circumstances the selection itself implied a rebuke to Webster, but that was minor compared to
what followed. There were the usual nominations — with
Davis again at the head of the ticket — and the usual declarations of party principle. Included among those, however, was a
ringing denunciation of John Tyler, his administration and all
his works, plus, which was worse still, a frank endorsement of
Henry Clay for the 1844 Whig presidential nomination.[29]

From Webster's standpoint nothing could have been more
devastating than the action of the state convention, or indicated
more clearly how far his control of the party had slipped under
Lawrence's offensive. Having always considered himself the
natural leader of the Massachusetts Whigs, Webster took it for
granted that one consequence of this position would be their
absolute obedience in matters touching his own interests. Indeed, it was a simple case of *quid pro quo.* For years he had
worked to make the local organization one of the few majority
Whig state organizations in the country; in return he expected
it to do everything possible to help him achieve his goal, the
presidency. If that sometimes meant supporting another man —

as it had in 1840 — it certainly did not mean supporting Henry Clay in 1844.

Up to a point Webster could ignore the efforts being made against him in Massachusetts. To act would only draw attention to the situation. As long as there was a chance it might take care of itself, that was foolish. Further, even after the completion of the Ashburton negotiations he had little enough surplus energy to spend in local political battles. California, Oregon, the special mission — these demanded his closest attention. On the other hand, the declarations of the convention could not be ignored. If nothing else they brought the state of affairs in Massachusetts into the open where it had to be dealt with.[30]

A public confrontation of some sort was necessary, which meant, logically, a speech. Even before the convention met plans had been made in Boston for a large dinner in Webster's honor, but he decided an ordinary meeting — without dinner — would better suit his purposes. In suggesting the change to the committee that issued the invitation he pointed out that more people could be present at a meeting than a dinner, that a meeting would "impose the least restrictions and best suit the convenience of all who may be disposed to attend it." [31] Whatever the committee thought of these reasons — and one of its members was Abbott Lawrence — Webster had others that he preferred not to mention. With his friend C. P. Curtis he was more candid. "There cannot be such a dinner without toasts," he observed, "and there cannot be toasts in which all would agree." [32]

Postponed until September 30, the meeting was held in Faneuil Hall. By then Webster had had ample time to determine his strategy. As always he appeared confident speaking from a familiar platform. It was a remarkable performance. The dinner had been planned originally to congratulate him on the treaty. Dismissing that subject in a few sentences, however, he spent the rest of his time bitterly attacking first all those who persisted in criticizing his connection with the administration, and second, the delegates, resolutions, and everything else connected with the recent state convention. The climax came when, drawing himself up to his full height and glowering down at his audience, he announced in measured tones: "I am a Whig, I always have been a Whig, and I always will be one; and if there are any who would turn me out of the pale of that communion, let them see who will get out first." [33]

These were strong words, indeed much too strong, it soon became clear. To Charles Sumner the applause when Webster had finished seemed "in rapture and spontaneousness . . . very unlike the echoes which he has excited . . . at other times." [34] Sumner may well have been right. Certainly the speech pleased few, if any, of the people who heard it. "Ephraim is joined to idols: let him alone" was the "severest sentence" Winthrop would pass, but coming from a friend that was severe enough. [35] As for Webster's enemies, they were beside themselves. "Boastful, cunning, jesuitical, fawning, and insolent," sputtered John Quincy Adams; [36] and Adams aside, there were even rumors that Tyler was displeased with his Secretary of State's outburst, that he was going about Washington making jokes at Webster's expense and would have dismissed him had he had an adequate replacement. [37]

Webster had made a serious mistake. Adams was angry because he supposed the speech was a personal attack on himself and because he disliked Webster anyway. Winthrop's attitude was another matter. Attempting to recoup his losses, Webster had managed only to alienate one of his most loyal lieutenants. Nor is it likely that Winthrop was alone in his defection. As he himself wrote Everett, "Nobody but W. could have taken the course he has taken with impunity," [38] which meant, if it was true, that even following Webster's lead would have been at best a perilous affair. In fact the only notable volunteer was Caleb Cushing, and all the while Cushing was moving nearer and nearer an open break with the Whig party — an event that was marked, when it finally occurred, by his appointment late in the spring of 1843 to the China mission Everett had turned down.[39] By then Webster had resigned and was on his way back to Massachusetts and into the bonds of Whig regularity.

### III

In most clubs it is considered bad form for members to air their differences in public, and the Massachusetts Whig party was no exception. By attacking Lawrence in the manner he did, Webster committed a serious breach of etiquette. The fact that Lawrence had been carrying on a full-scale offensive against him might have served as an explanation for the faux pas, but it was hardly an excuse. Lawrence's attack was a model of good clubmanship; quietly conducted, always kept behind the scenes, it could only be met on a similar basis. Everybody's sympathy was with Lawrence who, for his part, seemed in no hurry to cover his wounds. A year after the Faneuil Hall speech he had still to lose, Winthrop felt, "the chagrin produced by Mr. Webster's onslaught." [40]

Yet sympathy in this case — and the carefully tempered display of righteous indignation — proved to be a currency of limited exchangeability. In the normal course of events Lawrence should have benefited substantially from the general distaste that greeted Webster's attack, but the result of the state election that fall prevented him from turning sympathy into the more tangible stuff of political support.

In 1842, for the second time in four years, the Whigs lost Massachusetts to their Democratic rivals. As the principal architect of the party's strategy in the campaign, Lawrence was forced to shoulder a large part of the responsibility for defeat. Webster, on the other hand, left the party to fend for itself, with the net result that his stock rose while Lawrence's fell — in spite of Faneuil Hall. Whether Webster could have prevented the Democratic triumph was at best doubtful, but the point could still be argued since, conveniently, there was no way of disproving it.[41] It embodied, too, an obvious directive for the future: without "Jupiter to get our wheel out of the mire of locofocoism," as one good Whig put it, the party was sure to lose again.[42]

The outcome of the 1842 election improved Webster's case considerably, but the amount of leverage he had to work with when he returned from Washington the following May was still slight. However eloquently his friends might argue that the Massachusetts Whigs needed him, he was in no position to dictate terms to the party. John Quincy Adams thought otherwise, but in this opinion his son, Charles Francis, who was better acquainted with the situation in the state, believed him mistaken. "He appears to me," wrote the younger Adams of his father, "to overrate the influence of Mr. Webster at the present crisis, and not to come down sufficiently to the true level of Massachusetts politics, which are for the present purely local." [43]

The test came at the state convention in June. On the first ballot John Davis — the defeated incumbent of the year before and as much an ally of Lawrence's as ever — received 707 out of 787 votes for the gubernatorial nomination. Within a few hours, however, word came that Davis declined to run. The nomination then went to George Nixon Briggs of Pittsfield, a congressman of a dozen years past who was closely associated with neither Lawrence nor Webster. The whole proceeding was carried through with the sort of harmony that indicated a good deal of prearrangement.[44]

Webster did not participate in the planning, but he did make his feelings known in various quarters, and on that basis, mediating elements within the party were able to work out a satisfactory arrangement. Earlier in the year he had informed Winthrop that he "would attend any meeting where his presence

might be desired to aid in restoring the State to safe hands,"
providing the Whigs nominated someone "of not too acrimoni-
ous politics." [45] That obviously eliminated Davis, to say nothing
of Lawrence, who was also mentioned as a possible candidate.
Later Winthrop noted Webster had named Briggs "among the
first" of the men he would like to see nominated.[46] With Webster's position clear, all that remained was to convince Davis not
to run, and a promise of the state organization's support for the
Whig vice-presidential nomination the following year probably
accomplished that.

In all these transactions the principal loser was Lawrence. If
Briggs was not precisely Webster's man, neither was he Lawrence's as Davis had been, and barring Davis's nomination there
was every indication that Lawrence would have liked the honor
himself.[47] In the face of such a defeat he made up his mind, two
days after the convention, to travel to England for the summer
with his family. "He says he is ill," wrote his nephew A. A.
Lawrence, "and he cannot live as he does now, a contested election approaching, a crowd of strangers to whom he must pay
attention, a diseased liver and other things induce him to take a
journey to recruit himself." [48] Thurlow Weed was also in Europe that summer on one of his own periodic retreats from the
tribulations of New York politics. Weed, however, went supplied with letters of introduction from Webster, while Lawrence did not.[49]

Lawrence's absence left Webster free to play the role the Massachusetts Whigs had envisioned for him when they nominated
Briggs. There were, too, other considerations quite apart from
the matter of his reconciliation with the party compelling him to
"come out." As was so often the case, he badly needed money.

In its more immediate manifestations this need had involved
him, during the months just prior to his resignation, in a series
of rather complicated financial dealings with Baring Brothers
through their Boston agent, Thomas W. Ward. Ward did not

like Webster or trust him, but he had great respect for his ability and therefore believed it a wise policy to be generous when the occasion arose. His opinions in this respect were often repeated in letters to his English associates, and together those opinions form a picture of Webster that a good many Boston and New York businessmen of the period might have found accurate. In spite of Webster's self-seeking ambition, his "disregard to his moral obligations," and his "recklessness in pecuniary matters," he was still, Ward felt, "by far the greatest man we have," his views were generally "sound and comprehensive," and in "defending the true principles of the constitution and upholding the rights of property" he was unsurpassed. If this were not enough, one had only to imagine "the evil which might come from such a mighty intellect acting on the wrong side," to perceive the necessity of doing everything possible to keep Webster "right." [50] For the time being Barings agreed. They were less bothered by some of Webster's lapses than Ward, though one of the London partners did write that he thought it "a pity" Webster could not "be made to feel the value of money." In this case, however, it was not so much Webster's refusal to pay his debts as his ever-vigilant "eye to the gratification of his ambition" that rendered him only partially — and never wholly — useful to the firm.[51]

While he was still in the Cabinet Webster had borrowed a large sum of money from Barings, using some of his Western land holdings as security. Subsequently the land had proved to be "embarrassed" with prior claims and he never offered a substitute. The loan became, in effect, a gift.[52] Ward advised the partners to write the matter off, which they were willing to do, stipulating only that the whole business be kept quiet. "I dare say," one of them wrote, "the opposition papers on your side would attribute to some mercenary motive the change of the Diplomatic account." [53] Apparently the United States account had been awarded to Barings a short while earlier, with what motive it is impossible to tell. In any case, Webster had no further dealings with the firm while he remained in office, but soon after his resignation he began to receive regular payments from Ward. Among other things Barings had a substantial interest in American state debts, which a number of states were steadfastly refusing to honor. Here Webster, by bringing the issue before the public and putting it in proper perspective, could render an invaluable service, or so Ward thought, and to that end he was prepared to pay a sizable retainer.[54]

With both his own political interests and Baring Brothers pressing him to enter the field, Webster did so late in the fall of 1843. A major feature of the Whig campaign that year was a series of last-minute rallies staged throughout the state. At Andover Webster delivered the principal address, and by the time he had finished Ward and the Whigs had every reason to be pleased. If he ended by repeating — albeit in gentler terms — the threat from his Faneuil Hall address to all those who would cast him beyond the pale of true Whig brotherhood, he nevertheless managed along the way to endorse Briggs's candidacy and to insert an eloquent appeal for "the entire re-establishment of character and credit" by the states.[55]

For all its plain-spoken relevance Webster's Andover effort did little to help either Ward or the Whig cause. State credit policies underwent no dramatic transformation, and the eleventh-hour endorsement of Briggs can have changed few — if any — votes. But Briggs did win the election. The year before when Webster shunned the Whigs they had been defeated; now success crowned their combined efforts. Superficially the most striking point of contrast between the two canvasses remained the different roles he had played in them. As dubious as the connection was, it was easily made, and by the end of 1843 there were few Whigs in Massachusetts who would have denied Webster a place in the fold or refused to grant that the party was once again in his debt.

## IV

The Andover speech had restored Webster to Whig good graces at home. Considering the obstacles he faced, that in itself was a substantial accomplishment. In November 1843, however, the reconciliation remained only half complete. In spite of the difficulties his cause had suffered over the last three years, Webster's presidential yearnings were undiminished. Nor had the role he envisioned for the Massachusetts Whigs in that connection changed. The full status quo ante bellum — to be again the party's undisputed leader and to receive as a matter of course its wholehearted support for his national political ambitions — those were the goals he sought.

Achieving them would not be easy. Ultimately he would have to rally again a group of men who owed their primary allegiance to him rather than to the party, for there Lawrence — if somewhat daunted — was still powerful enough to bar the way. In the meantime Clay's claim to the nomination the following year seemed secure. Whatever hope there was would have to be for some distant future — 1848, or even 1852. But Webster could wait. For now, the important thing was to lose none of the momentum he had gained.

As Secretary of State Webster had become interested in the possibility of negotiating reciprocal tariff reductions with England. When the Whig tariff bill passed in 1842 he commented to at least one person that it was "too high." [56] Then shortly before his resignation he called an informal meeting in Boston to discuss the idea of a commercial treaty between the United States and Britain. According to Winthrop, the city's "free trade merchants relished his suggestions greatly," and before long a petition was circulating "calling upon him to carry out his views and to attempt the negotiation proposed." [57] As a de-

vice for building the kind of support Webster needed, tariff reduction had potential. In some quarters interest in it, as Winthrop's remarks indicated, ran high. It had, too, the great virtue
of defining ground on which Lawrence could never stand. No
one was more deeply committed to the principle of protection;
that summer in England he made a special point of sounding
out various people on the subject of Webster's "dangerous"
ideas.[58]

Though later Lawrence was happy to report "the question of
reciprocity treaties amounts to nothing," [59] he might have saved
himself the trouble — at least as far as Webster was concerned.
If the issue had potential, apparently it had too little, for he
soon dropped it. Boston's free trade merchants were not the
force they had been twenty years earlier. Massachusetts was
wedded to manufacturing, manufacturing depended on the
tariff, and no amount of political maneuvering could alter those
facts.

But tariff reduction was not the only available field for activity. There were other issues and other groups as the outcome of
the 1843 election made clear. The people of Massachusetts had
chosen to bestow a victory on the Whigs, yet the dimensions of
that victory were by no means wholly satisfying. The party
failed to receive a majority. Of a total of 121,000 votes cast,
Briggs netted only 57,000, or under 48 per cent. This was better
than the Democratic showing by 3500, or 3 per cent of the total,
but it left almost 9,000 votes, a striking figure, for Samuel E.
Sewall, the Liberty party candidate. With its unequivocal demand for abolition, in four years the Liberty party had increased its vote ninefold to the point where it held a balance of
power in the state. Moreover, the party's growing totals were
plainly coming from Whig voters and Whig strongholds.[60]

The situation, while disturbing, contained a number of intriguing possibilities for Webster. By the end of November he

was already discussing it with his close political associates as well as some of Boston's more influential citizens. To both groups he made the same point: unless something were done, the Liberty party would continue to gather strength at the Whigs' expense and end by becoming "the ruling party" in the state.[61] Nor were mere appeals for the Whigs to "come out" enough to prevent this from happening. The Whigs did come out, but all too often, he wrote Everett, it was simply to "go over" to the abolitionists. Although the party had always managed in the past, this was "a fragile basis to rest party hopes upon, for time to come." In the future more would be required. "We need counsels, mild, but comprehensive and long-sighted; such we have not." [62]

Though the future amply justified Webster's concern, it was at least arguable in 1843 that the antislavery vote in Massachusetts had reached its maximum strength at the level of 8 per cent; that the threat to the Whigs and the need for action were negligible. On the other hand, Webster had good reason for adopting the line he did. Whatever the future might hold, there had always been a decidedly moralistic quality to Bay State politics, and more and more in recent years that quality had focused on the issue of slavery. The kind of antislavery sentiment that turned to politics, futhermore, was generally a far cry from the stark radicalism of William Lloyd Garrison and his followers. Legalistic, committed to institutions and institutional restraints, it had all the earmarks and potential of respectability. It was best expressed in a series of resolutions passed early in the spring of 1843 by the state legislature. The first of these advocated amending the national Constitution to eliminate the advantage Southern states derived from being able to count three fifths of the slave population in computing representation in Congress, the second deplored the treatment of free Negro seamen in Southern ports, and the third voiced strenuous opposition to any and all projects for the annexation of Texas.[63]

Such an approach Webster could champion freely. He had reached a point, too, where everything in his own political situation argued in favor of doing so. Within the Massachusetts Whig organization there was already, and had been for several years, a group working to commit the party to a more advanced position on slavery: men like Stephen C. Phillips, a Salem businessman with a taste for politics, who had served two terms and part of another in Congress; Charles Allen of Worcester, at the time a judge in the state Court of Common Pleas; and Charles Francis Adams, the son of John Quincy and a leader in the fight for that year's antislavery resolutions in the legislature. Most of these men were young and they shared the characteristic enthusiasm of youth for a good cause. They also shared a youthful impatience with the older, more conservative leadership of the party, which too often seemed reluctant to reward talent in younger men. Though he considered the place his by right, Webster here at least had reason to be grateful that the prominent position in the older clique lay temporarily beyond his reach. The effect was to make the "Young Whigs" — Phillips, Allen, Adams, and others — his own natural allies, a potential nucleus for the group he would need to by-pass Lawrence in his drive for the presidency.[64]

An odd melange of principle and ambition, such an alliance in fact took place. The issue on which it was forged was Texas. Of the host of separate issues growing from the larger question of slavery this was the safest, and likely to have the widest appeal. It was also the one that Lawrence and his friends were most anxious to avoid. In principle they were as much opposed to annexation as Webster, or Adams and Phillips, but the issue was bound to embarrass Clay and hence they consistently tried to ignore it. Later, when he raised the hue and cry over Tyler's annexation schemes, Webster was accused of trying to sabotage Clay's candidacy and thereby win the nomination for himself. The charge was incorrect. He cared far less about Clay than he did about Clay's Massachusetts supporters, and it was against them that he used the Texas issue. He had long since given up all hope of the nomination in 1844.[65] When a group of New Hampshire Whigs offered him their support late in 1843 he thanked them respectfully but declined, noting that "the tendency of opinion" in the party was "generally and strongly set in another direction." [66]

In his annual message to Congress, delivered on December 5, 1843, Tyler made a veiled but nonetheless clear appeal for annexation.[67] By that time, spurred on by evidence of a rapidly developing entente between the Lone Star Republic and Great Britain, he was acting in earnest to open negotiations with the Texas government. Webster may or may not have known this. In any case the intimations of the message gave the Texas issue a clarity and force it lacked earlier. Webster had already discussed the subject with Charles Allen.[68] Now — no doubt by prearrangement with Allen — he received a letter from a committee of "Citizens of Worcester County" requesting his views on annexation. In his answer he dealt at length with the history of Texas, quoted from an 1837 speech opposing annexation on antislavery grounds, repeated the constitutional argument against admitting foreign territories as states, and ended with a ringing appeal for the nation as it was, without unwarranted additions or extensions. "We have a republic, gentlemen, of vast extent and unequalled natural advantages . . . Instead of aiming to enlarge its boundaries, let us seek, rather, to strengthen its union, to draw out its resources, to maintain and improve its institutions of religion and liberty, and thus to push it forward in its career of prosperity and glory." [69]

The reply to the "Citizens of Worcester" was dated January 23, 1844. On March 13, Webster wrote Allen and instructed him to have it published "at once" if this had not already been done. In the interim the entire complexion of the Texas issue

had changed. The change was not unexpected and later, explaining how he learned of it, Webster perhaps magnified his
shock at the discovery. Even if he knew, however — and had
from the beginning — what Tyler intended, he could not have
known much before the end of February how far matters had
progressed. "We have no doubt," he wrote Allen, "the annexation of Texas (and therefore the extension of slavery and the
establishment forever, of a predominance of the slave-holding
interests), is a matter in active negotiation at this moment." [70]

Any question Allen had as to the accuracy of this information
would probably have been eliminated by the fact that it came
from Washington. Webster had gone there in January on Supreme Court business and also, as Winthrop put it, "to rescue
his relations to the Whigs." [71] In the second of those enterprises
he apparently accomplished everything he could have wished.
To Everett, Winthrop wrote in glowing terms of the "reconciliation" that had taken place and of a dinner he himself had
given Webster and various "old friends" where "all went as
merry as a marriage ball." [72] This sort of political bridge-
mending took time and time spent largely in Whig circles where
little enough was known of the inner workings of the administration. But Webster did manage to see Abel Upshur, Tyler's
Secretary of State, and through Upshur he received the information he passed on to Allen.

When he returned to Boston Webster described this meeting
in detail to George Ticknor, who in turn wrote an account of it
after Webster's death. According to the account Webster had
long been on friendly terms with Upshur and so felt no com-
punction about advising him to leave Tyler's Cabinet. Upshur
replied that he was inclined to do so, indeed would have, had he
not "a particular object to accomplish." Webster saw in a moment what that object was: "I felt Texas go through me" was
the phrase he used. Once he realized Upshur's position he said
nothing more on the subject, but within forty-eight hours, Tick-

nor maintained, "he knew all about it" and "was astounded at the boldness of the government." [73] By then the treaty of annexation was virtually complete. A few days later Upshur was killed in a chance explosion while inspecting the U. S. S. *Princeton* with the rest of the Cabinet. When John C. Calhoun was appointed Secretary of State in Upshur's place, the final shred of doubt — if one existed — disappeared. The administration's commitment to Texas was now beyond retrieve.

With the issue about to explode in Washington, Webster lost no time in marshaling his forces there and elsewhere. He wrote Allen. He saw Winthrop and had him propose a strong anti-annexation resolution to the House. He also convinced Joseph Gales to run a number of editorials in the *National Intelligencer* that he himself had written hinting at Tyler's plans. Finally, at about this time, word first reached Boston — undoubtedly through Webster — of the growing magnitude of the crisis.[74]

In less than three months Webster, with a minimum of effort, had become the leader of the anti-Texas movement in Massachusetts. There had been no competition; no one had undertaken to challenge his activities. That situation was bound to change. Since the beginning of the year rumors had been circulating in Boston — usually traceable to one of several Washington sources — that Clay's supporters were prepared to let annexation pass rather than have it interfere with his candidacy.[75] In a city where feeling on Texas already ran high, those rumors were proving increasingly embarrassing to local Clay men. Up to a point they remained silent, but when it began to appear that annexation was imminent some concession to popular feeling became necessary. It was March 17 when Charles Francis Adams noted in his diary, "news received today of John Tyler's private intrigue to bring about the annexation of Texas," and added that the treaty was "already negotiated." [76] Three days later

Abbott Lawrence called an informal meeting at his house to consider, as Adams, who attended, put it, "whether any measures were expedient in regard to the annexation of Texas."

Specifically, Lawrence wanted a course of action that would prevent the Liberty party from making undue capital out of Texas. "His phrase," Adams observed, "was that they should circumvent the abolitionists." [77] This was the same line Webster had taken when he first suggested the Whigs adopt a stronger position on slavery. At the time it had stemmed from a genuine concern for the party's future. More important than that concern, however, had been the realization that the slavery issue also provided an excellent means of combating Lawrence's power within the Massachusetts Whig organization. Now Lawrence was attempting to use the issue in the same way. If he too wished to "circumvent the abolitionists," Webster must have figured in his calculation fully as much as Garrison or Samuel Sewall did. On the other hand, his commitment to Clay kept him from making any more than a token gesture toward the anti-Texas forces. In an all-out campaign aimed at undercutting Webster's position, the hastily called meeting of March 20 might have been a useful beginning, but Lawrence could go no further. Nothing tangible came of the meeting, with the net result that it accomplished more harm than good. "The truth really is that the wealthy classes have become inactive," Adams remarked in disgust.[78]

The indictment was accurate. While Lawrence was sounding his belated — and expediently weak — alarm over Texas, the other solid Whig businessmen of Boston were conscientiously ignoring the entire issue. Webster's attempts to interest them met with little success. To men like Nathan Appleton and Thomas Perkins the threat seemed, at most, a minor one.[79] Even when the treaty was signed and sent to the Senate, there remained the problem of getting the necessary two thirds of that body to agree to it — a doubtful eventuality. When the Senate voted annexation down early in June 1844, that prediction stood confirmed. Whether the danger had been eliminated thereby was another matter. The Democrats had already met and adopted a platform calling for the "re-annexation of Texas," and just before Congress adjourned Tyler tried to have Texas annexed by joint resolution of both Houses, a measure requiring only a simple majority to pass.

These were disturbing signs, but for the present Webster had other things to think of. May had brought the Whig convention, and now he was to be required to pay the final price that the party and the solid Whig businessmen of Boston demanded of him for having stayed too long in Tyler's Cabinet — to campaign for Henry Clay as President.

Clay's victory at the convention, never for a moment in doubt, had been Lawrence's trump card from the beginning. Whatever progress Webster had made in the months since his return, here lay a test of Whig loyalty that nobody, and he least of all, could afford to ignore. Traveling to Baltimore at the end of April, therefore, Lawrence was supremely confident,[80] and with good cause, as the results of the convention proved. If John Davis failed to become the party's vice-presidential candidate, there was still the fact of Clay's nomination and the platform that conveniently avoided any mention of Texas. On the subject of the tariff the platform was equally silent, but the tariff was already more than adequate. With obvious satisfaction and a veiled reference, perhaps, to Webster's recent maneuvers, Lawrence wrote his brother Amos: "I have been gratified to find that the people of the United States understand the motives that govern the prominent political men of the Union. The tariff and Texas are both dead and buried by common consent." [81]

While Lawrence attended the Whig convention in a mood of confidence and found much to approve in its deliberations, Webster — who was also there — must have had reactions of quite another variety. His only consolation was working for Davis' defeat, and even that required the utmost caution. Later there were rumors that he had made it the sine qua non of his support for Clay,[82] yet these were patently false. Webster was in no position to lay down conditions. He himself made that clear in Baltimore as soon as the convention was over by publicly endorsing Clay and again, a few days later, at a great "ratification assembly" in Faneuil Hall where he declared his "entire and hearty" approbation of the party's choice.[83] Such gestures impressed some people more favorably than others. To Winthrop, Webster's course had "reinstated him in the regards of our friends" and even given him "some hope of the succession." [84] Thurlow Weed felt differently. "What hard work it is for Webster to get back into the Party," he wrote Alvah Hunt. "His speech at Baltimore was unworthy of him, and that at Boston, just received is still worse." [85]

Throughout the summer and autumn Webster continued to campaign for Clay. On the assumption that a Whig victory would improve state credit policies, Ward kept up Webster's retainer, which may have accounted for the extra measure of energy he brought to the task.[86] Never in any previous campaign had he traveled so far or spoken so often. For a man of sixty-two the effort was remarkable.

In his speeches, Webster dealt most often with the tariff, but he never failed to mention Texas and invariably took a strong antislavery stand against annexation. So thoroughly did he cover that ground that Charles Francis Adams, who had an almost congenital tendency to doubt the party's soundness on the issue, felt by the end of the summer — largely, he noted, as a result of Webster's activities — that everything was going "for the present right." [87] Nor did Clay's attempt to temper his original opposition to annexation in a series of letters written and published expressly for that purpose in any way alter Webster's position. If Clay felt "the subject of slavery ought not to affect the question one way or the other," Webster disagreed. Speaking of annexation late in October at a Whig rally in Philadelphia, he declared: "Because it does increase the evils of slavery, because it will increase the number of slaves and prolong the duration of their bondage — because it does all this, I oppose it without condition and without qualification, at this time and all times, now and forever." [88] When the election was over, Webster maintained that the so-called Alabama letters had done as much as anything else to defeat Clay. [89]

The election of 1844 was close, so close that a shift of only 5000 votes in New York would have given Clay that state, and with it the victory. With so much at stake and such a narrow margin determining the outcome, there were a dozen explanations for the defeat. Clay's vacillation over Texas, however, remained one of the most convincing. The North was full of people who believed with Webster that the Alabama letters had cost the Whigs the election; that a sufficient number of New Yorkers who voted for James G. Birney, the Liberty party candidate, or simply stayed home in disgust, would have done otherwise if Clay had never put pen to paper.

The theory was plausible, but it depended on a number of totally unverifiable assumptions about how people in New York and elsewhere would have behaved in certain hypothetical situations. For example, it was essential to the theory that all electoral votes apart from those of New York remain unaffected by Clay's stand on Texas, yet if he had not written the Alabama letters, he might well have lost Tennessee, North Carolina, Delaware, and Maryland. As it was he carried those states by a combined total of only 7000 votes, and together they cast thirty-five electoral votes, or but one less than New York. Yet granting all this, people at the time still believed Texas — and ultimately slavery and Northern feeling about it — had decided the election, and in the long run the belief itself was more important than whether or not it was correct.

From Webster's standpoint the outcome of the election and

the theory devised to explain it definitely constituted an advantage. Above all the effect was to dramatize the need to accommodate politically the rising tide of Northern antislavery sentiment—a course he had been advocating for a year. In Massachusetts the issue was brought home with an extra degree of force, for the national ticket of the Liberty party had done better there than in any other state in the Union. Further, Clay had run a good 2500 votes behind Briggs, the Whig gubernatorial candidate.[90] Accordingly, it now became Webster's good fortune to find himself listened to with increasing attention, though Lawrence and his allies were no more inclined than ever to credit his predictions. Clay's defeat had substantially weakened Lawerence's position, however, and the renewal of the administration's attempt, as soon as Congress convened in December, to force the annexation issue did nothing to improve it.

During the months after the election Webster threw himself more strenuously than ever into the anti-Texas movement. His strategy seemed to be to press the issue at random from as many different sides as possible, but beneath the surface he was working constantly to cement alliances and build up his personal following. Throughout December and January he kept in touch with the situation in Washington through Winthrop and encouraged him to do what he could there. At the same time he was using his influence to have the Massachusetts legislature reaffirm its anti-Texas resolutions of the year before and making plans for the first Anti-Texas convention, which met in Boston at the end of January.[91]

The call for a convention had grown from a petition circulated by Stephen Phillips, now one of Webster's closest associates.[92] In spite of steady opposition from Lawrence the sessions were heavily and enthusiastically attended. At Webster's suggestion Phillips was made chairman,[93] while Charles Allen proposed the official address, which was all but unanimously adopted. Webster himself had written the address, however, which Charles Francis Adams considered a particularly fortuitous circumstance. He had never quite trusted Webster's motives in the Texas affair and often complained of his efforts "to keep control of the movement in his hands" and make it "subserve his projects for the future," [94] but the address itself he thought admirable. "It is," he wrote, "a strong paper and concludes in a very powerful and satisfactory manner on the subject of slavery. Considering his position I think this as connected with his future course is worth the whole convention." [95] Even John Quincy Adams was impressed. Upon reading reports of the convention he paid Webster one of the few compliments in a long acquaintance: "Webster's address is a full-length likeness of New England, or, rather, of Massachusetts. For Webster's mind, though a native of New Hampshire and graduate of Dartmouth, has been moulded by thirty years of association with Massachusetts to the Boston standard of thought and the mental scale of Harvard." [96]

## V

By the time the Boston Anti-Texas convention assembled Webster was on his way to Washington. Earlier that month the state legislature had voted to return him to his old seat in the Senate. Though officially his term did not begin until March 4, it was always useful to be on the ground beforehand.

Meanwhile the election itself was concrete proof of the distance Webster had traveled in two years. At the time of his resignation in 1943 the necessary votes might well have been lacking. At the very least his candidacy would have split the party in two. Now the Whigs were united behind him, and with their support his election was assured. Altogether it was a striking change, part of which Webster owed to circumstances beyond his control, yet only part, for he played the hand he had been dealt with surpassing skill. Nowhere was this more apparent

than in his handling of the Texas issue. With antislavery sentiment increasing steadily in the state and Lawrence committed to
Clay and Clay equivocating on Texas, a strong stand against annexation proved to be a highly effective device for combating
Lawrence and his allies. In the end the Senate seat had come
almost as a matter of course.

Amid the general success of Webster's policies, however, there
remained one question. In Massachusetts, presidential politics
and a moderate antislavery position had proved a profitable
combination, but to what extent would it be in Webster's interests to continue combining the two? If he had not already asked
himself that, the passage of the annexation resolution would
have forced him to do so. When Webster took his seat it had
already been law for four days. The address of the Boston Anti-
Texas convention may have been "a full-length likeness" of
Massachusetts, as Adams claimed, but it poorly reflected the feelings of most of the rest of the nation.

Argued in extreme terms, or to the exclusion of all else, antislavery was a poor guide to policy and utterly useless as a key to
national political success. That Webster understood only too
well. However useful the issue might have been in Massachusetts, it still had to be approached within a framework of reason
and established usage. On the national level slavery could only
be one among many different issues — issues that would be bar-
gained and traded in its behalf as the need arose. Like every
other component of the system, antislavery had to meet the test
of balance, and in Webster's hands it did. Opposition to the
annexation of Texas was an eminently reasonable position; it
was constitutionally correct, it jeopardized no interests in the nation, it was consistent with the standard Whig dictum against
expansion, and it was clearly aimed at maintaining the existing
national equilibrium. Indeed, except as conscience required,
there was no need even to mention slavery. Webster rarely

missed an opportunity to do so, but he was always careful to distinguish between slavery as it existed and the extension of slavery.

When the conscience of Massachusetts was presented in that light, it seemed to leave ample freedom for the pursuits of national politics. Webster's stand on Texas, after all, was nothing more than his general position on slavery applied to a specific issue, and that position had been for years the stock in trade of successful Northern politicians. If it was sometimes necessary to come down hard on the evils of slavery, slavery was evil, and those Southern politicians who disagreed would at least understand what compelled him to take the line he did. The pressures on them in connection with the issue were no less great. Finally, if antislavery did become too troublesome, there would always be other issues to soften the conflict, to shift the emphasis and build support around. A healthy national balance both insured and required this sort of adjustment constantly.

Returning to the Senate after five years' absence, then, Webster had little reason to believe his activities in Massachusetts would impair his national "availability." Presidential politics and antislavery were a difficult mixture but by no means an unworkable one, in spite of annexation. Logic and the experience of the past together confirmed the point, and what better guarantors were there than these?

None, perhaps, yet events can run counter to logic and the past is no warrant against change. The viability of Webster's situation depended on three separate conditions, any of which the events of a single hour might have transformed completely. As long as slavery remained but one issue among many, as long as Southern Whig politicians continued to make the expected allowances for his mild attacks on their peculiar institution, and as long as those attacks remained satisfactory to the group he was working with at home, Webster was on safe ground. The moment one of these ceased to be the case, however, the entire political spectrum would shift.

In the early months of 1845 there were already signs of change, but for the most part they were still too fleeting and indistinct to read with any degree of accuracy. The single exception was the situation Webster left behind in Massachusetts. From the beginning he had proceeded on the assumption that his views and those of the men he most relied on in the anti-Texas movement were identical, that they supported his moderate approach to slavery. And they did, at least insofar as their views were much closer to his than they were to those of the radicals, men like Garrison and Wendell Phillips. The mere fact of Garrison's presence at the Anti-Texas convention had thoroughly annoyed Charles Francis Adams, for example, and when Garrison took it upon himself to offer a resolution calling for the immediate dissolution of the Union, Adams was furious.[97] Yet curiously, he himself was advocating a course at that very moment which, pushed far enough, led to the same point.

Late in 1844 the governor of Massachusetts commissioned Judge Samuel Hoar to investigate the treatment of free Negro seamen in Charleston, South Carolina. He had been in Charleston less than a week when the South Carolina legislature voted to expel him from the state, by force if necessary. The Massachusetts legislature, in turn, responded with a report deploring Hoar's treatment. Adams was the author of the report. Faced with a clear issue, he had decided at the outset to draft as strong a statement as possible. His initial effort, which created a mild sensation among his colleagues in the legislature, eventually had to be modified. The principal source of difficulty was a declaration — according to Adams the "gist of the paper" — that South Carolina's action had voided all existing constitutional obligations between Massachusetts and her sister state.[98] If this was not precisely Garrison's call for disunion it was still a long way from what Webster would have considered reasonable, or expedient.

As approved by the legislature, Adams' report questioned whether South Carolina had not sacrificed its claims on Massachusetts, but offered no final decision on the point.[99] This was at least a partial victory for moderation. The whole passage, too, could have been an isolated incident and nothing more. Feeling in the state ran high over the Hoar business; a vigorous response of some kind was certain. The only trouble with this line of analysis was that it still left Adams and Webster miles apart on the fundamental issue, and Adams remained one of the leading figures in the group on which Webster had come to depend so heavily. As for the other "Young Whigs," it was too soon to tell whose lead they would follow, but their reaction to annexation was hardly an encouraging sign. For Webster — however much he opposed annexation — Tyler's signature on the joint resolution ended the argument. Adams and his friends took a different view. Texas had yet to be admitted as a state; therefore the question remained open, could still be agitated, and would be, they announced, as soon as word of Tyler's victory reached Boston, until the last vote was cast in Congress.

Together principle and ambition were creating a new political order in Massachusetts, and one that accorded ill with the tenets of balance.

# *Four*
# The Nation, 1845-1849

W<small>HEN</small> W<small>EBSTER</small> <small>RETURNED</small> to the Senate in 1845, Washington was still less than fifty years away from its founding. The city's rude, improvised character, its sundry inconveniences, and its climate were a source of constant annoyance to those who lived there and the butt of uniformly disparaging comment by foreign travelers. For as long as Webster lived, Washington would remain that "City of Magnificent Intentions" — and little else — which Charles Dickens had seen in 1842. Trying to describe the American capital for his British readers, Dickens had arrived at a graphic formula for recreating it: Take the "straggling outskirts" of any large European city; "burn the whole down; build it up again in wood and plaster"; make the houses as undistinguished as possible and the roads nonexistent or impassable; "make it scorching hot in the morning and freezing cold in the afternoon, with an occasional tornado of wind and dust"; and finally, erect a few, very grand public buildings "anywhere, but the more entirely out of everybody's way the better." [1]

There was a good deal of humorous exaggeration in the picture Dickens painted, but it also contained a healthy measure of truth. Even the romantic engravings of the period show roads still unpaved, lined with raw wooden buildings and open fields. In the midst of all this the stately elegances of the Capitol Building and the White House must, in fact, have seemed incongruous.

Yet here perhaps there was a kind of appropriateness, a parallel — at least in 1845. The hectic rate of political change in the preceding decade had exacted a heavy toll in political careers. New names and new faces were everywhere in Washington. In the four years since Webster had left the Senate to become Secretary of State, fully three quarters of its membership had changed. Of the entire body only three men — John Berrien of Georgia, Thomas Hart Benton of Missouri, and Levi Woodbury of New Hampshire — had been there twenty years earlier when Webster first entered the Senate. Even Clay and Calhoun were, for the moment absent.

If those who remained sometimes felt themselves out of place in a scene where so much had changed, they had little choice but to accept the situation. The business of government might be rendered more complicated by such rapid turnovers in personnel, but the functions of government did not cease. Whatever adjustments were necessary would have to be made, and made in spite of all the other difficulties of the period. In the meantime the process of adjustment was nothing aided by the rate at which new congressmen continued to replace old ones. By the end of 1850 there were only seven men left in the Senate who had been there longer than a decade, and the average age of senators had fallen from fifty-one to forty-seven — a full twenty years younger than Webster was at that point.

II

The special session of the Senate at which Webster took his seat was over in less than three weeks. The signal event of the year — the annexation of Texas — had already taken place. Nothing would match it in importance, or indeed could have. Webster's sole effort in the session was a brief eulogy of Isaac C. Bates, his colleague from Massachusetts, who died four days before adjournment.[2] Successful Northampton lawyer, state legislator, congressman, and senator for five years, Bates had managed to steer clear of the disputes that plagued the Massachusetts Whig party during the period. With the stature that feat earned him, and his steady, country ways, he would have been a valuable associate for Webster.

The man who replaced Bates belonged in quite another category. Before the month was out the Massachusetts legislature elected John Davis to fill the vacancy. For three years Davis and Webster had not spoken, or even met. Whatever friendship may have existed between them, the 1842 Clay endorsement and Webster's Faneuil Hall address had ended — permanently. Of all the men the legislature might have chosen, barring Lawrence, Davis was the least likely to please Webster. As for Lawrence himself, he was delighted. "The people of this commonwealth will not heed the advice or remonstrances of that eminent individual as in former years," he wrote Everett speaking of Webster. "Circumstances have transpired since his election which would now make it difficult for him to secure an election if it were to take place now. It was *shown up* in the election of Governor Davis." [3]

An impartial observer might have pointed out that Lawrence was in no position to judge, that his view of the matter too obviously reflected his personal feelings; still what he said contained a grain of truth. The election of Davis was fair warning that — for all Webster's recent gains — there remained points in the system capable of resisting his will. Davis proved to be one of them and by no means the only, or even the most bothersome one.

On his arrival in Boston that spring, Webster found the political scene little changed from when he left, but elsewhere his affairs had run into considerable difficulty. The year before when the possibility of his returning to the Senate was first broached, he had made it quite clear to a number of people that, financially, he could not afford to do so. [4] His legal practice was thriving, but he needed every cent he earned, and being in Congress would reduce the number of cases he could accept. To solve the problem a group of his friends had set about collecting a large fund in his behalf. The figure projected was $100,000 — half to be raised in Boston and half in New York — the income from which was to go to Webster during his lifetime.[5] Designed to free both his benefactors and Webster from the embarrassment attendant upon the constant appeals for small loans and gifts that had been his practice in the past, the plan had at least the merits of humanity and efficiency. On the other hand, the size of the sum involved and the nature of the undertaking itself shocked many people.[6] Lawrence's remark about "circumstances" transpiring since Webster's election no doubt referred to the proposed fund.

Far more distressing than the general public reaction to the plan, however, was the reaction among those who should have been most concerned. Contributions were surprisingly slow in making their appearance.[7] Part of the problem may have stemmed from Webster's handling of the Texas issue. Further, to support the fund when it was under attack took more courage than a conservative business community could be expected to muster without good cause. This was supposed to be a good cause of course; the fund's promoters spoke of it as a wise investment, and most State Street merchants — in spite of Texas — probably agreed. But there were other difficulties. Within the year Webster had won a striking political victory from Lawrence, yet Lawrence's economic power remained undiminished. He was still the "leading man" in Boston, still very much a person to stay on the right side of. The fact that he and Webster were openly at odds with one another must have dimmed enthusiasm more than a little when it came to contributing money for Webster's support.

Early in August 1845, Nathan Appleton wrote Webster urging him to make up his differences with Lawrence. If Webster was agreeable he had only to write Appleton stating his willingness "to let bygones be bygones" and Appleton, in turn, would pass the information on to "the other party."[8] Under ordinary circumstances Webster would probably have refused such a propositon since it required him to make the first move. Now he hastened to comply. There followed a series of letters to Appleton — one that Lawrence apparently considered unsatisfactory and then a revised copy of it.[9] In the end a kind of reconciliation was achieved, though at best a very partial one. "The intimate and cordial personal relations heretofore existing between Mr. Webster and Mr. Lawrence are thus restored," Adams noted in his diary after a conversation with Lawrence in September; "but," he added, "it is very apparent that confidence between them never can be restored."[10]

Still, Appleton's good offices had secured what Webster wanted. By March 1846, contributions from Boston totaled $37,000, an impressive figure even if it was short of the original goal. Lawrence's name was absent from the list of donors,[11] but a liberal sprinkling of Appletons and Lowells nicely balanced the omission; Thomas Perkins had contributed, and so had William Amory, Josiah Quincy, Jr., and William H. Prescott.[12] Altogether the list contained forty names — a generous tribute both to Webster and to the timeliness of Appleton's intervention.

Appleton was not a politician, either by training or inclination, but he was a shrewd judge of men and situations. Webster's predicament made an understanding with Lawrence imperative; Appleton provided the entrée. The question was why. In his initial letter to Webster, he had spoken of "many reasons both public and private" for a reconciliation, but what those reasons were he left unsaid. Vague as this seemed, Appleton was not acting simply out of a disinterested desire to see harmony restored. His "public" reasons were urgent, as Webster well knew.

With a Democratic administration in Washington and James K. Polk at its head, a revision of the tariff was certain. How serious a revision remained in doubt. Polk's majorities in Congress were not large and there had always been a small but powerful pro-tariff wing in the Democratic party. In this situation, with a sufficient degree of effort and cooperation, the friends of protection might still accomplish wonders. Effort and cooperation were essential, however, and the outlook for either was slight as long as Webster and Lawrence continued to quarrel.

Given Appleton's interest in the tariff he could be expected to do whatever the situation required. On the other hand, if that was his sole concern when he began his peacemaking activities he might easily have waited. In August 1845 the threatened revision was still a long way off. Congress would not be in session again until December, and there were other matters for it to consider before the tariff. Since Appleton knew this it was safe to assume he had something else on his mind — in addition to the tariff — when he wrote Webster.

In the history of the Massachusetts Whig party the summer of 1845 stands as a major point of demarcation. For better than a decade the organization had succeeded in spite of its defects — its fundamental lack of structure, its too-casual way of proceeding, its internal divisions and quarrels. Now those defects were coming home to roost, and not just for a season as they had in 1839 or 1842, but permanently. The full extent of the danger was still unclear in 1845; there were indications, however — indications that even a man as sanguine as Appleton could ill afford to ignore.

The crux of the problem was that group of earnest, ambitious young men who had joined Webster in the anti-Texas movement. With the annexation resolution through Congress, much as Appleton opposed it, he — and the rest of the Boston business community — considered the matter settled. To continue to agitate it, and the slavery issue that lay behind it, would only anger Southerners whose support was needed elsewhere: on the tariff, for example. When Charles Francis Adams and his friends announced that they would carry on the fight against Texas, then, Appleton grew concerned.

As long as nothing more serious than irate newspaper articles came of the affair, the threat remained minor. Late in June, however, Adams, Stephen C. Phillips, and Charles Allen, who together had been appointed a "committee of correspondence" at the anti-Texas convention in January, sent out a circular appealing for advice and cooperation to meet the new Texas "emergency." In answer to the argument that Congress had settled the issue, the circular pointed out that Texas had as yet to be admitted as a state, therefore the question remained open.[13] The results of this initial effort were negligible, but the Young Whigs had no intention of giving up. By October they had joined forces with Garrison and Wendell Phillips, and a new circular as well as a second mass protest meeting at Faneuil Hall were in the offing.[14] Asked to sign the circular, both Appleton and Abbott Lawrence refused, and lest anyone miss the point they wrote letters roundly criticizing the entire enterprise.[15]

Despite the growing division in its ranks the Whig party achieved a victory in Massachusetts that fall with all the perennial signs of party unity on display. Adams attended the state convention determined to support its nominees, and his young friends followed his lead to a man.[16] The time was not far off when such a result would seem a major accomplishment, but for now it hardly offset, in Appleton's opinion, the damage Adams was doing in other areas. Of all his blunders the worst was his open association with "those who have distinguished themselves as members of the Abolition party." The effect was to taint the whole of Massachusetts Whiggery with abolitionism. Granted that Adams and his associates were acting on their own initiative, many of them held prominent positions in the party; the connection was unavoidable.

To deal with the situation Appleton evidently decided it was imperative to unite the rest of the party in opposition to the Young Whigs, and with that in mind, along with the tariff, he proceeded to write Webster in August just as the second phase of the anti-Texas movement was gathering momentum.

Appleton's motives were sufficiently obvious to leave Webster little doubt about what would be expected of him in the future. What he could perform was another matter. On the subject of the tariff he agreed wholeheartedly with Appleton, but beyond that point any accord between them stretched thin.

The Whig campaign in Boston that year climaxed as usual with a rally at Faneuil Hall. Introduced as "the Defender of the Constitution," Webster spoke briefly about those "urgent national questions" that made a Whig victory in Massachusetts essential. His principal topic was Oregon — just then developing into a major crisis — but he also had a word or two to say about Texas. He noted and then deplored the tendency toward separate action that the issue had produced. If this approach seemed contrived to please Appleton, however, the appearance was misleading, for Webster confined his rebuke wholly and explicitly to the Liberty party. Further, in discussing the current status of annexation, he said nothing to discourage the idea that it might still be prevented. In fact, he pledged himself to just such a course. "I can only say for one, that if it should fall my lot to have a vote on such a question, and I vote for the admission into the Union of any State with a Constitution which prohibits even the legislature from ever setting the bondman [sic] free, I shall never show my head again, depend upon it, in Faneuil Hall!" [17]

In essence, Webster had offered the Massachusetts Whig party and his own influence in it as rallying points in the continuing struggle against annexation. If this was precisely what Appleton wished to avoid it must have suited Webster himself even less, yet he had no alternative. Unquestionably he was annoyed and embarrassed by the line the Young Whigs had taken. His every instinct and belief would have argued that Texas was now an accomplished fact. But instincts and beliefs aside, he was in no position to alienate the leaders of the anti-Texas movement by denouncing their activities; he owed too much to their support and needed it still. The most he could do was try the middle way: denounce "separate action" if it meant joining a third party, yet ignore the growing indications of separate action within his own fold.

On December 29, 1845, the state of Texas formally entered the Union. The week before, on the day the bill admitting Texas passed to a third reading in the Senate, Webster rose and uttered a final, solemn protest. One by one he stated the reasons for his position, briefly and without equivocation: here was a bill he could never approve, it transgressed every principle of justice, it violated the conscience and interests of his state, it ran counter to all his own beliefs and principles. "I agree with the unanimous opinion of the legislature of Massachusetts; I agree with the great mass of her people; I reaffirm what I have said and written during the last eight years, at various times, against this annexation. I here record my own dissent and opposition; and I here express and place on record, also, the dissent and protest of the State of Massachusetts." [18]

Among Webster's shorter speeches few were as powerful, or moving, as this one, and doubtless he was sincere in what he said. Considering the turn events had taken in Massachusetts, however, he was probably also relieved to have the long crusade against Texas over. With his own position relatively secure, divisions in the local party organization had lost their usefulness. Whether they could be thus easily wished out of existence was something else again. The day Webster spoke, General Zachary

Taylor with half the United States Army under his command was camped on the south bank of the Nueces River near Corpus Christi. Within three weeks Taylor had been ordered by President Polk to advance to "positions on or near the left bank" of the Rio Grande.

## III

Beginning with the admission of Texas, the first session of the Twenty-ninth Congress was destined to be one of the most momentous in the century. In rapid succession it was called upon to witness the resolution of the Oregon question, to reduce the tariff along "free trade" lines, to reenact the subtreasury system, and finally to declare war on Mexico. Amid all this activity the problem of assigning priorities taxed many men, including Webster. In a year, no one would doubt the future waited on events along the Rio Grande, but in December 1845, or even as late as June 1846, that was still unclear. Other matters seemed more pressing: to Webster Oregon did, and so did the tariff.

The demand for the whole of Oregon in the 1844 Democratic platform had been a convenient counterweight for Texas, but it left Polk in a difficult position once he took office. For years the United States had expressed its willingness to settle with England along the 49th parallel; now the line moved north all the way to 54°40′ — "or fight," said the democrats of the land-hungry Northwest. A thoroughly practical man, the President knew that any thought of obtaining all Oregon was foolish. England would never agree to such an arrangement; the only possible solution was a compromise. At the same time the only compromise possible was one that followed the 49th parallel, and as long as England remained opposed on that point nothing could be done. To bring pressure on the British government, as well as to quiet the more fervent members of his own party,

Polk had adopted a stiffly bellicose tone on Oregon. In his annual message in December he reasserted the United States claim to the entire territory and recommended that Congress vote at once to end the joint occupation agreement of 1818.[19]

Polk's statements produced a fresh outbreak of anti-British efforts among his supporters in Congress. Within a few days a resolution was before the Senate directing an "Inquiry into the Condition of the Military Defenses of the Country," and talk of war had become commonplace. Such violence, Webster felt, was not "altogether pleasing to Mr. Polk." [20]

From the outset Webster had understood Polk's motives in Oregon; he knew that the President was aiming only at a compromise settlement and that he had no intention of provoking a war with England over the issue.[21] If Polk was "safe," however, his overzealous friends in Congress were still a danger; after all Madison had been forced to go to war in 1812 against his will, and largely because of pressure from his own party. In the early months of 1846, then, Webster threw his energies into the battle for peace, calm, and diplomatic reasonableness. When warlike measures were spoken of in the Senate he ridiculed them; when the resolution for giving notice that the United States wished to terminate the Convention of 1818 came up, he argued against it; and finally, when it became clear that "notice" in some form was bound to pass, he tried to have it postponed.[22] By June he could congratulate himself that any time he may have gained with these efforts had paid off handsomely. The British government had decided to settle along the 49th parallel. Transmitted by the President to the Senate, the offer was promptly accepted.

The Oregon settlement pleased Webster immensely, but for all his pleasure the episode had cost him something. His steady opposition to the 54°40' men had made him a target for every conceivable kind of abuse. As time passed the insults, charges, and accusations came more and more to center on the Ashburton negotiations and Webster's use of the so-called "secret service fund" in connection with the treaty. For weeks charges and countercharges, investigations, explanations, reports, and testimony multiplied in dizzying profusion. In the end — thanks largely to the generous support of John Tyler — Webster managed to clear himself of the worst of the charges. There were those who remained unconvinced, however, and the resulting blot on the treaty, which he considered one of his finest accomplishments, was disheartening.[23]

Peace with England — in fact peace in general — had always played a major role in Webster's thinking. Nothing was more likely to raise havoc with national balance than the clash of arms across national borders. On a more mundane level, war unsettled commercial values and it confused the normal operation of domestic politics. For all these reasons a peaceful resolution of the Oregon dispute seemed essential — even if it meant a rough fight.

Webster's thinking on tariff reform — which in June of 1846 promised an equally difficult struggle — was no less emphatic, but it ran along different lines. In his view the tariff was above all a political issue. Its economic consequences were not to be scoffed at, of course; the rate at which foreign textiles were taxed was a crucial issue in Massachusetts. Far more important than anything affecting the price of cotton cloth, however, was the fact that, from the moment the Whig party first drew breath, the tariff had been — in spite of everything tending to divide the party — a vital adhesive, a rallying point, and the issue that most clearly set the Whigs apart from their Democratic rivals. Every good Whig was a high tariff man. Polk's challenge to the Whig tariff of 1842 threatened them all alike, and logically the man who took the lead in resisting that challenge belonged at the head of the party.

With so much to be gained from a vigorous stand on the tariff, Webster had the added satisfaction of knowing his efforts would meet with warm approval at home. For all those who might have feared — watching his conduct in the anti-Texas crusade — that he had become just another abolitionist agitator, here was tangible proof to the contrary: proof that he stood firm both on the interests of his state and on the eternal Whig verities. This view Webster himself cultivated with some energy, writing often to leading businessmen for advice and information and keeping them constantly mindful of the dangers ahead. "I wish I felt no more alarm about the Tariff, than I do at the present moment about war," he remarked to Nathan Appleton in January having just observed of the Oregon crisis: "We grow daily more pacific." [24]

The administration's tariff bill, which not only reduced rates but worked a major revolution by abolishing the sine qua non of protection — specific duties — in favor of a system of graded, ad valorem duties on broad categories of goods, passed the House easily on July 3 and moved on to the Senate.[25] There the friends of protection had two choices, Webster pointed out: they could either try to defeat the bill "just as it is" or amend it with an eye to eliminating some of its more objectionable features. Of the two approaches he favored the former, initially.[26] By the middle of July, however, it had become clear that the proposed tariff — if it passed the Senate at all — would need every vote the administration could muster for it. In this situation the chances of effecting a compromise seemed much better than they had earlier, and Webster accordingly reversed his positon.[27]

The spectacle of the archdefender of protection working to pass a compromise tariff was an odd one, but Webster knew what he was about and why. To defeat the administration bill outright would have been a purely negative gesture. To stand between the opposing forces, on the other hand, and manage both to lower duties a little and still salvage the principle of protection from the threat of "ad valoremism" — that was an accomplishment any man could point to with pride: "a proper & *permanent* tariff" as Webster described it. What he envisioned was a reduction of existing duties, under the act of 1842, by at least 20 per cent — or more if necessary. Such a plan had the approval of every businessman he talked to; it had the grudging consent of his Boston correspondents; even Robert Walker, the Secretary of the Treasury and author of the administration bill, declared himself "satisfied with it," according to Webster, and agreed "in his next official communication, to say, that this ought to be considered the *settlement* of the Tariff controversy." [28] Thus supported, the compromise proposal needed only the sanction of Webster's colleagues. "If *all* the Whig Senators go for this, I have great hopes of carrying it," he wrote on July 21.[29]

Within a week those hopes had flickered out to nothing. In spite of Webster's best arguments, his most energetic efforts, a group of Whig senators remained opposed to any kind of compromise. Led by John J. Crittenden of Kentucky, who claimed "he wished the administration to make its own Bill, and to make it as bad as it pleased," these men, Webster felt, were acting with little more than their own selfish ends in mind.[30] "The true difficulty here — or at least, one of them," he wrote, "is that there are those on both sides, who think much is to be made, hereafter, out of the Tariff as a *political topic*." [31] He himself was deeply concerned with the political implications of the tariff, of course, but only in rather long-range terms. Less ambitious and more narrowly wedded to the problems of the moment, the anticompromise group took a shorter view: the abandonment of protection by the Democrats would make a handy issue for Whig congressmen in the coming fall elections.

With half the Whigs in the Senate opposing him, Webster had no choice but to retreat. On the twenty-fifth and twenty-seventh, in a speech on the tariff that proved to be the longest one he ever gave in the Senate, he avoided the subject of compromise entirely.[32] By then he was doing everything possible to defeat the administration bill as it stood.

Ultimately even that failed, but for a while the chances

looked quite good. The week before, the President had felt it necessary to ask one Democratic senator who was on the verge of leaving Washington on urgent private business "to remain and vote for the bill"; another, who announced himself unable "on principle" to approve the administration's tariff reduction, was harried into resigning his seat.[33] In spite of such efforts, the issue still hung in the balance; one vote, either way, would settle it. The vote everybody focused on belonged to Senator Spencer Jarnagin, a Whig from Tennessee who was currently standing for reelection. Jarnagin's legislature had instructed him to support tariff reform. With his Whig colleagues pulling one way and the administration and his instructions the other, rumors about the state of Jarnagin's intentions circulated constantly. By the morning of the twenty-seventh, however, Webster — who superintended the negotiations with the Tennessean for the Whigs — felt confident that Jarnagin would stand by his party. Then everything went wrong. Scheduled for a vote that day, the bill was suddenly returned to committee.[34] The next morning it was out again, but in the meantime Jarnagin had changed his mind. When the final tally was recorded later that day, the bill passed by one vote — his.[35] "I would not impute any corrupt motive to Mr. Jarnagin," Webster wrote, "but he falsified his promises, & has thoroughly disgraced himself, forever." [36]

Disgraced or not, Jarnagin had given the administration the tariff it wanted. For the moment Webster could only assume that Polk himself had engineered the senator's last-minute change of heart.[37] As it happened, however, Polk did not see Jarnagin on the crucial evening of the twenty-seventh, or the next day; if anybody tipped the scales, someone other than the President did. Later Webster discovered this, for in a letter to the *National Intelligencer* about the incident, written early the following year, he could find nothing more tangible to rail at than *"Legislative Instructions,* an authority, which in forty years experience, we have hardly known to be once used for any real good purpose or object." [38]

Under the circumstances, to be left condemning the practice of legislative instructions was cold comfort. The real difficulty had not been legislative instructions at all, but the Whig party. Presented with a splendid opportunity for rallying the Whigs to his standard, Webster had found them both divided and unwilling to accept his lead. He counseled compromise and half of them opposed him; he coaxed promises from Jarnagin and Jarnagin promptly broke those promises to carry the day for the Democrats. With so little accomplished where so much had been hoped for, the future must have seemed less promising than before. By now, too, it was most emphatically that future which looked southward — to the march of troops across the Rio Grande — for its shape.

## IV

Spare and remote almost to the point of asceticism, James K. Polk hardly seemed the sort of man to cherish vivid dreams of empire; yet he did. Further, to the chagrin of his opponents, he invariably managed to make those dreams come true. In large part his success was due to the all-embracing character of his vision. Where another man might have concentrated his efforts in one direction, only to lose the prize down a bottomless well of sectional jealousy, Polk was prepared to move on every front — from the 49th parallel on the Pacific to the Gulf of California and Vera Cruz.

When Taylor was ordered south from the Nueces to the Rio Grande in January 1846, the order constituted a tacit admission that ordinary diplomacy had failed to achieve Polk's objectives in that quarter. He wanted a favorable settlement of the longstanding Texas boundary dispute, and he wanted California plus whatever else he could secure of Mexican territory. Though he preferred other means, he was perfectly willing to go to war to obtain those things. By January war had become his only available instrument. But starting the war presented something of a problem; if Polk was to carry Congress with him, the first move must seem to come from Mexico. Weeks passed. Slow to begin, Taylor's march was even slower in progress, and when he arrived the Mexicans for some time did nothing. Finally the necessary skirmish took place. Word reached Washington early in May, and a jubilant President hurried to inform Congress that American blood had been shed on "American soil." When the Walker Tariff passed the Senate the Mexican War was already two and a half months old.

The climax of Polk's Mexican diplomacy happened to coincide with Edward Everett's installation as President of Harvard, so Webster was relieved of the necessity of voting on the war message. He had gone north on April 19 and did not return to the capital until mid-May. If his absence at such a juncture seemed unfortunate, he quickly discovered otherwise. The scene he left behind in Massachusetts was proof enough that some historic moments were better missed.

The trouble began the moment news of the vote on Polk's message reached Boston. The President had asked for money and troops, and the bill that provided them stated flatly in its preamble that war existed "by the act of the Republic of Mexico." In the strictest sense that was true, yet the preamble ignored the extent to which the United States had provoked Mexico by sending troops into the disputed territory. Almost to a man the Whigs rose in protest, but attempts to alter the preamble failed in both the House and Senate. As a result Polk's opponents were left in the unenviable position of having to choose between accepting his version of events and refusing to aid a United States Army under attack in the field. In the end there were Whigs voting on both sides of the issue, with varying consequences. Few men, however, found themselves as hard-pressed for justifications — or as roundly criticized — as Robert Winthrop, the Representative from Boston.

Winthrop had voted for the bill. All his Massachusetts colleagues in the House save one and the only Massachusetts senator present — John Davis — had voted against it. In the hectic hours before the bill passed Winthrop had done everything in his power to change the preamble, but failing that he felt obliged to vote with the majority; regardless of how, war had come and Taylor's troops needed provisions and reinforcement. This kind of reasoning made sense to men like Appleton and Lawrence; it even satisfied Webster, who privately praised Winthrop for his stand.[39] One group remained unconvinced, however. With the Texas question dead and buried the Young Whigs needed an issue; Winthrop's vote was tailor-made for the purpose.

The mere fact of the war was an issue of course, and recognizing that Charles Francis Adams and his friends had promptly acquired control of the near-defunct Boston *Daily Whig* to air their particular point of view. Edited by Adams, the *Whig* made a practice from the beginning of treating its readers to simultaneous attacks on the Democratic administration in Washington and the conservative leadership of the Whig party in Massachusetts. In the latter category Lawrence and Appleton came in for a good deal of abuse, but neither one of them held elective office. Winthrop — whose position and close relations with the older ruling group in the party gave him both the shadow and the substance of power — was a much better target. The attack began in July with an editorial by Adams accusing Winthrop, among other things, of having "set his name in perpetual attestation of a falsehood." [40] A week later this was followed by an article even more vitriolic in tone. In voting for the war bill Winthrop had "told a lie" — been guilty of "gross disloyalty to Truth and Freedom" — declared "Boston," as the author styled himself.[41]

"Boston" was Charles Sumner. Throughout the long struggle against annexation the Young Whigs had grown steadily in number and many of the new recruits were men of singular ability — Henry Wilson, for example, and John G. Palfrey, Secretary of State of the Commonwealth and a former professor of theology at Harvard. None of the new men, however, and only Adams from the original group, could match Sumner for sheer brilliance. Darkly handsome with a gift for vivid prose and a style in everything uniquely his own, he had won the patronage of many of Boston's leading citizens. Yet for all Sumner's dinners at the Appletons' and his friendship with Longfellow and Prescott his future remained uncertain. At thirty-five the only occupation he could claim was a desultory law practice. In this situation he had drifted almost by accident into the inner councils of Young Whiggery; his interest in politics and the slavery question were both of very recent origin in July 1846.[42] But Sumner did nothing by halves. If the fate of the Whig party or the plight of the Negro were problems he had given scarcely a thought to two years earlier, they now aroused his deepest concern — as anybody reading his attacks on Winthrop would have discovered.

For his part, Winthrop lost no time in ferreting out the identity of "Boston." Surprised and hurt because his relations with Sumner had always been cordial, he at first did nothing, waiting for the other man to offer some explanation. The explanation, which Sumner eventually sent in a personal letter, spoke in rather grandiose terms of "duty" and ended with the hope that their friendship would continue.[43] Winthrop was not to be so easily won. He considered the "Boston" articles a personal affront and told Sumner as much.[44] More letters followed, and then another installment in the "Boston" series that finally brought matters to a head. "Blood! blood! is on the hands of the representative from Boston. Not all great Neptune's ocean can wash them clean," declared Sumner, using an image he later made famous.[45] Winthrop, appalled, wrote Sumner at once terminating all relations.[46]

Sumner wanted Winthrop's seat in Congress: Winthrop himself could think of no other way to account for the younger man's behavior. It was a plausible explanation certainly and true or not found a good many adherents among Sumner's former patrons — those who did not simply believe he had lost his reason. The consequences were striking. One by one the doors in Boston and Cambridge Sumner had fought so hard to open were closed to him. At the same time many of his compatriots among the Young Whigs were meeting with a similar experience. From State Street to Beacon Hill and on beyond to the farthest corners of Massachusetts, lines were being drawn that only a generation — and a war — would erase.

While polite Boston and the Whig high command were reverberating from the shock of Sumner's tirades, Webster was in Washington laboring over the tariff. Beyond telling Winthrop he himself would have voted for the war bill he took no part in the controversy. To choose publicly for one side or the other would have been foolish as long as his absence afforded him the luxury of not having to do so. But the session could not go on indefinitely. By August 6 the Independent Treasury Act — the last of Polk's major legislative projects — had become law. Within five days more Webster was on his way back to Marshfield.

When he arrived party affairs were already in a critical state, with the annual Whig convention still a month away. Assuming nothing happened before then, a showdown at the convention seemed inevitable, especially since Phillips, Adams, and Sumner would all be attending as delegates. "Being forewarned, we should be fore-armed," wrote Winthrop, who thought the selection of the Young Whig leaders as delegates "perhaps politic, & perhaps unavoidable." [47]

With the same forewarning as Winthrop, Webster faced a substantially more difficult task at the convention. For most of the men assembled in Faneuil Hall, including Winthrop, the issue was clear; one made a choice and acted accordingly. Webster, too, would have to choose. The circumstances no longer permitted the studiously cultivated appearance of neutrality. On the other hand, how to express his choice, once he had made it, was a problem of major proportions. In the end he decided to appear before the convention, but purposely timed his arrival for a point after all the impassioned speeches and the predicted fight over the platform had taken place.

The final act planned, Webster was free to watch the rest of the drama from the wings. A thoroughly discomforting spectacle it was. As a rule Massachusetts Whig conventions were sedate affairs, even decorous by the standards of the period, but this one broke every precedent. Time and again competing demonstrations bellowed up from the floor, and the more the chairman gavelled for order the worse the confusion became. In the midst of one such outburst, triggered by the announcement that Winthrop was about to speak, Sumner charged to the platform and delivered an elaborate plea for the party to accept as its standard THE REPEAL OF SLAVERY UNDER THE CONSTITUTION AND LAWS OF THE NATIONAL GOVERNMENT. While cheer after cheer rose from the Young Whigs, he concluded with a personal appeal to Webster, imploring him to join their ranks, adding to his renown as "Defender of the Constitution" and "Defender of Peace" a third and far greater distinction, "never to be forgotten on earth or in heaven — Defender of Humanity." [48] It was a difficult moment; had Webster followed Sumner the results would have been disastrous. Fortunately the chore fell to Winthrop, who managed to spend most of his time discussing such safe, if uninspiring, topics as the tariff and the subtreasury.

When Winthrop had finished, the convention turned to the business of framing a platform, and the maneuvering began in earnest. At the last minute the regular leadership had drafted a set of unusually stiff antislavery resolutions, but the Young Whigs had a set of their own, drawn up by Stephen Phillips, which were stiffer still and a good deal more specific: henceforth the party would adopt as primary objectives three things — the prohibition of the interstate slave trade, the exclusion of any additional slave states from the Union, and the abolition of slavery in the District of Columbia and the territories; every candidate receiving a Whig endorsement would have to go on record as a sponsor of those objectives; no man could claim the party label who did not campaign openly for abolition by "all Constitutional measures." No sooner had Phillips presented his resolutions than a motion was made to table them. There followed two speeches, one by Adams and the other by Charles Allen, both in favor of the resolutions. Then, just as the vote was about to be taken, Webster appeared on the arm of Abbott Lawrence.[49]

It could hardly have been a more dramatic entrance. For those who wondered what he thought of the proceedings of the convention, the fact that Webster had accepted Lawrence's escort spoke volumes. Yet he himself said nothing at first — waiting for the vote on Phillips' resolutions. In the general confusion, recording the vote proved almost impossible; only after two attempts by voice had failed and the chair had resorted to a show of hands was there anything like a clear decision: 91 delegates for the Young Whig platform amendments and 137 against. The result was announced and Webster rose to speak. "Mr. Chairman and Fellow Citizens: I deem it a great piece of good fortune to be for a few moments in so large a body of the Representatives of the Whigs of Massachusetts. Wherever they are assembled, there is an odor of liberty about them that I love to inhale." [50]

Neatly sidestepping the obvious difficulties of his subject

Webster proceeded to trace that "odor of liberty" to its source. It was not only the party's avowed attachment to "the progress of human liberty . . . at home or abroad" he cherished, but the good will and tolerance with which it greeted differences of opinion within its own ranks. In any group "composed of intelligent, honest, patriotic and conscientious men and masses of men" absolute unanimity was impossible, yet toleration and "a community of feeling and a community of purpose" together could still bring about the cooperation "necessary both for action and result." From there Webster moved directly to the heart of the matter — a statement of his own position and a prescription for the future. "There are important topics in relation to which gentlemen here present, whom I hold high in my regard, and warm in my affection, differ from me; and as to which they see a line of duty not apparent to me." The word "duty" was the key; if Sumner and his friends felt duty compelled them to transform the Whig party into an instrument for freeing the Negro, Webster disagreed. But that was all. The party by implication remained as he had cast it — flexible, tolerant, fully capable of encompassing and reconciling such disagreements. "I see in the dark and troubled night which is now upon us, no star above the horizon, but the intelligent, patriotic, *united* Whig party of the United States."

"A few generalities intended as a soother," commented Charles Francis Adams in disgust.[51] He was right; Webster had set out to soothe, and generalities were the principal coin expended in the effort. Taken together, however, those generalities amounted to something more than a simple palliative — something that Adams in his disappointment at the outcome of the convention probably missed. Faced with a situation where choice had become imperative, Webster had abandoned the uneasy middle ground of the year before and openly opposed his former Young Whig allies. This was the most striking fact about the performance in Faneuil Hall, but there were others equally worth considering: the matter of emphasis and tone, for example. With dozens of ways of saying what he had to say, nothing could have been milder than the way Webster chose. So even-tempered, so free of rebuke was his statement of opposition that it hardly merited the term at all.

To espouse a position in one breath and retreat from it in the next may have seemed so much wasted effort, but for the moment Webster had no alternative. From his standpoint what the Young Whigs proposed was clearly impossible. Opposition to slavery could never become the sole objective of the Massachusetts Whig organization; the result would have been its political isolation and an end to his own hopes for the nomination two years hence. On the other hand, the fact that the issue had hung so evenly in the balance — 91 votes to 137 — was proof enough that Webster's one-time associates deserved the gentlest possible treatment. Their strength might still be turned to useful ends. Events had temporarily eliminated the middle ground, but nothing yet suggested this was a permanent arrangement. Best then to temporize; to be firm where necessary but contrive at the same time to leave every door open. A few days after the convention Sumner wrote Webster, repeating the invitation he had issued in Faneuil Hall: "I have long desired, in public as in private, to approach you with the sentiments which I then expressed, believing that there now lie before you fields of usefulness & glory which you have not yet entered." [52] Webster's reply was a triumph of gracious refusal. He had "ever cherished high respect" for Sumner's "character and talents" and "seen with pleasure" the promise of the younger man's "future and greater eminence and usefulness." At present they happened to entertain "a difference of opinion respecting the relative importance of some of the political questions of the time." Webster regretted this deeply, but he had no intention of allowing it "to interfere with personal regard, or my continued good wishes for your prosperity and happiness." [53]

Surveying the tangle of Massachusetts Whig politics after the

convention John Quincy Adams remarked, "there are two divisions in the party, one based upon public principle, and the
other upon manufacturing and commercial interests." [54] When
Adams wrote, the terms "Conscience" and "Cotton" Whigs were
already in use, and to the casual observer the divisions they
connoted had become an established fact. But the situation remained more fluid than such labels implied. Webster was a case
in point. In a particular set of circumstances he had opted for
one side in the struggle, but he made no permanent commitment — at least in his own mind. Even his appearance with
Lawrence had to be read in this light. If the two found it expedient to wear the cloak of friendship in public, the old enmity
remained.

## V

When the Whig state convention met in September 1846, the
presidential election was still two years away. This length of
time might have seemed ample for the adjustments Webster was
laboring over, yet he himself knew better. The havoc wrought
by the Mexican War in Massachusetts politics was not an isolated phenomenon; everywhere in the nation old alignments
were shifting. Out of the prevailing rush and disorder, furthermore, tendencies were emerging that Webster in particular
had cause to guard against if he could. The future would define
those tendencies more fully, but for the time being two names
pinpointed the difficulty with telling precision: Zachary Taylor
and David Wilmot.

The United States commander in Mexico and an aspiring
Democratic congressman from Pennsylvania, Taylor and Wilmot were an odd pair to have marked an era so deeply. As
different from one another as two men could be, they were both
destiny's children — both more shaped by than shapers of the

events that brought them prominence. In a war it would have been difficult if not impossible to lose, Taylor played a major role that in turn, due to the conditions of the time, thrust him into politics virtually against his will. No less the victim and beneficiary of happenstance, Wilmot, in August 1846, found himself faced simultaneously with an election and a constituency grown restive under the administration's apparent disregard of Northern interests. He needed an issue: the proviso which bore his name gave notice that he had found one.[55]

As it happened the Wilmot Proviso might have been called by any one of a dozen other names, but the honor fell to Wilmot. In the final days of the session Polk had asked Congress for $2 million to facilitate negotiations with Mexico over territorial adjustments. Offered as an amendment to the necessary appropriation bill, the Proviso required the express prohibition of slavery in any territory acquired from Mexico as a result of the War. Wilmot had won the right to present his version of the amendment over the claims of his competitors because he had not previously taken a strong stand on slavery. With the support of most of his Northern colleagues — Whigs as well as Democrats — the measure passed the House easily. In the Senate, where adjournment cut short the discussion before a vote could be taken, it fared less well, but that hardly ended the matter.

Throughout the initial debate in the Senate on Wilmot's proposal Webster remained silent. Had the issue come to a vote he would have cast his lot with the Proviso men, but not without considerable misgiving. In his request for funds Polk for the first time had hinted publicly at his larger aims in the War. Most people had long since guessed what those were, but no official confirmation had been forthcoming. Now, with the President talking openly of "territorial adjustments," the issue was clear. One consequence was to give instant support to the theory that the administration was waging war to "expand the area of slavery." This was the standard Conscience Whig interpretation in Massachusetts and the origin of much of the opposition to Winthrop's vote. It was also the chief rationale behind the Wilmot Proviso. As an explanation of Polk's war aims, the antislavery view may or may not have impressed Webster; the antislavery remedy as embodied in the Proviso he almost certainly considered partial and misdirected.

To begin with there were two questions involved: slavery and expansion. The two were related but separate in the vital sense that they could be treated independently of one another. The Whig party — North and South — had always opposed territorial expansion; its record on slavery was far less unanimous. The Democrats tended to divide on both issues. For anyone wishing to prevent the spread of slavery, then, one simple solution suggested itself immediately: let the slavery question per se go and take a stand against expansion. Such a course would draw the support of a united Whig party as well as large numbers of Democrats. Insisting on the Proviso, on the other hand, would only drive Southern Whigs into the arms of the expansionists, an arrangement bound to prove disastrous for the party, for the country, for the cause of antislavery, and for Webster personally.

Because he said nothing at the time, it is difficult to know precisely how far Webster's thinking had progressed along these lines by August 1846. The question was important. Six months later he argued the anti-expansionist position at length in the Senate, offering it explicitly as an alternative to the Proviso. If in fact the alternative occurred to him earlier, he made what amounted to one of the major blunders of his career by waiting as long as he did to announce it. When the Proviso reached the Senate its siren call had already attracted most Northern Whig representatives. In the months that followed it became a rallying cry for Northern politicians everywhere; local platforms were built around it; all but one of the free state legislatures passed resolutions favoring it. The net effect was to crystallize the lines of debate to the point where no alternative — however promising — seemed likely to win many supporters.

At the end of a long and particularly trying session with all the vagaries of Massachusetts politics still before him to be dealt with, Webster's lapse in the case of the Proviso, if serious, was at least understandable. He was tired; he had a great deal on his mind. Nor did the events of the session and affairs at home constitute the sole items in that category. As each day brought fresh word of Zachary Taylor's triumph in Mexico, the national political situation — already overburdened with complications — seemed about to acquire another.

Clay's defeat in 1844 had left Webster a leading contender for the Whig nomination four years hence, but at no point could his claim to the nomination have been labeled secure, even before Taylor burst on the scene. Outside of New England the time-honored objections to his candidacy were as strong as ever. Though for the moment people seemed willing to forget them, it was only because the other possibilities — Clay, General Winfield Scott, or Judge John McLean of Ohio — offered even less to hope for. Taylor changed all that. At the end of the first summer of the War, "Old Rough-and-Ready" was still a stranger to politics, but his victories in Mexico had made him a national hero. It remained to make him a Whig, and that task Webster's old associate Thurlow Weed had already cheerfully adopted.

In the best of all possible worlds Weed might well have preferred Webster's name at the head of any Whig ticket. The editor of the Albany *Evening Journal* was a realistic man, however; he lived in the world as he found it, not as he thought it ought to be. In the world of 1846 Webster's chances against whomever the Democrats might nominate were poor. The party needed a fresh face and one with a good deal of popular appeal. Weed had every reason to be delighted, then, with what he learned from a chance meeting early that summer with Colonel Joseph P. Taylor, the general's brother. According to Colonel Taylor, Old Zack "had no politics," but he did harbor a healthy dislike for Andrew Jackson and felt so strongly about foreign manufactures that he insisted on American-made cloth for his coats. The general was a Whig after all! Back in Albany, having suggested that Colonel Taylor advise his brother to keep silent on political topics and concentrate on the War, Weed confidently predicted Taylor would be the next President. September brought word of the great American victory at Buena Vista, and Weed repeated his prediction with gusto.[56] He also found himself joined by a growing number of like-minded Whigs. There were problems of course: the hero of Buena Vista was a Southerner and a slaveholder, which was bound to cause trouble in the North; he was also the commanding figure in a war the Whig party opposed. Yet none of these circumstances seemed to bother the enthusiasts; for every entry on the debit side of the balance they stood prepared to point out ten across the page.

With state legislatures gathering across the country to debate the Proviso, and Taylor's name on everybody's lips, it scarcely seemed an auspicious moment for Webster to begin his own campaign in earnest. The longer he waited, however, the worse the results were likely to be. Having already accepted an invitation to an enormous public dinner in his honor at Philadelphia on December 2, he made that the scene of his first major effort.

True to the conventions of the period Webster concentrated on issues at Philadelphia — even to the extent of never once mentioning the Whig party. On the other hand, the sentiments he expressed could hardly have been called lofty. For two and a half hours he harangued the deeds and policies of the Polk administration with merciless energy. His chief target was the tariff, but he also managed to suggest that the President had been guilty of an impeachable offense in bringing on the War as he had.[57]

The Philadelphia speech was not a particularly noteworthy piece of oratory, the more so because it avoided any mention of the chief issue of the moment — the Proviso. It was at least a beginning, however, and under the circumstances perhaps the best one Webster could have managed. With the opening of Congress only a few days away, the political scene offered more than the usual number of pitfalls.


## VI

The distance from Philadelphia to Washington was not great, but to Webster the two cities must have seemed worlds apart in December 1846. In Philadelphia the subjects he discussed were of his own choosing; if he wished to ignore a troublesome issue like the Proviso he could. Washington was another matter. There the agenda of debate lay beyond his control, and as it turned out the men of the second session of the Twenty-ninth Congress spoke of very little else but the Proviso.

No sooner had the session begun than Polk renewed his request for funds, adding $1 million to the original figure. On February 15 the so-called "Three Million Bill" passed the House — with the Proviso attached. The proceedings had gone on at near white-heat intensity, and whatever degree of conviction or emotion had been lacking, the Senate was sure to provide.

The day the final vote was taken in the House, Webster offered a pair of resolutions in the Senate, pointing out as he did so that "it was not his purpose to interfere, by any proposition of his own, with . . . the three million bill, either by way of amendment to that bill or otherwise." The resolutions were to be considered separately at some appropriate time in the future.

For the present he simply wanted them read and laid on the table. Of the two, the first was the more important: *"Resolved, That the war now existing in Mexico ought not to be prosecuted for the acquisition of territory to form new States to be added to the Union."* The second resolution, growing logically from the first, called upon the administration to signify its desire not "to dismember the Republic of Mexico" and to begin peace negotiations at once.[58]

What would the fruits of the Mexican War be — slave or free? Webster's answer was simple: eliminate the problem by insuring the War would bear no fruit, at least of a territorial variety. When he presented his resolutions this position — "no territory" as it came to be called — was already well defined, thanks to the efforts of another Whig senator, John M. Berrien, of Georgia. In order to expedite matters during the short session, administration forces in the Senate had decided to draft their own $3 million appropriation without waiting for the House bill to pass. On February 2 Berrien offered an amendment to the Senate bill incorporating the gist of Webster's later resolutions.[59] As opposed to the amending tactic Webster's preference for keeping "no territory" distinct from the Three Million Bill made better sense since the appropriation itself was clearly for the purpose of territorial acquisition. But time was too short for a separate debate, so in the end Webster threw his support behind Berrien's amendment, regardless of the logical inconsistencies involved. Moreover, if time was running out on the session, it was also true that response had long since hardened around the issue to the point where new solutions faced obstacles enough, without requiring a whole new set of ground rules.

Meanwhile, the full magnitude of the obstacles confronting "no territory" became clearer every day. For two weeks after Webster presented his resolutions, debate in the Senate dealt almost exclusively with the territorial question. Calhoun, back in his old seat, made a brilliant speech condemning the Proviso and demanding equal rights for Southerners in the territories. Without such parity, he hinted, the days of the Union were numbered.[60] Other Southerners made the same point, often in even plainer terms, while Northerners were just as emphatic in defense of the Proviso. Each day brought a new series of accusations and counteraccusations, threats and counterthreats. Yet through it all the focal point of the dispute remained the same. The proviso was the issue; the Webster-Berrien alternative was scarcely mentioned.

With the debate careening so far from the course he hoped it would take, Webster apparently decided it was useless to try to affect the outcome by further elaborating his position. Having promised such an elaboration at the time he offered his resolutions, he waited to present it until after the Senate had taken final action on both the Proviso and Berrien's amendment.[61] Then, faced with the fact of defeat, he too rose to point the finger of blame and pronounce warnings for the future.

By the time the roll was called for the Proviso it was already near midnight with the end of the session less than two days away. Webster could not say a great deal, but in the short time allotted him he managed to make his point abundantly clear. His principal quarrel was with the Northern Democracy — "I so denominate the party only because it so denominates itself." Here were men who professed themselves enemies of slavery, who voted for the Proviso, and yet who — when a far more promising means of limiting slavery presented itelf — turned the other way. "Every member of the Senate belonging to the Democratic party, in the Northern states, however warmly he might have declared himself against more slave States, yet refused to vote against all territorial acquisition, a measure proposed and offered as a perfect security against more slave states." Given a choice between principle and territory, the Northern Democracy had chosen territory, with all the consequences that choice implied. "They are for acquiring territory; they are for more States; and, for the sake of this, they are willing to run the risk of these new States being slave States, and to meet all the convulsion which the discussion of that momentous question may hereafter produce. Sir, if there be wisdom, or prudence, or consistency, or sound policy, or comprehensive foresight in all this, I cannot see it." Nothing had been settled; the end of the War would only give rise to a new chapter in the same debate. "Will the North consent to a treaty bringing in territory subject to slavery? Will the South consent to a treaty bringing in territory from which slavery is excluded?" As matters stood the future seemed "full of dangers" to Webster and his coleagues' blunder in "suffering to pass the golden opportunity for securing harmony" something "not unlikely to attract the attention of the age." "We appear to me to be rushing upon perils headlong, and with our eyes wide open." [62]

These were solemn words, but the senators had little opportunity to ponder their meaning. As soon as Webster took his seat the roll call on the Three Million Bill began. The result was a foregone conclusion; without the Proviso or Berrien's amendment to encumber it, the bill passed easily in a straight party division. For the third time that evening Webster found himself voting with the minority.[63]

No stranger to defeat, Webster might have been content with warning his colleagues of the danger they courted in annexing new territory to the Union. Indeed there was little else to be done, but warnings like the one he issued that night in the Senate left the problem at best half defined. He had spoken movingly of national disharmony and the "convulsion" that further discussion of the slavery issue might produce. Unquestionably this generalized concern for the nation was real, yet the threat to the Whig party and to his own standing in it must have troubled him no less deeply. To a man the Whigs had supported Berrien's amendment, and Webster duly noted the fact. Unmentioned, however, was the party's behavior in the face of the Proviso, which had been anything but harmonious or unified. Only one Southern Whig senator, John Clayton of Delaware, had voted for the Proviso; not a single Northern Whig senator voted against it.

Once the Berrien amendment had been defeated, Webster himself had no choice but to vote for the Proviso. To thus align himself with the Northern cause, on the other hand, was hardly a course calculated to appeal to Southern Whigs, whose support he needed for the nomination. Further, the longer the territorial question continued to divide the nation and the party, the worse the consequences would be. With so much pending, Taylor — a Southerner and a slaveholder — was bound to seem more attractive to his fellow section men than someone of Webster's ilk, and the better Taylor's chances became in the South, the more steadfastly Northern politicians like Weed would hold to him, despite the rising chorus of opposition within their own ranks. It was a matter of simple arithmetic: no Whig could be elected President in 1848 who failed to command at least a measure of Southern support.

## VII

All of which must have been very much on Webster's mind as he set out, late in April 1847, for an extended tour of the South.

Beyond Virginia he had no firsthand knowledge of the section, and the purpose of the trip, ostensibly, was to remedy that deficiency. As originally planned his route lay through the coastal states, then west to New Orleans from which point he would travel north up the Mississippi by steamboat. For a man of Webster's age this was a strenuous undertaking, and it is little wonder he failed to complete it — even without the added considerations that may have induced him to call a halt. In the end he got no farther than Atlanta, Georgia.

For weeks before his departure invitations to speak had poured in from every part of the South. He chose carefully: a public dinner at Richmond where he toasted the memory of John Marshall, a greeting to the citizens of Charleston and in the same city dinners in his honor given by the New England Society and the Bar Association, a reception at Columbia for the student body of South Carolina College and another in Savannah held near the base of a monument honoring the revolutionary heroes Nathanael Green and Casimer Pulaski — all occasions admirably suited to the themes he meant to develop. For the moment any discussion of concrete political issues was out of the question. Even if such a course had been appropriate, the difficulties involved were overwhelming. The only solution was to concentrate upon the general, which meant, above all, the nation.

The definition of the nation Webster offered his Southern hosts differed little from what he had said on similar occasions in the past. His major theme was balance and the factors that operated to maintain it. Nor had those factors changed. Addressing the Charleston Bar he derived them in a near-perfect duplicate-in-miniature of the speech he had given four years earlier at Bunker Hill. Here was the same unique combination of British culture and American institutions developing organically over time. "The establishment of our free institutions is the gradual work of time and experience, not the immediate result of any written instrument. English history and our colonial history are full of those experiments in representative government which heralded and led to our more perfect system." Here, too, was the same parallel between conditions in the United States and those to the south, particularly in "unfortunate, miserably governed Mexico," with its vast revenues all spent "in putting up one revolution and putting down another, and in maintaining an army of forty thousand men in time of peace to keep the peace." What accounted for the difference? Continuity but also, as before, character — though this time Webster chose as his model not Washington, but the "independent . . . enlightened judge," the man at the center of the system working actively to balance it by balancing the minute, individual interests within it.[64]

Institutions, the shared culture, and character — the instruments of balance had not changed; yet at odd moments on the Southern tour Webster did depart from the standard formulation, and the departure was significant. In the first of his three short speeches at Charleston he referred to "differences of opinion on many subjects . . . between your fellow-citizens and myself and between South Carolina and Massachusetts." Under the circumstances this might have seemed a rather hazardous line to take, but the sequel proved safe enough for in the next instant Webster was declaring that such "differences of opinion" were only natural. Moreover in spite of them — and this was the important point — the peoples of Massachusetts and South Carolina remained united in "spirit," in "mutual esteem," in "the sense of common brotherhood," and in their determination to serve the nation "to the utmost of their power . . . with filial reverence and patriotic devotion." Ultimately, such bonds transcended everything else. "If we do not always think alike, we all feel alike. We feel that much of the individual happiness, as well as the national renown, which belongs to us now, or may belong to us hereafter, does and will attach to us as the undivided, and I hope always the indivisible, members of the great American republic."[65]

The striking feature in all this was the importance Webster placed on emotion and feeling. A viable national balance depended on the proper functioning of the instruments of balance — institutions, culture, and character. Those instruments, in turn, could be made to function successfully only when men applied them in the right spirit, and the right spirit had always included, in Webster's view, certain definite emotional qualities. The emotional components of the system, however, had never before received such heavy emphasis. In the past, reason made the essential translation from private interest to national allegiance; the heart may have aided in the process, but its role was distinctly secondary.

Charleston saw the beginning of the shift; Savannah its completion. "Others may value this union of confederated States as a convenience, or an arrangement or a compromise of interests," Webster informed the crowd in Monument Square, "but I desire to see an attachment to the Union existing among the people, not as a deduction of political economy, nor as a result of philosophical reasoning, but cherished as a heartfelt *sentiment.*" [66] Three months earlier in the Senate, Calhoun, asserting that Southern "interests" were being sacrificed by a Northern-dominated national government, had predicted dire consequences unless the process were stopped. Implicit in the argument was the assumption that the Union was valuable, above all, precisely as "an arrangement or a compromise of interests." Always before when confronted with such an analysis Webster had accepted the basic assumption but challenged the argument drawn from it. Now apparently he felt obliged to take issue with the assumption itself. Whether he was prepared to grant the argument was another question, but to the casual observer it might almost have seemed so.

In the meantime the new line, whatever its other merits, made possible a host of graceful allusions to the glories of Southern hospitality and the virtues of travel as a means of "cultivating reciprocal feeings of kindness and courtesy." [67] On both points Webster could speak with sincerity. Always curious about the way other people lived and thought, he studied everything and filled long letters home with information on such diverse topics as the turpentine industry, the origin of the word "cotton," the architecture of Charleston, and the number of acres planted with rice one "hand" could cultivate "when they wish to make work easy." As for the people, he found them "excellent" and noted often how "very kindly" he and Mrs. Webster were treated, how "handsomely" they were entertained. And handsomely in this case was no exaggeration. Everywhere along the way people turned out to cheer, and city fathers lavished compliments on "the Defender of the Constitution." At Wilmington, North Carolina, he was met and escorted into the city on a special train; farther south there was a dinner at General Wade Hampton's "magnificent establishment," a torchlight parade staged by the students at Columbia, and a ball in Charleston for 1200 people.[68]

It was all very gratifying. It was also, unfortunately, quite exhausting. In poor health to begin with, Webster found it more and more difficult to cope with the elaborate attentions paid him. Finally at Augusta a "bilious and feverish" attack forced him to cancel his engagements altogether. He took to bed and remained there for a week. At the end of that time he felt "pretty well over" his "ill turn" but had definitely decided not to continue the tour.[69] Hot weather had never agreed with him, and the prospect of hazarding his weakened condition against the combined rigors of a Southern June and more Southern hospitality evidently settled the issue.

Or at any rate health was the official reason given for cutting short the tour. Quite possibly there was another. "I feel now a great deal better then [sic] when I left Washington," Webster wrote on the final day of his stay in Atlanta.[70] If this was so, and he had been well enough to set out in the first place, then presumably he might have continued — had there been anything to gain by doing so. In fact there was not. "Webster began making his circuit against the Taylor current, but judging it too strong, I am told, has now turned his head down stream," remarked John Pendleton Kennedy to Robert Winthrop, adding; "he was a little *disgruntled* to find his political reconnaissance turned into a civil and social affair 'without respect to party.' " [71]

Author, politician, and a long-time friend of Winthrop's, Kennedy had a passion for gossip that sometimes outran his otherwise acute perceptions, but not in this case. The Southern tour had been undertaken as a "political reconnaissance," and on that basis its results were discouraging indeed.

In every city, however warm its welcome, there would have come that moment when Webster sat down with the leaders of the local Whig party to discuss the future — a future in which they saw the figure of Zachary Taylor looming daily larger. Granted that Old Zack was a Johnny-come-lately to the Whig fold, he still represented the surest hope for victory in Georgia, or South Carolina, or Virginia. That condition no amount of rhetoric could overcome, and to proceed in the face of it when health and comfort together dictated a retreat would have been foolish. Shortly after Webster's departure, Berrien summarized the entire refrain: "Although the great majority of our people are I think opposed to the war — still military candidates are all the rage." The Georgia Whig convention that was about to assemble would almost certainly, Berrien felt, "nominate . . . General Taylor for the Presidency." [72]

## VIII

After leaving Atlanta Webster returned to Savannah and from there went directly to Boston. By the end of the first week in June he was settled at Marshfield, where he remained for the rest of the summer. The world heard little of him during those months; except for an occasional law case he spent his time fishing and otherwise enjoying the bucolic pleasures of his "place of places." [73] It seemed a peaceful interlude. Yet behind his placid, confident exterior Webster himself was anything but placid or confident. Writing his sister-in-law Harriette Paige late in August he observed, "we had a dull & lonely day yesterday. I sat on the Piaza, almost all day, *thinking.*" [74]

Brooding might have been a better word. Webster had gone south hoping for a vigorous movement in his behalf. Given such a movement he could have appealed to Whig leaders elsewhere in the country without embarrassment as a national candidate. But then for every one of his own he found ten Taylor banners flying below the Mason-Dixon line. The conclusion was obvious: if the South was to be won at all, some other section of the country would have to act so decisively and persuasively that its lead became at once irresistible.

That left New England and in particular Massachusetts — the point from which Webster had always begun in the past. Even though the results thus far had been something less than satisfactory, the old formula might yet work. On the other hand just how fully could Webster count on the united support of his section? And assuming that the Whigs of New England were prepared to back his candidacy, just how much was that backing worth? In Massachusetts the Whig organization ought to have endorsed him as a matter of course, but so divided was the organization and such was the strength of the antagonisms — old and new — which plagued it, that every inch of the way had to be fought for, and the victory once won was scarcely a victory at all. The climax came at the state convention in September.

A year had produced some strange configurations in Bay State politics. For all the gentleness with which he stated it, Webster's rejection of their position at the last convention had left the Conscience Whigs hurt and angry. His support of "no territory" as an alternative to the Proviso they liked even less; to men like Adams and Sumner "no territory" seemed at best a sorry evasion of principle. [75] As a result they were anxious to do anything they could to scuttle Webster's cause. Meanwhile Abbott Lawrence had definitely decided to back Taylor for the nomination, and though Taylor was anathema to the Conscience men the two groups could at least make common cause against Webster, and did.

The convention opened with the usual speeches and local nominations. The next item on the agenda was to have been an endorsement of Webster's candidacy. Before the necessary motion could be made, however, Stephen Phillips offered another stating that it was "inexpedient to recommend a nomination of candidates for the Presidency and Vice Presidency." Taken by surprise, Webster's forces promptly moved to table the suggestion, but then when Chairman George Ashmun — an ardent Webster man — awarded the first vote on the tabling motion to the "ayes," his decision was challenged and a regular division demanded. Opinions differed as to what happened next. According to the four tellers the "ayes" carried the second vote, yet Charles Francis Adams was convinced they falsified the count. It hardly mattered; between them the Conscience men and Lawrence had come so close to defeating Webster that the damage was done. Out of a total of 500 votes the official tally gave him a bare majority of ten.[76]

When it came to the actual endorsement the delegates behaved with greater unanimity. The vote in Webster's behalf was impressive. Indeed had there been less at stake he might have let matters rest at this point, but not now; too much hung in the balance.

Called upon to speak, Webster did his best to combine a stiff attack on slavery with an equally vigorous defense of "no territory" as the best and most workable means of preventing the institution's further spread. As for the Proviso, he alternately claimed it as his own "thunder" and argued that in the hands of the "Northern Democracy" it represented the poorest sort of security. "Are we quite certain that they will abandon the Administration and support the proviso against the slave power?" The answer was obvious: "the very last subject on which I should dare to venture a prediction would be the course of the Northern Democracy on this subject of the extension of slavery." "No territory," on the other hand, had the sanction of the United Whig party "North and South" to draw upon.[77]

Ultimately, Webster argued, it was a question of what kind of issue slavery would become. Beyond a doubt they all agreed "that we are to use the first and last, and every occasion that offers, to oppose the extension of slave power." Given such a program the Proviso had the advantage of embodying an unequivocal statement of both their paramount goal and the moral principle that underlay it. Slavery was more than a moral issue, however: "I speak of it here, as in Congress, as a political question, a question for statesmen to act upon." This did not mean it was "less important in a moral point of view," only that, Webster explained, "as a legislator, or in any other official capacity, I must look at it, consider it, and decide it, as a matter of political action." Within the context of political action the Proviso — in spite of its obvious merits — was bound to fail. There were too many votes against it; it was "not a sentiment to found any new party upon."

Later Webster was accused of having drastically altered his position at the convention in order to court back the support of the Conscience element in the party; "he who had gone up, as men thought, the Oldest of Old Whigs, came down again Younger than the Youngest," jeered *The Liberator.*[78] But the charge was only half correct. Unquestionably Webster did direct his appeal to the Conscience men. Their opposition had very nearly cost him the endorsement and promised to work still more damage in the future unless something were done. But there was a limit to what could be done. Webster went out of his way to condemn slavery and committed himself unequivocably to opposing its extension; yet on the fundamental issue of "no territory" versus the Proviso he stood firm. Even if he had not believed the Proviso was a poor device for accomplishing the end assigned it, he could scarcely have abandoned "no territory." Such a volte-face would have ended all remaining hope of Southern support. With his position thus determined, the most he could do was attempt to defend "no territory" by illustrating its basic compatibility with a strong antislavery stand.

Whether he convinced the Conscience forces was another matter, but before the convention was over they had at least discovered the perils of an alliance with Lawrence. As always the final piece of business was the platform, and to forestall any opposition the predrafted version included a particularly rigorous antislavery declaration. The same tactic had been tried the year before, and the Conscience men had still come forward with objections; the pattern repeated itself now. No sooner was the platform read than John G. Palfrey rose and offered an amendment stating that the Massachusetts Whig organization would support no candidate for the presidency who was not on record as an opponent of slavery. Since this clearly eliminated Taylor it might have appealed to Webster, but the Lawrence faction carried the issue easily; the amendment was defeated and the platform passed intact.[79]

From the Conscience standpoint the convention had proved a devastating experience. With Lawrence and Webster once again at odds, Adams and his friends held a potential balance of power within the party. Still they failed utterly to capitalize on that advantage; having allowed Lawrence to use them as a cat's-paw against Webster, they came away at the end of the day empty-handed. Logically the result should have been to drive them nearer Webster again, and there were indications of such a movement. Yet nothing came of it — for one good reason. If the Conscience men found scant comfort or profit in an alliance with Lawrence, they had already tried a similar arrangement with Webster to no better effect. By September 1847 a growing number of them had come to feel that the only reasonable course was to abandon the party completely. The debacle at the convention strengthened their arguments a dozenfold.[80]

For Webster the convention had been no less a debacle, though his wounds were perhaps less apparent. Needing the unqualified endorsement of a united organization, he had at least been granted the form. In substance the endorsement he received was far from unanimous and the organization that tendered it scarcely united. At the time he did the obvious thing and turned to rebuilding the bridges he had destroyed the year before. But it was too late for the obvious — the tried or the tested — in Massachusetts politics. The bridges Webster was laboring over all led to the Conscience forces, and they for their part were on the way out of the party forever.

## IX

A dispassionate survey might have convinced Webster that his chances for the Whig nomination had, by the end of 1847, fallen to virtually nothing, but still he persisted. With the War drawing to a close and the Whig's position in Congress strengthened as a result of the 1846 elections, there was always a possibility something more could be done with "no territory." That left Massachusetts, however, where the rift in the party seemed to grow wider daily.

To make matters worse, in December the situation in Massachusetts became the subject of national attention. The problem was the election of Robert Winthrop as Speaker of the House. The congressional contests the year before had given the Whigs a slight majority in the House, and Winthrop — with seven years of service, an impressive manner, and the good opinion of most of his colleagues to his credit — was a logical choice for the speakership. The issue was settled easily in caucus. Then when it came to a vote before the House as a whole several Whigs, including John G. Palfrey of Massachusetts, voted against Winthrop. To break with his party in this fashion was spectacular enough, but the fact that Palfrey was a representative from Winthrop's own state made it seem doubly so. Even John Quincy Adams, for all his opposition to slavery and the War, voted for Winthrop. But Adams belonged to an older generation; he had never really been a member of the Conscience group, and to those who were, Winthrop's stand on the War bill had placed him forever beyond the pale. In voting as he did Palfrey gave notice of that view and also, in the process, presented the country with a rather telling picture of Massachusetts Whig politics.[81]

Doubtless Palfrey's action annoyed Webster, yet he took no part in the ensuing controversy. Even if there had been a position he could safely assume — which there was not — his attentions for the moment were concentrated elsewhere. Besides New England, he had always relied, in his presidential calculations, on a solid bedrock of support in New York. Weed's early defection to Taylor had dimmed prospects in that direction considerably, but up to the beginning of 1848 an influential group of New York City merchants and bankers continued to express a preference for Webster. Late in January word came that most of the members of this group had signed a petition calling for a Taylor rally. Furious, Webster demanded an explanation.[82] In fact the men in New York had lost confidence in his chances, though to smooth matters over a polite fiction was manufactured about the necessity of cooperation to stop Clay. There was also a good deal of talk about mending relations with the pro-Taylor faction in order to secure Webster the vice presidency should Old Zack prove invincible after all.[83]

Whatever else he thought, Webster was not interested in the vice presidency. In wishing it for him his New York friends were undoubtedly sincere. Weed, too, approved of the arrangement,[84] yet Webster himself remained adamant. Considering how long he had waited for "first place" his attitude was understandable, but it did have one rather striking result. By disclaiming any ambition for the vice presidency Webster left the field open to a variety of other contenders, not the least of whom was Abbott Lawrence.

As anxious for political power and distrustful of Webster as ever, Lawrence had gravitated early to the Taylor camp. His relations with its leading figures were excellent. As a potential vice-presidential candidate he had far less appeal than Webster, but everyone agreed a Massachusetts man would be an invaluable addition to the ticket, and with Webster out of the running who better than Lawrence? To put that question as effectively as possible Nathan Appleton traveled to Washington in April where — at Lawrence's request — he saw and spoke with some of the more influential Taylor men, including John J. Crittenden.[85] By the middle of May groups were working actively in New York and Boston to organize and finance a movement in Lawrence's behalf at the convention. "We are now ready to strike for our friend & your friend, for the V. Presidency, and we write for the purpose of asking you to unite with us in furnishing the sinews of War" ran the refrain from one city to the other.[86] Ironically the Lawrence faction in New York included a fair share of Webster's own former supporters.

While the lines of political accord were stretching outward from Weed's New York and Lawrence's Boston to Washington and Crittenden's Kentucky, Webster, in the Senate, was suffering another, even graver setback — the final defeat of "no territory." The session had opened with a bitter debate over the continuation of the War. Without exception the Whigs favored calling a halt, and they were supported by enough Democrats, including such luminaries as Calhoun and Benton, to have posed a serious problem for Polk had not Nicholas Trist rescued the President at the eleventh hour. Trist had been dispatched late the year before to discuss peace terms with the Mexican government. Subsequently his authority was withdrawn, but he went on to negotiate a treaty anyway. Polk took a dim view of both Trist's independence and his treaty, and there was strong sentiment in the Cabinet for prosecuting the War until all of Mexico had been conquered. As it was, with Mexico City in the hands of Scott's army, the settlement Trist agreed to provided for the annexation of only California and New Mexico. If confirmed expansionists like Secretary of the Treasury Robert Walker thought this was too small a price, however, Polk recognized that anything more would require another year of fighting. Mindful of the growing weight of antiwar feeling in Congress and the nation at large, he finally decided to try the treaty in the Senate regardless of his own objections or those of his Cabinet. By the end of February the debate over Trist's handiwork was in full swing.

As long as it was simply a question of whether or not to continue the War Webster found himself acting with a comfortable majority of his colleagues. The treaty altered that circumstance. On the peace issue those who favored limited territorial gains could join the "no territory" forces without embarrassment. Trist's settlement, by contrast, offered precisely what most of the limited gains men wanted, which left "no territory" bereft of allies except for those few senators who still harbored designs on all of Mexico. It was a strange fate that placed Webster and the most dedicated of his expansionist opponents in harness together, but at the time it appeared eminently logical, even to Polk.[87] The arrangement also had a fair chance of working — or seemed to. As the debate progressed from the Foreign Relations Committee to the Senate as a whole, Webster might have longed for the security of January's antiwar majority, but it took only a third of the Senate — in this case nineteen votes — to defeat a treaty.

In the end the nineteen votes did not materialize. Polk at first was sure they would, but by March 2 he was writing of the treaty, "the prospect now is that it may be ratified, but by a very close vote." [88] The issue was settled eight days later, and as the President predicted the treaty passed, though the vote was hardly close. With four senators absent or abstaining the tally read thirty-eight for and only fourteen votes against Trist's settlement.[89]

If Polk was delighted, Webster had every reason not to be. The year before the Whigs had come down solidly in favor of "no territory"; a repetition of that performance would have defeated the treaty. Then, with the party united behind the doctrine he had championed and the treaty beaten, Webster could have gone before the convention — and the nation — promising peace. As things turned out, however, not only did the treaty pass, it split the Whigs in the Senate completely; indeed a majority of them voted with the administration. It was harder, after all, to turn down territory you actually possessed than territory you might one day acquire, and much more difficult to justify such a course to one's constituents.

In the aftermath Webster had ample opportunity to express his views on the treaty and did so, though by then the question had become in every way academic. Late in March two bills came before the Senate, one creating ten new regiments for the army and the other appropriating funds for their support. Both bills had originated before Trist completed his negotiations. They were war measures and presumably the ratification of the treaty had rendered them unnecessary, but they were still being urged as a precaution in case Mexico decided to back down on her word. Having spoken briefly against the first bill,[90] Webster used the second as an excuse for a full-scale attack on the War and its fruits. Was there a danger Mexico would refuse to let herself be stripped of her territories? He welcomed such an eventuality. The treaty was an unjust treaty, the War had been waged for territory, and his own position on that point had never changed. "I am against all accessions of territory to form new States . . . I yield nothing to the force of circumstances that have occurred, or that I can consider as likely to occur. And therefore I say, Sir, that if I were asked today whether, for the sake of peace, I would take a treaty for adding new States to the Union on our southern border, I would say, *No!* distinctly, No!"

Webster added that he "wished every man in the United States to understand . . . my judgment and my purpose" in the matter.[91] In truth few Americans probably either understood or cared. The War was over, California and New Mexico were secure, and most of Webster's countrymen were happy enough things had ended as they had. It was a sad defeat in a season full of sad defeats for Webster — quite apart from those of politics. At the end of April he buried both his only daughter and the youngest of his two surviving sons. Julia Webster Appleton was thirty and the mother of five children. Edward Webster, twenty-eight, had died while on duty with the army in Mexico.

# X

Webster remained at Marshfield for a month after the funerals of his children, but the week before the Whig convention found him back in Washington. With delegates pouring through the capital on their way to Philadelphia, the stock of individual candidates rose and fell by the hour. Confusion and rumor were everywhere. Yet above it all one word could be heard over and over again — "availability." To Webster "availability" had been from the beginning the paramount threat, an enemy to be beaten before all others; to the men who assembled in Philadelphia at the Chinese Museum on June 7 it became something quite different.

The idea that the party's presidential nomination ought to go to the man most likely to succeed with the national electorate — the core of the availability principle — scarcely constituted an innovation in 1848. It was as old as the two-party system. On the other hand, the basic concept had been given a rather novel pair of interpretive twists by Taylor's supporters in the months since his rise to prominence. The first was that potential success at the polls ought to be the only criterion for choosing a candidate, while the second held that Taylor was the only Whig sufficiently available to be elected. Both of these propositions were debatable, but judging from the results on the first ballot the Taylor men had already won the lion's share of whatever arguments were to be had.

Taylor's total on that first ballot was 111 votes as opposed to 168 for his five opponents — Clay, Scott, Webster, John M. Clayton, and McLean. Of the 168 Webster's share amounted to only 22. On the second ballot that figure remained constant while Clay's fell and Taylor's inched perceptibly upward. Delighted, the prophets of availability were ready for the final effort when the convention adjourned that evening. By all accounts they performed admirably. The next morning the third ballot showed a substantial increase for Taylor and by the fourth, with Old Zack's total standing at 171, it was all over. Webster's count, in the meantime, had fallen to a mere 13.[92]

As news of events in Philadelphia reached Washington it may have afforded Webster some small consolation — in an otherwise thoroughly depressing scene — that Massachusetts had remained loyal to the end. Appearances here were deceptive, however. The fact that the men from Massachusetts stood firm by no means proved they shared a common commitment to the cause. The group had its quota of diehard Webster men, but the Lawrence faction was also well represented and Henry Wilson and Charles Allen were on hand for the Conscience forces.

In this situation Webster, whose chances of winning were minuscule, offered a convenient rallying point, indeed the only point on which the Massachusetts delegation could unite at all, as became clear once Taylor's nomination was secure.

Having thrown away their votes on Webster to keep peace in the delegation, Lawrence's Massachusetts supporters doubtless expected an even return in the vice-presidential contest. Thanks to his friends' maneuvering Lawrence entered the convention a heavy favorite for second place on the ticket. In the normal course of events he ought to have won it easily and probably would have had it not been for the efforts of Charles Allen. Opposed to Taylor from the start, the Conscience men were equally opposed to Lawrence as a Taylor supporter. Allen lost no time in announcing this view. With cheers for Taylor still rocking the hall he rose to deliver an impassioned speech against making the nomination unanimous. "We spurn the nominee," he informed his fellow delegates; Taylor's election would only "continue the rule of slavery for another four years." As for the vice presidency: "Massachusetts will spurn the bribe." [93] The reference was oblique but clear enough for Allen's listeners. By the time the balloting began Lawrence had already fallen behind his strongest rival, Millard Fillmore of New York. On the second ballot Fillmore swept to victory with only a scattering of votes against him.

For Webster, who had good reason to rejoice at Lawrence's defeat, the convention's action ought to have come as a pleasant surprise. Inevitably, however, he was charged with having engineered the affair, and any pleasure he felt soured at the necessity of producing a defense. The defense was genuine. Aside from disqualifying himself, Webster had remained out of the vice-presidential contest altogether. "There are twenty falsehoods in circulation about letters, said to be written to Phila. by me, interfering with Mr. Lawrence's prospects etc.," he wrote Richard M. Blatchford. "I have written no such letters nor any letter with such design, at anytime, nor to any person." Should Blatchford think it likely that "false rumors may reach Mr. Lawrence's ears, on this subject" he was free "to make the contents of this known." [94] In due course Webster's letter found its way to Nathan Appleton with instructions that it be passed on to "Mr. L." who at that point was about to depart for an extended trip to Canada.[95]

If Lawrence preferred to contemplate his defeat somewhere other than Boston, Webster was even less inclined to remain in Washington. Congress was still in session, but as soon as he decently could he left for Marshfield. There, all during the early part of the summer, he stayed, wondering what to do next. Taylor's nomination and his own wretched showing at the convention had shaken him to the core. The normal impulse would have been to shut the world out, yet the delegates at Philadelphia — along with the pain they caused Webster — had released a host of other shock waves that sooner or later would have to be dealt with.

The immediate problem Webster faced — and in a sense the sum of all the others — was what to do about Taylor's nomination. There were three possibilities: he could either support Taylor or oppose him, or he could remain uncommitted. Of the three his own preference lay somewhere between the first and the third. Within a week of the convention he was writing his son, "I can see no way, but acquiescence . . . not enthusiastic support, nor zealous approbation; but acquiescence, or forbearance from opposition." [96] In theory simple "acquiescence" and "forbearance from opposition" were fine; practically speaking they left the major part of the issue unsettled. People expected to hear from Webster, and the real question was what — if anything — he would say. Those closest to him, including his son, urged silence.[97] On the other hand, old friends like Edward Everett argued that such a course "would place you in a false position in reference to the future." [98] Webster seemed inclined to agree, conceding privately, "I must say something, somewhere soon." [99] Yet at the end of August he had still said nothing.

To further complicate matters, all the while he waited the long-standing crisis in Massachusetts Whig politics was approaching its denouement: the Conscience forces were bolting the party. For over a year they had been threatening to do so if Taylor was nominated; now the drama played itself out in rapid sequence. On June 10 the *Whig* carried a circular announcing a mass meeting for all the "true hearted" at Worcester eighteen days later. The Worcester convention, which was attended by over 5000 people, formally rejected Taylor. No alternative nominations were made, but those present did pledge themselves to support only candidates who were "known by their acts or declared opinions to be opposed to the extension of slavery." In the meantime the question of where those candidates might come from had aleady received one compelling answer. On June 22 a splinter faction of the New York Democratic party nominated Martin Van Buren for the presidency on an antislavery platform, and the day before in Columbus, Ohio, a convention had sent out a call for a general gathering of all antislavery groups to meet at Buffalo in August. Throughout July Charles Francis Adams and his friends worked at organizing the state to choose representatives for the Buffalo convention. When the matter of who its nominee should be arose, most of them balked at Van Buren, but it was difficult to settle on anyone else. By the time the convention met they were resigned, and the choice of Adams as Van Buren's running mate on the new Free Soil party ticket went far toward quieting any lingering doubts.[100]

All of these proceedings involved Webster deeply. At the time he said no more about them in public than he did about Taylor and never once did he encourage, discourage, or even communicate with his former allies in the Conscience junto. They communicated with him, however, and more than once in the unmistakable tones of political courtship. If Adams managed to quash Sumner's persistent inclination to place Webster at the head of the antislavery ranks, there were others who shared Sumner's dream. Shortly before the Philadelphia convention Henry Wilson, who was slated to attend as a delegate, wrote Webster explaining what he and his friends intended to do if Taylor won the nomination. "Last week several gentlemen from Boston and the towns in the vicinity met and agreed if Taylor should be put in nomination to organize an opposition to him in the state and country if possible." They would need, the letter continued, "a great Man to lead us for we *never shall surrender.*" In fact they needed "just such a man as you are," to which Wilson added, "I have wished for years that you would feel it to be your duty to take the lead in a movement of this kind." [101]

Wilson might have saved himself the trouble. Some of Webster's younger supporters did attend the Worcester convention, though they refused to sign the "call" that preceded it. At the same time Fletcher Webster seemed anxious to have his father give serious attention to overtures from the antislavery forces. Yet despite his friends' enthusiasm and the continuing signs of interest from the antislavery camp, Webster himself remained unconvinced. "Northern opposition is too small & narrow to rely on," he wrote his son, and that apparently settled the argument.[102] Later, when the antislavery men had settled their own argument and accepted Van Buren, Webster denounced the arrangement. In answer to a letter from E. Rockwood Hoar begging him to speak just "one word" in behalf of "the cause" he replied, "it is utterly impossible for me to support the Buffalo nomination; I have no confidence in Mr. Van Buren, not the slightest." [103]

Whatever else he accomplished, in declaring his opposition to Van Buren Webster left himself without a political leg to stand on. The time had come to make that long-delayed statement about Taylor. The occasion he chose was Marshfield's annual Whig rally held that year on September 1. There, surrounded by his neighbors, Webster informed the world in plain language that he considered Taylor's nomination a mistake. "I know enough of history to see the dangerous tendency of such resorts to military popularity." But, he hurried to add, there was "another side to this account." As poor a choice as Taylor was he had more by far to recommend him than either of the other candidates. Van Buren could be discounted since he had no chance of winning. Lewis Cass, the Democratic nominee, on the other hand, was very much in the running, and his election would be an unrelieved disaster. To prevent such a contingency, and for that reason only, Webster was prepared to cast his ballot for Taylor and advised the Whigs of Marshfield to do the same.[104]

"Was ever anything so cold as Webster's Marshfield pronunciamento?" remarked Robert Winthrop.[105] A recent Taylor convert who stood solidly by Webster before the convention, Winthrop perhaps had a right to complain. Still the wonder was that Webster managed to say anything at all. At the time few people bothered to ask why he had "come out," yet the answer was simple. "The future," Everett urged, think of the future, and when the moment came Webster did. What future a man of his age and in his position could look forward to was something else again.

## XI

For the time being the future could only be read in the present and there one fact emerged with a clarity that gainsaid all dispute. Webster had failed, and behind his failure lay the failure of his approach. In 1844, in the period just prior to his return to the Senate, he had banked everything on a judicious mixture of presidential politics and opposition to slavery. The results at that point were more than satisfactory, indeed so satisfactory that there seemed every reason to suppose the same formula would continue to work wonders. But then all too soon Webster found himself in the position of trying to ride two horses at once. Antislavery and presidential politics had ceased to be a workable combination, even in Massachusetts.

The source of the difficulty was obvious. From the beginning Webster's approach had required that certain basic elements in the situation not change, when in fact everything during those years changed constantly. It was vital to Webster's plan, for example, that slavery continue to function as part of a wide spectrum of political issues, yet one by one the old issues like the tariff seemed to fade in the developing quarrel over the South's peculiar institution. No less troublesome — and just as contrary to all past experience — was the growing rigidity of attitude everywhere. In 1844, a moderate, reasoned opposition to slavery extension seemed nicely tailored to fit the demands of the Young Whigs at home in Massachusetts. It also promised to offend only the most narrow-minded of Southern politicians. Both groups were essential to Webster and both disappointed him profoundly. Every month the Young Whigs grew more radical, and every month Southerners became more nervous and more defensive on the subject of slavery. In the end moderation satisfied no one.

Between his own miscalculations and the prophets of availability Webster stood defeated long before the Philadelphia convention began. Here was one explanation of what had gone wrong, yet at best it represented only a partial accounting. Ultimately the problem reduced itself to a consideration of change — rapid, sweeping, unexpected change — and its causes. Moreover, explaining the change from the perspective of 1848 involved special difficulties because the full dimensions of what had happened were still unclear. Two factors could be isolated, however: one had to do with the stakes men played for during the period, the other with generations.

The point about generations was simply that new men were assuming positions of power within the American political hierarchy. Weed, Polk, Adams, Wilmot, Sumner, the young senators and representatives who flocked to Washington — they were all Webster's juniors by at least ten and more often twenty or thirty years. What they lacked in experience they compensated for with ambition, yet experience in this case remained crucial. It was not that the new men were less well trained than Webster and his contemporaries; they were differently trained. Their lives had been lived at a time when the nation was free from serious external threats, when its institutions were securely established, and when the danger of division from within seemed minimal. They tended to take such a state of affairs for granted; they were less cautious, less inclined to compromise, less concerned with maintaining any sort of day-to-day political equilibrium than many of their seniors. When the War of 1812 began Thurlow Weed was fifteen years old; Sumner was nine the year the Missouri Compromise passed.

Schooled as it had been, the new generation was bound to alter the tone and substance of American politics, but there was more to it than that. Alone, a hundred Polks or Sumners could never have accomplished the change of those years. The essential ingredient that did was the prize at stake — millions of acres of unsettled territory. The federal government had always had quantities of land to distribute, but the basic terms of distribution had long since been settled in 1844. Then came Texas — to say nothing of the rest of the North American continent, which "Destiny" now decreed should gravitate to American hands. Here every question was open for debate, and above all slavery. In 1843 discussions of slavery offered little tangible profit to anybody. Five years later the profit potentially was enormous, and precisely because the stakes were so high neither side seemed willing to compromise.

With a sure instinct for the source of the trouble Webster worked steadily after 1846 to lower the stakes. The result was "no territory" — a solution to his own problems as well as the nation's. On either count "no territory" made good sense, but logic in this case proved a poor currency. Better timing might have helped — Webster waited too long to present his solution, yet even had he come forward earlier the chances of success would have been slight. Too many Americans were delighted with their new territorial riches, too few saw the problems they raised. When Congress adjourned that summer its members were already wrangling bitterly over the question of slavery in the Mexican cession. In those debates lay ample confirmation of the warning Webster had issued the year before, and for some people, perhaps, a clearer view of what he had tried to accomplish. By then, however, the issue was settled. Whatever else the future held, "no territory" had become a dead letter; the stakes in the game were beyond lowering.

Shortly after the Philadelphia convention John Berrien wrote Webster of his regrets and misgivings at Taylor's nomination. The whole debacle could be traced, he felt, to that "moment when the Whig party of the Senate faltered in the discharge of what I supposed to be its plain and obvious duty, in the matter of the Mexican treaty." A united rally on "no territory" would have defeated the treaty, which in turn would have enabled the party to choose a candidate "with a just reference to his merits and qualifications and not solely on the grounds of his supposed 'availability.' "

Berrien's preference for Webster was obvious, but the convention having made its choice he fully intended to support Taylor and advised his colleague from Massachusetts to do the same. Like Everett he pointed to the future — with one important difference. Where Everett's entreaties had been vague, Berrien's were detailed and specific. More than any other single group in the party, he argued, Southerners had united behind Taylor. His nomination was their doing, and the man who came to their aid "in this hour of need" could not but "be gratefully remembered by them." In Webster's case the rewards promised to be especially handsome, provided certain other, essential conditions were met. "If as I hope and believe the unhappy question which fanatics, and minor politicians are constantly thrusting into our councils shall be disposed of within the next four years, I think there is no portion of the Union in which your talents and public services will be more and more justly appreciated than that with which my local position renders me most intimately conversant." [106]

Besieged as he was with appeals to come out for Taylor, Webster probably paid little attention to Berrien's letter. The Georgian did make one interesting suggestion, however, and that was his last. For all the baroque courtesy surrounding the point its logic was inescapable: as long as slavery remained a national political issue Webster's interests would continue to suffer.

If the events of 1848 taught anything, then Berrien was right. Reason, moderation, the tenets of balance, the time-honored verities of American politics — all of the canons Webster lived by had failed in the face of slavery; further agitation of the issue would only make matters worse. On the other hand, disposing of Berrien's "unhappy question" presented so many problems, in September 1848, that it hardly seemed a solution at all. Who could say how it was to be done? Certainly Berrien himself offered nothing on this score, and any ideas Webster himself may have had he kept well concealed.

# *Five*
# March 7, 1850

On November 7, 1848, Zachary Taylor was elected President of the United States. Sixteen months later to the day, Webster gave a speech in the Senate that became at once, and has remained ever since, the most controversial of his career. Between the two events lay not so much a change in the complexion of affairs, as the continuation — albeit at sharply accelerated rates — of tendencies already well established in the years before 1848. If the Seventh of March Speech signaled a radical departure for Webster it also stood as the logical culmination of those tendencies.

What made the speech so controversial then and afterward was the question of Webster's motivation. When he rose to speak that day in the Senate the air was heavy with crisis; there were those who believed the Union trembled on the brink of collapse. But the crisis in Webster's own affairs — if of longer standing — was no less real and deep. Noting that either situation might have led him to take the line he did, men tended to assume it had to be one or the other. In the long debate that followed, each position found its legion of zealous supporters.[1] Largely ignored, however, was a third possibility: that self-interest and concern for the nation together, operating in something like equal measure, had settled the issue. Ultimately this explanation was the only one that made sense.

## II

The effect of Taylor's victory on Webster's situation was predictable. Having supported the Whig candidate with the faintest possible praise, and then only at the last minute, he expected little in return and got less. The party's new high command — men like Weed and Seward of New York, Truman Smith of Connecticut, Crittenden, and John Clayton of Delaware — had debts enough to honor without rewarding the halfhearted gestures of elder statesmen. His friends had hoped Webster would be Secretary of State, but what little support for the idea materialized quickly faded. Nor was lack of "a place" in the new administration the only index of Webster's status; he was equally without influence — an outsider in every way.

The liabilities of his position were apparent even before Webster left Massachusetts that December. For some time it had been the custom for the state's presidential electors to meet at a dinner in Boston after the elections. It had always been a Whig affair with the local party leadership out in force. That year both Webster and Abbott Lawrence attended. As the Bay State's foremost Taylor man — even if he had lost the vice presidency — Lawrence was delighted with the outcome of the election and evidently wanted no confusion on that score. All of the men speaking that night had kind words for Taylor, but many of them — including Governor Briggs — had also taken the opportunity to regret that the state's electoral vote could not go to "its own great statesman." Lawrence followed a very different line. "My candidate is in," he announced rising to toast the President-elect. "I repeat, that I have no regrets; for my candidate is in." Other men were just discovering Taylor's merits; Lawrence had been aware of them from the start. Indeed not since "General Washington, the father of his country, filled the

Presidential chair" had any "more worthy or fit person" been chosen "to fill that chair than General Zachary Taylor." [2]

Lawrence had obviously intended an insult; Webster was on his feet at once. He did not enjoy speaking of himself, he began, "but there are times when a public man may so speak." He had been a candidate for the Whig nomination in the recent election; he was also "a man of considerable public importance, not only within the boundaries of Massachusetts, but without her boundaries, and throughout the length and breadth of this continent." His opinion of Taylor was common knowledge: he believed the general was an "honest man" and that "with the aid of abler men whom he may call around him, he may administer the government on Whig principles." On that basis Webster was prepared to support the new President, but there he drew the line. "Having said this much, I will not so far forfeit my self-respect as to say that I think this man fitted for this high trust. He is not fitted for it. He lays claim to no high qualifications himself. No intelligent man lays any such claim for him." [3]

Under the circumstances Lawrence's challenge had to be met and the approach Webster chose suited the occasion admirably. Yet no approach, however well conceived, could alter the basic facts of the case. As a result of Taylor's victory Lawrence held the balance of power within the Massachusetts Whig organization as well as a clear track to the source of authority in Washington. It was Lawrence — not Webster — who figured prominently in countless rumored versions of Taylor's Cabinet; it was Lawrence who would distribute federal patronage in Boston and throughout the state.[4] If he wished to insult Webster he could do so with impunity.

Back in Washington for the short session, Webster found a scene fully as discouraging as the one he left behind. At the last minute Lawrence was maneuvered out of his prospective secretaryship only to be made minister to England — a plum of rare value, even if it removed him temporarily from the political stage.[5] As for the men who did go into the Cabinet, not one was a close associate of Webster's; in fact he barely knew several of them. "I am not of the councils of those who hold and exercise executive power," he answered one man who wrote asking for help in securing a minor federal appointment.[6] With old friends he was even more outspoken: bemoaning the low "tone of character" in the new administration, he talked of retiring from Congress altogether.[7] "I am willing to stay in the Senate, if that should be thought desirable, though I should prefer to leave it. What I sincerely wish, and all that I wish respecting myself, is to see Fletcher placed in a position to support his family, and myself left to my profession, my studies, or my ease." [8]

Webster's interest in retirement proved short-lived, and in time the mood of depression passed. The conditions that produced it, however, remained the same. "I am on friendly terms with all the members of the administration," he wrote early in March,[9] but several weeks later, when he tried to turn those "friendly terms" into something more concrete for his son, he faced a solid wall of opposition and prior commitment.

Intelligent, hardworking, and by all accounts a dutiful son, Fletcher Webster had nonetheless failed to make his mark in life. At thirty-six he had a large family to support and no certain means of doing so beyond a mediocre law practice. His demands on his father's generosity were constant, and considering Webster's own strained circumstances, a decided burden. With a Whig administration in power Webster looked forward to lightening that burden. Specifically he wanted Fletcher appointed federal district attorney for Boston — a respectable post carrying a good income with it. The only difficulty was that George Lunt had already been promised the appointment. As the sole Massachusetts delegate to vote for Taylor at Philadelphia, Lunt had a strong claim on the President. He also had powerful backing. "I have no doubt A.L. has had a hand in the whole matter," Webster wrote his son.[10]

At first there seemed reason to hope in spite of Lunt. Webster marshaled his forces with care. Seward, already one of Taylor's closest advisers, rallied around, as did Clayton and Thomas Ewing in the Cabinet. Letters were written by Rufus Choate and other prominent members of the Massachusetts bar questioning Lunt's professional qualifications, and Webster himself told the President on several occasions that Lunt "was not fitted for the office," arguing that if Fletcher would not do some third party ought to be appointed.[11] The affair dragged on for months, but in the end Lunt and "those other gentlemen" who supported him had their way. Taylor felt obliged to honor the promises made on his behalf and the Cabinet concurred. Early in 1850 the President did appoint Fletcher surveyor of the port of Boston, which was a profitable office, though hardly as prestigious as the district attorneyship would have been. "To say truth, I do not wish to see him dependent for his bread on the income of a subordinate place in the customshouse," Webster remarked when the idea was first broached. "I would rather starve with him." Apparently the younger Webster disagreed, for he accepted the post.[12]

Long afterward Peter Harvey recalled a drive he had taken with Webster to a place called "the Falls" on the Virginia shore in June 1849. The conversation ranged widely, but Webster seemed depressed and Harvey had hard work to keep him from brooding. What particularly rankled was how seldom politics rewarded honest effort. His whole career had been proof of this, "but the unkindest cut of all," Webster cried out at one point, "the shaft that has sunk deepest in my breast, has been the refusal of this administration to grant my request for an office of small pecuniary consideration for my only son." [13]

If the words seemed strong, the feeling they expressed was understandable. Nothing could have demonstrated more clearly what Webster's situation had become than the business of Fletcher's appointment. By itself that situation was bad enough, but its implications for the future were even more disheartening. In two years Webster would be seventy; his health was at best uncertain. If he was ever to realize his great ambition, 1852 stood as the last reasonable opportunity. Yet how was he to proceed? When a Whig administration denied him such a modest request, what possible grounds were there for hoping the Whig party would nominate him when the time came? The answer was none — unless things changed.

### III

While Webster struggled with the realities of his new position, the affairs of the nation were progressing from bad to worse. The problem was the same: slavery, and particularly slavery in the territories. In August 1848 Congress had finally provided a territorial government for Oregon — outlawing slavery in the same act — but this was accomplished only after weeks of bitter dispute, and it by-passed the far more difficult question of California and New Mexico completely. Altogether over two years would pass before that question was settled.

In his last annual message, delivered in December 1848, Polk had dealt at length with California and New Mexico: both areas were still under military rule; it was imperative that some other arrangement be made. As for slavery, the President suggested extending the Missouri Compromise line to the Pacific.[14] The plan had the virtue of simplicity, but it satisfied few people. In the North adherents of the Proviso continued to insist on absolute exclusion, while Southern extremists demanded just as adamantly that slavery be given free access everywhere in the Mexican cession. Both groups, moreover, were growing.

In the short time before Taylor's inauguration a half-dozen proposals were made for organizing California and New Mexico; none of them, however, gained anything like the necessary support to pass. Instead Congress distinguished itself with an unprecedented show of violence. Toward the end both houses were meeting round the clock, and the strain on tempers already stretched thin proved overpowering. Threats flew back and forth, and at one point a fistfight broke out on the floor of the Senate.

In the midst of all this Webster offered his own version of "the most expedient course to pursue at the present moment in regard to the Territories of California and New Mexico." Basically it amounted to the recognition of whatever law existed in the area as a temporary basis of authority.[15] Since the law in question was Mexican law and Mexican law prohibited slavery, the plan would have had the same effect as the Proviso — a fact that escaped no one. Polk made it clear he would veto such a measure, and in the Senate Calhoun — who was then supporting a move to "extend" the Constitution to California and New Mexico — met Webster head on in debate.[16] With each man challenging the constitutionality of the other's position the exchange was sharp, but little came of it. When Congress finally adjourned at dawn on March 4 nothing had been done beyond applying federal revenue laws to California and New Mexico.

At the time he clashed with Calhoun, Webster had made no general statement of his position, nor did he during the remainder of the session. Calhoun, on the other hand, had repeatedly set forth his views, general as well as specific. Through constant "acts of aggression" the North had grown in wealth and power at the expense of the South, argued the South Carolinian; unless the process were stopped Southerners would be left with no alternative but to submit completely or take "independent action." Under the heading "acts of aggression" came the whole abolitionist menace, the exclusion of slavery from the territories, and the failure of Northerners to return fugitive slaves as the Constitution specified.

Believing that a united stand by the South was the only way to impress the North, Calhoun had tried in December 1848 to rally Southern congressmen, in a body, behind his position. The results were mixed. Two addresses were drafted, one by Calhoun himself and another, much milder in tone, by Berrien. At the final meeting of the Southern caucus in January the Berrien version was rejected in favor of Calhoun's. When the time came to sign the document, however, only forty-eight senators and representatives stepped forward; the rest — twenty-four Whigs and seventeen Democrats — refused outright.

The fact that only two Whigs endorsed Calhoun's "Address of the Southern Delegates" robbed it at once of much of its force. What was to have been a vigorous defense of Southern rights had become a mere party gesture. Or so it seemed. Actually Southern congressmen were less divided on fundamental issues than they appeared to be. Disagreeing over means, they tended to see eye to eye in the matter of ends. When the "Address" affirmed the right of slaveholders to take their property into the territories, for example, it stated a proposition that few Southerners would have disputed. The question was how to secure that right. Calhoun's appeal for concerted action — transcending party lines — in the face of the exclusionist threat was one way, but men like Robert Toombs and Alexander Stephens were banking on another. As Whigs they looked forward confidently to the day when a Whig administration, with a Southerner at its head, would take command. Then surely the appropriate adjustments would be made, the necessary guarantees offered.[17] That faith brought Taylor into office in March with a healthy measure of Southern support, but it also visited certain clear obligations upon him — in the eyes of his Southern supporters, if not his own.

Meeting Taylor for the first time shortly before the inauguration Webster found him "pleasant and conversable enough, and by no means of such a harsh and stern countenance as the pictures represent him." [18] Other judgments were less favorable. To many the new President seemed stiff and awkward, and his difficulties with English grammar provoked comment everywhere.

In the weeks when Old Zack was still a stranger to Washington such things mattered a good deal, but the great question — always — was what he would do. With California gold attracting settlers by the thousands the problem of the territories was becoming daily more acute. In his Inaugural Address the President promised Congress a free hand in regulating "matters of domestic policy." [19] This was standard Whig doctrine, but in the case of the territories it clearly would not work. Congress remained hopelessly divided over California and New Mexico; if anything was to be done Taylor himself would have to act. And act he did — in his straightforward, soldierly way.

Early in June, T. Butler King arrived in California with instructions from the President to encourage the people to form their own government as quickly as possible. Behind those instructions lay a bold plan. If California and New Mexico could be made to organize as states, without waiting for congressional action, then the whole territorial issue would be neatly circumvented. In California there was already a strong movement in this direction, making King's task a relatively simple one. New Mexico presented more of a problem. Not only was the population smaller and less well organized, but Texas had claimed a substantial slice of New Mexican territory and was threatening to back up its claim with force if necessary.

By the end of the summer the situation in New Mexico was no better. California, however, had met the President's expectations handsomely. A constitutional convention was called for September 1 and would almost certainly decide for statehood. Meanwhile Taylor had said nothing to the nation of his plan beyond a single statement in a speech at Mercer, Pennsylvania, late in August: "The people of the North," he promised, "need have no apprehension of the further extension of slavery." [20] Brief as this was, it nonetheless covered what to most people was the essential point.

From the beginning Taylor had recognized that his plan, in all probability, would bring both California and New Mexico in as free states. Evidently he found nothing to object to in such an arrangement. His Southern supporters, on the other hand, were bound to object — and strenuously. Even before the Mercer speech there were signs of discontent among prominent Southern Whigs; in the weeks that followed those signs coalesced into an unmistakable pattern.

The trouble had begun with the Cabinet. Though it included more Southerners than Northerners, Taylor's official family was not popular in the South. Too many of its Southern members were suspect. Secretary of State Clayton had been the only slave-state senator to vote for the Wilmot Proviso in 1847. This was the most dramatic example, but there were others, and added to them was the fact of William Seward's growing influence over the President. An outspoken opponent of slavery extension, Weed's long-time New York ally had just arrived in Washington to begin his career in the Senate. Charming, talented, and deeply ambitious, he lost no time in cementing relations with Taylor. Within a few months their association had become so close that rumor had Seward sitting regularly with the Cabinet, which was not far from the truth.

Had Southern Whigs been under less pressure at home they might have viewed the apparent Northern bias of the administration more calmly. In time a concerted effort could have altered the balance. Time was at a premium in 1849, however, and the political climate of the South offered little opportunity for calm reflection. Everywhere Calhoun's appeal for a united front seemed to be gaining ground. Having refused to sign Calhoun's Address the previous winter, Whig senators and representatives found themselves explaining their action to increasingly hostile constituencies. At the polls the trend was clear. In state after state moderate Whigs went down in defeat to Democratic extremists. The only Whig elected in Virginia that fall was one of the two who had signed the Address. And where their power was already established, the radicals were becoming bolder every day. Secession was talked of openly in more than one state legislature, and October saw a Mississippi convention — working closely with Calhoun — issue a call for a convention of all slave states to meet at Nashville in the spring.

The situation was unprecedented. Southerners of every persuasion had difficulty finding their bearings, but the problem was doubly acute in the case of the Whigs. Fighting for their political lives, they looked to Washington only to be confronted with the President's Mercer declaration. For many the conclusion was unavoidable: whatever its details, the discernible outlines of Taylor's policy made a break with the administration imperative. Stephens and Toombs were typical. The winter before they had refused every appeal to abandon the party; by the time Congress assembled in December they were determined to act independently of the President.[21]

While the Whigs of the South were preparing their volte-face, the Northern wing of the party, for the most part, stood firm. The decision to do so was tentative, however. Political affairs in the North were fully as unsettled as they were below the Mason-Dixon line. The election of 1848 had revealed deep reservoirs of anti-extensionist sentiment. In many states the Free Soil party held the balance of power, and coalitions were already emerging. It mattered little what form a coalition took in a particular state — Free Soil–Whig or Free Soil–Democrat, the result was the same: a heightened competition for the antislavery vote. As long as Taylor continued to provide the Whigs with ammunition in that contest their support was assured, but there could be no mistaking the condition involved.

## IV

When Zachary Taylor's first annual message was read before the combined House and Senate on Christmas Eve 1849, the most striking piece of information in it had long since become common knowledge. The people of California were about to apply for statehood. A convention had met and drafted a constitution. Though the official version of the document was still en route to Washington, the fact that it prohibited slavery surprised no one. As the hotels and boardinghouses of the capital filled late in November, the news was everywhere, and everywhere too was a growing sense of crisis.

The impact on Taylor's relations with his party alone would have been enough to disorder the normal operations of government, but that was just the beginning. Ultimately California crystallized the entire sectional controversy. Slavery in the District of Columbia, the fugitive slave issue, New Mexico, and beyond it the whole territorial question — overnight all of these grew a hundredfold in importance.

For many people, particularly Southerners, the problem reduced itself to simple arithmetic. There were fifteen slave and fifteen free states in the Union; the addition of California would place the slave states in a minority. Practically speaking they were already outnumbered in the House, in the Electoral College, and in the nominating conventions of the major political parties. Only in the Senate had they retained an equal footing, but that made all the difference. Granted that no mere act of Congress could abolish slavery, with nothing to stop them, Northerners could harm the South in countless other ways — and would, argued Southern congressmen with growing vehemence and unanimity as 1849 drew to a close.

In the meantime Northern senators and representatives seemed less inclined to speculate about the broad implications of admitting California, but very few of them showed any willingness at all to let the prize slip through their fingers.

Whatever hope there may have been of avoiding a full-scale sectional confrontation died quickly in the opening days of the session. For three weeks Congress did nothing, paralyzed as it was by the inability of the House to organize. The elections the year before had deprived the Whigs of their majority, but the balance of power lay with a handful of Free Soil representatives, not the Democrats. Meeting in caucus the Whigs picked Winthrop to stand for the speakership again, while the Free Soilers chose Wilmot and the Democrats Howell Cobb of Georgia. Of the three only Wilmot had the united support of his party. A group of Southern Whigs — including Stephens and Toombs — refused outright to vote for Winthrop, and Cobb's totals were similarly cut by defections among the Northern Democrats. On the first ballot Cobb led, but no one had a clear majority. Twenty days — and sixty ballots — later there was still no majority. In the interim each of the three original candidates had been replaced by several alternatives, party groups had caucused for hours on end trying to resolve their differences, and national opinion had run the gamut from amusement to disgust.

It began to look as if the contest might go on indefinitely. On December 22, however, the House finally voted to abandon the majority rule and elect a speaker viva voce. The honor fell to Howell Cobb on what would have been the sixty-third regular ballot. At that point his total vote was smaller than when the balloting began.

The end of the speakership struggle surprised Webster by coming "sooner than I expected." The reason, he supposed, was "that many members wished to go home for the Holidays." These observations he passed on to Franklin Haven in a letter dated December 25, noting at the same time, "the message is regarded here as a good Whig Document, written in a plain and simple style." [22]

As a description of Taylor's style, "plain and simple" was accurate enough, but to imply that the message — once Congress was ready to receive it — struck men generally as "a good Whig Document" fell rather wide of the mark. In the eyes of some Whigs nothing could have been further from the party's proper stance than the policy the President outlined.

Basically that policy was as uncomplicated as the language that expressed it. On the subject of California Taylor saw no alternative: the area had met the requirements for statehood; Congress ought to admit it forthwith. The same approach should be taken in the case of New Mexico when the time came. But that was all. "With a view of maintaining the harmony and tranquility so dear to us all," the President cautioned, "we should abstain from the introduction of those exciting topics of sectional character which have hitherto produced painful apprehensions in the public mind." There followed a warning against the formation of parties based on "geographical discriminations," and at the end of the message Taylor made clear his intention to resist any attempt at dissolving the Union "to the full extent of the obligations imposed and the powers conferred upon me by the Constitution." [23]

Admit California, and as soon as possible New Mexico; beyond that let the sleeping dogs of sectionalism lie: that was the President's policy and the advice he offered Congress. In January in special messages to both the House and the Senate he spelled out in detail what he meant, but the basic plan remained the same.[24] It was still the same seven months later when Taylor went to his grave. Meanwhile Henry Clay had reappeared on the scene and the entire situation had changed.

The initial response to the "President's plan" was not encouraging. What support it had in Congress came almost exclusively from Northern Whigs; Southern Whigs and the Democrats generally were opposed. There was no common line of opposition, however: each group had factions within it arguing for different approaches. Northern Democrats disagreed among themselves as well as with Southern Democrats, and Southern Democrats were equally at odds with Southern Whigs. As a result the early weeks of 1850 found a furious debate raging in both the House and Senate, but very little concerted action of any kind. It was against this background, on January 29, that Clay presented his plan to save the Union.

Having left the Senate in 1842, Clay had only just returned when Taylor took office. He owed his election to Crittenden, an old friend and staunch ally in Kentucky politics. The two men had fallen out over Taylor, but when Crittenden resigned his Senate seat to become governor he promptly threw his weight behind Clay in the legislature. Rumor claimed that the Kentucky Whigs were less than enthusiastic about the arrangement, and Taylor men everywhere tended to view Clay's return to Washington with deep misgivings; his assault on the Tyler administration was only too well remembered.[25]

Finding himself the object of so much speculation, Clay behaved with characteristic nonchalance. In seven years he had grown thinner, but time had dimmed none of his legendary charm. He was pleasant to everyone and went out of his way to be cordial to Taylor. What his intentions were, on the other hand, few men knew. He associated with no group in particular and was clearly outside the inner councils of the administration. Indeed in that sense his position seemed strikingly similar to Webster's. For years the two had been bitter rivals, but now, ironically, they stood together — deprived alike of power and influence.

By the beginning of the last week in January it was generally understood that Clay had conceived a plan of his own and would present it soon. The details of the plan remained a mystery, but

Harry of the West had built his reputation on compromise, and a compromise proposal of some sort was what everybody expected when he finally rose to speak on the twenty-ninth.

The plan Clay offered took the form of eight resolutions. Together, he argued, they dealt with every one of the causes of sectional discord over which Congress had any control. Briefly they provided that: 1) California should be admitted as a free state, 2) the remainder of the territory acquired from Mexico should be provided with territorial governments with no provision made as to slavery at all, 3) Texas should relinquish its claim in New Mexico, 4) by way of compensating Texas, the federal government should assume part of the state's unpaid debt, 5) slavery should be left alone in the District of Columbia, 6) the slave trade in the District, however, should be abolished, 7) a more effective fugitive slave law should be enacted, and 8) Congress should declare that it had no power to interfere with the interstate slave trade. Holding his explanation of each of these points to a minimum Clay requested that debate on them be postponed for one week. At the end of that time he spoke again and over a period of two days discussed his plan at great length.[26]

Clay's argument on both occasions, though complex in detail, came to a simple point: the conflict between the North and South had reached a juncture where it threatened dire consequences for the entire nation; if those consequences were to be averted both sides would have to make concessions. The plan he proposed, Clay freely admitted, required more of the North than it did of the South, but the North — richer and more powerful — could afford to be generous. On another point he was less candid. Of his eight resolutions, only the one calling for the admission of California coincided with the administration's announced policy. Taylor had urged Congress to avoid "exciting topics of sectional character"; Clay evidently felt such an approach was inadequate, or undesirable, or both. He said nothing of his disagreement with the President, but the magnitude of the gulf between them hardly required elaboration.

V

Early on the evening of January 21 — the day Taylor's special message on California went to the House — Clay had paid an unannounced call on Webster. His purpose was to gain support for his plan. The night was chilly and Clay had a bad cough, yet apparently he thought enough of his chances to venture out in spite of the elements — and everything in Webster's career that might have kept a more cautious man at home. In thirty-five years in national politics the senator from Massachusetts had shown scant sympathy for the type of sectional compromise Clay was advocating.

But Clay came anyway, and not without profit as it turned out. After he had left Webster spoke of him "in words of great kindness," according to an anonymous "gentleman" who was present "during and after the interview." He added that "he agreed, in substance, with Mr. Clay" and that "he regarded Mr. Clay's plan as one that ought to be satisfactory to the North and to the reasonable men of the South." He had not studied the proposals in detail, but if after doing so "he should hold his present opinion," he fully intended to champion them in the Senate, "no matter what might befall himself at the North." As for the Proviso, which Clay's plan clearly precluded, Webster was emphatic, "that was no shibboleth for him." [27]

Altogether between his interview with Clay and the day Webster finally declared himself in the Senate more than six weeks passed. During that time the signs of crisis in the nation at large multiplied steadily. Throughout the South state legislatures and special conventions were meeting to select delegates for the proposed Southern convention at Nashville. In Boston, Garrison and his followers demanded the immediate dissolution of the Union, and if Garrison could be dismissed as a crank, legislatures and hastily called rallies everywhere in the North continued to appeal for the admission of California "at once" and the application of the Proviso to New Mexico.

In Washington matters progressed no more calmly than elsewhere, but Clay's proposals at least provided a focus for debate. In what remained of February after the Kentuckian had finished presenting his plan, the question was discussed from every side and the first tentative lines of accord began to emerge. Generally moderate Southern Whigs and Northern Democrats favored the compromise plan, while Northern Whigs stood by Taylor and Southern extremists continued to oppose every variety of concession to the North, including Clay's. On February 13 Jefferson Davis put the case for the Southern ultras with vigor and precision. The North alone was responsible for the current crisis; the South would yield nothing. On the contrary the South demanded justice — "full justice" — and if the North refused, "we will claim from this government, as the barons of England claimed from King John, the grant of another Magna Carta for our protection." [28]

If Davis's predictions sounded grim, Calhoun's, issued two weeks later, had an even more somber ring. The senator from South Carolina was deathly ill. Sickness prevented his attendance in the Senate much of the time. On the day he was scheduled to speak — March 4 — he was present but so weak his address had to be read for him. Still his point was clear. Clay's compromise would not do. If the Union was to be saved, argued Calhoun echoing Davis, the South must have complete justice. Every advantage of wealth and power had passed to the North; nothing less than a constitutional amendment could restore the balance. The admission of California would be a test case. If that were accomplished by the North it could only be "with the intention of destroying irretrievably the equilibrium between the two sections," and the South would have no choice but to leave the Union.[29]

Calhoun's speech climaxed the first month of debate on the compromise; by the end of the second he was dead.

Except for an occasional remark, Webster said nothing in the Senate during February or the first week of March. In private he was more communicative, but his utterances were surprisingly inconsistent. Having tentatively approved Clay's plan, he later left Robert Winthrop — after several interviews — with the distinct impression "that he would go with us for Taylor's plan." [30] As late as March 3 Winthrop was writing Everett, "I speak without any private knowledge of what Webster's speech is to be. But I have every reason to think that it will look to the President's plan." [31] On the other hand, William Plumer, a former congressman from New Hampshire and long-time friend of Webster's, noted in his journal after a meeting on February 9, "I am not without some fear that Mr. Webster has got some scheme of compromise in his mind." [32]

Clay had argued that the Union was in grave danger. Throughout the early part of February Webster saw no such danger, or if he did he went out of his way to play it down. "The Union is not in danger," he had written Franklin Haven on January 13.[33] A month later he said essentially the same thing to Peter Harvey: "Things will cool off. California will come in. New Mexico will be postponed. No bones will be broken — & in a month all this will be more apparent." [34] A second letter to Harvey, written the following day, reiterated the point: "I do not partake in any degree in those apprehensions, which you say some of our friends entertain of the dissolution of the Union." [35] Four days later there were similar assurances for Everett. "I think the clamor about disunion rather abates," Webster wrote, "and I trust that if, on our side, we keep cool, things will come to no dangerous pass." [36]

Webster's silence in the Senate evidently bothered his friends almost as much as the state of the Union did, and he took pains to reassure them on that point as well. In his second letter to Harvey he noted that though up to then he had "thought it advisable for me to hold my peace," he might yet have something to say. "If a moment should come, when it shall appear, that any temperate, *national,* and practical speech, which I can make, would be useful, I shall do the best I can." [37]

The "moment" came soon enough. Within a week Webster had definitely decided to speak.[38] Moreover on the twenty-fourth he wrote his son a singularly gloomy letter, suggesting that his entire view of the situation had changed. "I am nearly broken down with labor and anxiety," ran the letter in part. "I know not how to meet the present emergency, or with what weapons to beat down the Northern and the Southern follies, now raging in equal extremes." [39]

When Webster wrote this, Washington was filled with news of a particularly stormy interview that had taken place the day before at the White House. Attempting to convince the President of the wisdom of Clay's plan, Toombs and Stephens left him with the impression that disunion was the only alternative they saw if he refused his support. Furious, Taylor denounced the representatives from Georgia to Weed — who came in shortly afterward — as "traitors," adding that "if they were taken in rebellion against the Union, he would hang them with less reluctance than he had hung deserters and spies in Mexico." Even without the embellishment Weed doubtless gave the incident, Webster's concern was understandable.[40]

It was also short-lived. By March 1 he was already talking of a "lull in the storm of angry words, reproaches and threats," which he thought would provide a better atmosphere for his speech.[41] Four days later Charlotte Everett, who was staying with the Websters for the season, wrote her father, "Mr. Webster thinks now the whole noise about dissolution is over, & that there will be no more trouble." [42]

*

Anyone attempting to form a coherent picture of Webster's point of view on the basis of his remarks prior to March 7 would have been hard put to do so. He had been unusually generous with his impressions, but those impressions changed as often as the situation did. In the end only a small circle of intimates knew, or could have predicted, what he would say in the Senate — and why. By March 6 several old friends, especially summoned for the occasion, had arrived in Washington. That evening Peter Harvey, Edward Curtis, and Fletcher Webster met at Webster's house. Together the four men discussed the speech, wondering what reaction to it would be.[43] Calling after dinner, Winthrop found Webster busy with preparations and went away convinced the President's plan was about to acquire a most powerful and eloquent ally.[44]

## VI

With Webster at long last scheduled to speak, the seventh of March became, perforce, an historic occasion, even before he uttered a syllable. Webster felt it, and the crowds of people who filled the Senate chamber and the corridors outside felt it — along with the crush and the heat. Arriving well beforehand Charlotte Everett was lucky enough to find a seat but later gave it up to Mrs. Winthrop and stood for four hours, "leaning against one of the columns." [45] When Clay first presented the compromise resolutions, Webster recalled afterward, the mercury in the Senate stood at 100°.[46] Six weeks later it was probably at least as warm.

At twelve o'clock the special order of the day was read. Isaac Walker of Wisconsin, who still held the floor from the day before, graciously offered to relinquish it. "Mr. President, this vast audience has not come together to hear me, and there is but one man, in my opinion, who can assemble such an audience. They expect to hear him, and I feel it to be my duty, therefore, as it is my pleasure, to give the floor to the Senator from Massachusetts." Webster rose, thanked Walker, and began. He spoke for three hours and eleven minutes. The address fills forty-two pages in his published works.

"Mr. President, I wish to speak today, not as a Massachusetts man, nor as a Northern man," Webster announced at the outset, "but as an American, and a member of the Senate of the United States." [47] And a little further on, "I speak today for the preservation of the Union. Hear me for my cause."

After announcing that his motives — his "sole motives" — were the preservation of the Union and the restoration of "quiet and . . . harmony," he recounted briefly the events that had brought the nation to its "present political condition." He spoke first of the war with Mexico and then of the difficulties produced by the settlement and organization of California. The problem raised thereby was an old one: "the question of slavery in these United States." Partly because of its genuine importance, but also, "perhaps mostly, in consequence of the manner in which it has been discussed," slavery had become a source of "much alienation and unkind feeling" between different portions of the country. With an eye to determining why, Webster proposed to "review historically" the entire subject.

He began with slavery among the ancients and their attitudes toward it. From there he moved to a consideration of the various attitudes toward slavery in the United States and the differences in those, North and South. Calhoun had referred to the division in the Methodist Church. Webster deplored that division. There was no real reason for it. Both sides had displayed a "want of candor and charity," he felt. "There are men who, in reference to disputes of that sort, are of the opinion that human duties may be ascertained with the exactness of mathematics." Such opinions were dangerous. "Thus wars are waged, and unjust wars." Indeed uncompromising, oversimplified moral attitudes toward slavery were the cause "of a great part of those unhappy divisions, exasperations, and reproaches which find vent and support in different parts of the Union."

The conflict over slavery found its chief support in the realm of human emotion: that was the proposition with which Webster began his historical résumé of the slavery issue. It was also the burden of his argument throughout the entire speech. To prove it he turned to a view of "things as they are."

The fact was slavery existed in the United States. It had existed when the Constitution was adopted. At that time the people of the South were if anything more opposed to it than the people of the North. The Ordinance of 1787, which prohibited slavery in the whole of the Northwest Territory, was approved by every single Southern state. The only vote against it had come from a Northerner. The Constitution, drafted the same year as the Ordinance, recognized slavery, but the hope was that through the prohibition of the slave trade it would gradually be eliminated. The South, argued Webster, fully concurred in that hope.

Before long, however, a change began to manifest itself: "the South growing much more warm and strong" in support of the institution. The cause of the change, clearly and simply, was the spread of cotton cultivation. Cotton made slavery "a cherished institution" in the eyes of Southerners, "no evil, no scourge," as it had been formerly, "but a great, religious, social and moral blessing." Cotton too had given birth to "an eagerness for other territory, a new area or new areas," until finally the "whole interest of the South became connected, more or less, with the extension of slavery."

This brought Webster to the territorial question — a topic that occupied him for some time. In their efforts to acquire new land for cotton cultivation, he argued, Southerners had been singularly successful. First the Louisiana Territory, then Florida, and finally Texas had been added to the United States for the benefit of the South's cotton interest. In each case the area of slavery had been extended. It was an impressive achievement, but, Webster hastened to add, the annexation of Texas "pretty much closed the whole chapter . . . settled the whole account."

In other words the territorial question no longer existed. It had been settled in 1845 and nothing since had reintroduced it. If this assertion surprised Webster's listeners, he promptly restated it for emphasis.

> And I now say, Sir, as the proposition upon which I stand this day, and upon the truth and firmness of which I intend to act until it is overthrown, that there is not at this moment within the United States, or any territory of the United States, a single foot of land, the character of which, in regard to its being free territory or slave territory, is not fixed by some law, and some irrepealable law, beyond the power of the action of the government.

That he would demonstrate.

He started with Texas. His purpose — aside from proving that the issue of slavery had been forever settled there — was to show that without Northern support annexation could never have been accomplished. Here was ample evidence to refute the charge that Northern majorities had consistently blocked the path of Southern interests. At the same time Webster took the opportunity to explain what his own position on Texas and related issues had been. He asked Senator Albert C. Greene of Rhode Island to read aloud sections of his Niblo's Garden speech of 1837.[48] At that time he had opposed annexation and all further extension of slavery. Now, thirteen years later, he had "nothing, Sir, to add to, or take away from, these remarks." He also asked to have read the portion of the speech he gave at the Massachusetts Whig convention in 1847 accusing the Proviso men of stealing his thunder.[49]

Returning to the present, Webster explained that though he

had opposed the annexation of Texas he saw no way — the Republic having been admitted as a slave state — of touching slavery there. Nor, should it come to pass, could they prevent the state from being divided into four separate states, each permitting slavery, since that was part of the agreement under which Texas entered the Union. Thus had the issue of slavery been settled with respect to Texas.

In California and New Mexico matters had been arranged altogether differently, but the result, Webster argued, was just as final. There slavery was excluded, and "by a law even superior to that which admits and sanctions it in Texas." The law he referred to was "the law of nature, of physical geography, the law of the formation of the earth." With due caution he added that he meant only "slavery as we regard it; the slavery of the colored race as it exists in the Southern states." Granting that qualification, however, the law of nature had settled "forever, with a strength beyond all terms of human enactment, that slavery cannot exist in California or New Mexico." That this was true of California they already had proof in the state's constitution, and it was even more demonstrably so in the case of New Mexico. "What is there in New Mexico that could, by any possibility, induce anybody to go there with slaves?" Webster asked.

> There are some narrow strips of tillable land on the borders of the rivers; but the rivers themselves dry up before midsummer is gone. All that the people can do in that region is to raise some little articles, some little wheat for their tortillas, and that by irrigation. And who expects to see a hundred black men cultivating tobacco, corn, cotton, rice, or anything else, on lands in New Mexico, made fertile only by irrigation?

The corollary of Webster's application of the law of nature to California and New Mexico was obvious. If slavery — the only kind of slavery they had any experience of — was already outlawed by nature in the Mexican cession, what useful purpose could the Wilmot Proviso serve? None, Webster declared.

"Such a prohibition would be idle, as it respects any effect it would have upon the territory; and I would not take pains uselessly to reaffirm an ordinance of nature, nor to re-enact the will of God. I would put in no Wilmot Proviso for the mere purpose of a taunt or a reproach." For whatever reason, and regardless of what they expected to gain, Southerners were opposed to the Proviso, saw it as an "indignity," something "taking away from them what they regard as a proper equality of privilege." To force their acquiescence when the issue was already settled would be worse than foolish. Three times in the space of a paragraph Webster repeated his point, and with each repetition it grew stronger.

> I repeat, therefore, Sir, and as I do not propose to address the Senate often on this subject, I repeat it because I wish it to be distinctly understood, that, for the reasons stated, if a Proposition were now here to establish a government for New Mexico, and it was moved to insert a provision for a prohibition of slavery, I would not vote for it.

On the fundamental issue of slavery, Webster said, he stood where he had always stood. He opposed its extension and would continue to do so, but this was a question of means, not ends. Slavery was already prohibited in New Mexico by nature; the Wilmot Proviso made no more sense there than it would in Canada.

> Sir, wherever there is a substantive good to be done, wherever there is a foot of land to be prevented from becoming slave territory, I am ready to assert the principle of the exclusion of slavery. I am pledged to it from the year 1837; I have been pledged to it again and again; and I will perform those pledges; but I will not do a thing unnecessarily that wounds the feelings of others, or that does discredit to my own understanding.

Unequivocably and without reservation Webster had opposed the application of the Wilmot Proviso anywhere in the Mexican cession. He said nothing of how or when the area should be organized and argued for the admission of California only very obliquely if at all, but on this one point his position was clear beyond all doubt. Later his critics would find that position glaringly inconsistent with his past performance and utterances and damn him as a traitor to his principles. Anticipating the charge Webster pointed to his consistency on a still deeper level of principle: opposition to the extension of slavery itself. That, he argued, was the goal; the Proviso was simply one means of achieving it. He might have added that he had never been a Proviso man in the strictest sense of the term. For two years — from 1846 until the issue was finally settled in 1848 — he had advocated "no territory" first and supported the Proviso only as a last resort. Yet once "no territory" was defeated his support of the Proviso had been prompt and unqualified. To that extent his critics were right; his position did represent a departure, and a significant one.

Webster's rejection of the Proviso ended his discussion of the territorial question. From there he moved to a general consideration of the grievances, "real or supposed," which tended to divide the two sections of the country. Beginning with the fugitive slave issue he noted "at the North, among individuals, and among legislators, a disinclination to perform fully their constitutional duties in regard to the return of persons bound to service who have escaped into the free States." Here obviously the South was right, and the North wrong. The Constitution left no doubt in the matter. He desired "to call the attention of all sober minded men at the North, of all conscientious men, of all men who are not carried away by some fanatical idea or some false impression, to their constitutional obligations." There was a bill before the Senate on the subject that, "with some amendments," he would support "with all its provisions to the fullest extent."

Southerners complained of petitions to Congress from Northern legislatures advocating the abolition of slavery in the states. Webster opposed such petitions. He would be unwilling to receive one from the legislature of Massachusetts for two reasons: "first, because I do not consider that the legislature of Massachusetts has anything to do with it; and next, because I do not consider that I, as her representative here, have anything to do with it."

On the subject of abolition societies he was even more outspoken. "Their operations for the last twenty years have produced nothing good or valuable," he declared. Granted their members were "honest and good men, perfectly well-meaning men," anyone could see "what mischiefs their interference with the South has produced." As late as 1832 abolition was still being discussed in the Virginia House of Delegates. Then came the rise of the abolition societies in the North and "public opinion, which in Virginia had begun to be exhibited against slavery, and was opening out for the discussion of the question, drew back and shut itself up in its castle." Clearly the abolitionists were to blame for the change.

> We all know the fact, and we all know the cause; and every thing that these agitating people have done has been, not to enlarge, but to restrain, not to set free, but to bind faster, the slave population of the South.

Webster referred next to Southern complaints of the violence of the Northern press. This charge he dismissed. "The press violent! Why, Sir, the press is violent everywhere." Returning to the South's more legitimate grievances — fugitive slaves, petitions for the abolition of slavery in the states, and the abolitionists — he noted that only one of these lay "within the redress of the government." That was the want of an effective fugitive slave law.

The grievances of the North Webster dealt with more summarily — "I need not go over them particularly." He mentioned first the change in attitude toward slavery in the South. Beyond that there were the unfortunate comparisons made by Southerners between their slaves and the laborers of the North. Such comparisons were patently absurd; "five sixths of the whole property of the North is in the hands of the laborers of the North." Later, in the printed speech, the list of Northern grievances was expanded to include the imprisonment of Negro seamen in Charleston and the treatment of Hoar's mission to South Carolina five years earlier, but Webster said nothing on either subject in the Senate.

Of the grievances of the two sections in general, Webster felt that those which had their foundation "in matters of law" could be and "ought to be" redressed. For those which were founded in "opinion, in sentiment, in mutual crimination and recriminations," they could only "endeavor to allay the agitation and cultivate a better feeling and more fraternal sentiments between the South and the North."

And that, he implored his colleagues, ought to be their business — their primary concern. Their mission was to heal; anything else was beside the point, especially talk of breaking up the Union. "Mr. President, I should much prefer to have heard from every member on this floor declarations of opinion that this Union could never be dissolved, than the declaration of opinion by any body, that, in any case, under the pressure of any circumstances, such a dissolution was possible."

Secession! He heard the word with "distress and anguish." And as for peaceable secession: "Sir, your eyes and mine are never destined to see that miracle." War would follow disunion as surely as day followed night.

The breaking up of the fountains of the deep without ruffling the surface! Who is so foolish, I beg every body's pardon, as to expect to see any such thing? Sir, he who sees these States, now revolving in harmony around a common centre, and expects to see them quit their places and fly off without convulsion, may look the next hour to see the heavenly bodies rush from their spheres, and jostle against each other in the realms of space, without causing the wreck of the universe.

What was to become of "the great Constitution under which we all live?" Was it simply to be "thawed and melted away by secession, as the snows on the mountain melt under the influence of a vernal sun?" Where would the line be drawn? Which states would secede? "What is to remain American?" What would become of Webster himself? "Am I to become a sectional man, a local man, a separatist, with no country in common with the gentlemen who sit around me here?" Where would the flag remain? "Where is the eagle still to tower? or is he to cower, and shrink, and fall to the ground?" What would happen to the army? The navy? The public lands? How would each of the thirty states defend itself?

With question after question Webster deepened the picture of chaos, of balance destroyed. In the end he called upon the geography of the continent itself to bear witness to the wisdom of his argument. Before long "the strength of America" would lie in the Valley of the Mississippi. "Well, now, Sir, I beg to inquire what the wildest enthusiast has to say on the possibility of cutting that river in two, and leaving free States at its source and on its branches, and slave States down near its mouth, each forming a separate government?" Obviously such a thing could never be done. "No, Sir! no, Sir! There will be no secession! Gentlemen are not serious when they talk of secession." He had heard of a convention at Nashville. He hoped the object would be to "adopt conciliatory counsels." If the case should prove otherwise, he pointed out the ridiculousness of "concerting for the overthrow of this Union over the bones of Andrew Jackson."

Just before concluding Webster spoke briefly of the Texas–New Mexico boundary dispute and of the possibility of freeing the slaves. He thought the proposal to compensate Texas for ceding its New Mexican claims "well worthy the consideration of Congress." With respect to slavery he had no plan to offer or support, but, he added, "if any gentleman from the South shall propose a scheme, to be carried on by this government upon a large scale, for the transporation of free colored people to any colony or any place in the world, I should be quite disposed to incur almost any degree of expense to accomplish that object."

The peroration began on a note of appeal — "instead of groping with those ideas so full of all that is horrid and horrible, let us come out into the light of day" — and ended as a celebration of the nation and its accomplishments. With deftness and economy Webster restored the balance that secession had shattered a moment before.

> We have a great, popular, constitutional government, guarded by law and by judicature, and defended by the affections of the whole people. No monarchical throne presses the States together, no iron chain of military power encircles them; they live and stand under a government popular in its form, representative in its character, founded upon principles of equality, and so constructed, we hope, as to last forever. In all its history it has been beneficent; it has trodden down no man's liberty; it has crushed no State. Its daily respiration is liberty and patriotism; its yet youthful veins are full of enterprise, courage, and honorable love of glory and renown.

Here too nature, the land and the sea, pointed the way. "This republic now extends, with vast breadth, across the whole continent. The two great seas of the world wash the one and the other shore." And thus had they come to realize, Webster observed, "the beautiful description of the ornamental border of the buckler of Achilles:

> 'Now, the broad shield complete, the artist crowned
> With his last hand, and poured the ocean round;
> In living silver seemed the waves to roll,
> And beat the buckler berge, and bound the whole.' "

## VII

Writing Everett late in 1851 Webster observed of the Seventh of March Speech, "Mr. Clay's Resolutions were rather the occasion than the subject of the speech." [50] The distinction was accurate perhaps, but it hardly altered the fact that the speech was a compromise speech and the broad outlines of the compromise Webster advocated were Clay's. At the time there were two other possibilities: Webster could have sided with Taylor, or he could have taken some altogether different tack of his own. Admit California and leave all other sectional topics alone, the President had advised. Though Webster never said so explicitly, every line of the Seventh of March Speech implied he thought such an approach inadequate. As for striking out on his own, he called for little enough specific action, but those things he did mention — his rejection of the Wilmot Proviso, his appeal for a more effective fugitive slave law, his formula for settling the Texas–New Mexico boundary dispute — were all part of Clay's larger plan.

They also represented, in conjunction with one another, that part of the plan most likely to please Southerners. The major benefits Clay offered the North — statehood for California and an end to the slave trade in the District of Columbia — Webster left undiscussed. His principal appeal throughout was to the South.

"The Speech would have killed any Northern man except himself," Winthrop wrote Everett ten days after the Senate drama. "If Gen. Taylor had said the same things precisely in his Message we should all have said — 'so much for having a Southern President' & W. himself would have led off in denouncing him." [51] Surprised and annoyed at what he considered Webster's eleventh-hour abandonment of the administration, Winthrop may have overstated his case. On the other hand he had built his reputation on moderation, and his remarks were mild compared to the abuse dedicated antislavery men like Theodore Parker and Horace Mann heaped on the speech.

In the resulting furor, three points — Webster's position on the Proviso and fugitive slaves and his criticism of the abolitionists — bore the brunt of the attack. In fact, however, his concessions to the South went far beyond the level of specifics. The whole tone of the speech, as well as the assumptions that underlay it, were aimed at soothing the Southern mind — soothing it and banishing the fears that plagued it.

Traveling in the South in the summer of 1847 Webster had spoken often of "mutual esteem," "filial reverence," "patriotic devotion," and a "sense of common brotherhood" as vital adhesives binding the nation together. Others might value the Union "as a convenience, or an arrangement or a compromise of interests," he had declared at Savannah, "but I desire to see an attachment to the Union existing among the people, not as a deduction of political economy, nor as a result of philosophical reasoning, but cherished as a heartfelt *sentiment*." At the time this emphasis on feeling and emotion represented a significant departure for Webster. An appreciation of the nation as "a compromise of interests" had always played a far greater role in his nationalism than emotion; reason, not the heart, provided the essential motive power behind the system.[52]

In 1847 the shift in emphasis showed itself only as an occasional nuance. Three years later, in the Seventh of March Speech, it formed the basis of Webster's entire argument. If Southerners claimed the balance of power hung heavily in favor of the North, Webster seemed inclined to agree, but against the balance of power he projected a balance of national feeling. The quarrel over slavery had its origin in the realm of emotion, and its chief support still lay there, he argued; if harmony was to be restored they must heal the breach at its source. This meant a regime of restraint for both sides, but particularly the North.

Were Northerners threatening to outlaw slavery in New Mexico? Webster scorned such "evidence of the votes of superior power, exercised for no purpose but to wound the pride, whether a just and a rational pride, or an irrational pride, of the citizens of the Southern States." Calhoun had demanded a constitutional amendment restoring the equilibrium between the two sections of the country. Time and again addressing himself directly to "the honorable Senator from South Carolina," Webster offered Southerners the protection of an equilibrium that had nothing to do with constitutional amendments.

And for those who doubted whether their Northern brethren could muster the necessary self-restraint, he had only to point to his own performance that day in the Senate. Here was proof of just how much a "solicitous and anxious heart" could accomplish. Arguing often in clear opposition to his past and the interests and opinions of his section, he spoke — he announced at the outset — "not as a Massachusetts man, nor as a Northern man, but as an American." His views were generous, his manner throughout calm. "I have sought to enliven the occasion by no animated discussion," he declared near the end, "nor have I attempted any train of elaborate argument. I have wished only to speak my sentiments, fully and at length." If there was "any future service" he could render the nation on the basis of those sentiments, he would render it cheerfully. If not, "I shall still be glad to have had an opportunity to disburden myself from the bottom of my heart, and to make known every political sentiment that therein exists."

The magnitude of Webster's concessions could only be explained in one way, his opponents claimed. Anticipating their argument and perhaps leaning toward it himself, Winthrop wrote Clifford on March 10, "I greatly fear he will be suspected of having been tempted into a new position by Southern overtures in regard to 1852." [53] Two weeks later at a meeting in

Faneuil Hall, called for the express purpose of considering Webster's speech, Theodore Parker put the case more bluntly. The speech was "a bid for the Presidency," and he could think of "no deed in American history" to compare with it "but the act of Benedict Arnold." Parker did grant there was an alternative hypothesis; that necessity — the danger to the Union — might have determined Webster's stand. But, he hastened to ask, did anyone seriously believe Webster thought the dissolution of the Union imminent, or at all likely? "I will not insult the foremost understanding of this continent by supposing he deems it possible." [54]

Parker's analysis presented a clear choice; it was simple and to the point. It also ignored the fact that men in general act most often out of a complex of motives. The Seventh of March Speech could be read as a "bid for the Presidency," but with the same amount of effort and a different point of view it became a piece of disinterested statesmanship of the highest order. In truth it was neither.

At the beginning of 1850 Webster stood virtually alone in national politics. A Whig administration controlled the national government, but he had long since discovered he was out of place and out of power in Taylor's Washington. Unless that situation changed any hope of the nomination in 1852 was idle. In the meantime the sectional controversy had reached new heights of intensity. Party lines — already overstrained — were disintegrating completely, and the Whigs fared rather worse in the general scramble than the Democracy. By the end of January the Southern wing of the party was in open revolt against the President. With the administration barring his way to power, what better for Webster than to ally himself with the administration's enemies? And if his position at home suffered as a result, what good had been all the support Massachusetts could give in 1848 — or ever, for that matter?

So ran the argument from pure expediency, but the same

kind of calculation on Webster's part could have led to a very different result. Faced with a full-scale revolt among the Southern Whigs to say nothing of Clay's blanket rejection of his policy, Taylor would doubtless have welcomed any help he could get. For Webster, in turn, here was an excellent opportunity to improve his standing with the administration. Considering the President's predicament, the rewards for a sufficiently vigorous effort might well have been substantial.

Yet Webster chose to oppose Taylor, and when the time came he made that opposition abundantly clear. The question was why. Clay based his plan on the need for extreme measures to preserve the Union. Taylor saw no such need. Webster's decision to back the compromise seemed to imply that he accepted Clay's view of the situation and rejected the President's. From there it was a short step to arguing — as Webster's friends did — that the Seventh of March Speech represented an earnest attempt to save a nation on the verge of collapse.

The only trouble with this line of reasoning was that Webster perceived no threat to the Union, at least of the sort men feared in 1850. His pronouncements on the subject prior to March 7 varied from week to week, but the total impression they left was one of optimism. If the end of February found him momentarily discouraged, the mood soon passed. Never once did he mention secession as a tangible danger. Even before the Senate, when he finally spoke his piece, he devoted far more attention to "talk of secession" than secession itself.

At the time of Taylor's nomination John Berrien had written Webster of the possibility of eliminating the slavery issue from national politics. In the last analysis the Seventh of March Speech was an attempt to do just that. It also stood as the ultimate expression of Webster's nationalism, and whatever lay uppermost in his mind that day in the Senate — his own interests or those of the nation — nationalism for him had always been an amalgam of both.

In January, two weeks before Clay presented his compromise, Webster wrote Franklin Haven that he feared the prospect of a "useful session" was "not encouraging." The reason was obvious. "There is so much excitement and inflammation on the subject of Slavery, Dissolution, etc., as that it overwhelms, or threatens to overwhelm all really important measures." [55] Five months later he was still lamenting the fact that "all important public measures" were "worse than stationary." "The tariff, for instance, is losing important friends through the irritation produced by these slavery debates." Webster's next remark was particularly illuminating. "I suppose no history shows a case of such mischiefs arising from angry debates and disputes, both in the government and the country, on questions of so very little real importance." [56]

Webster did not mean that slavery was unimportant in any absolute sense. On the contrary, slavery was unimportant only in that the national government, operating properly under the Constitution, could have very little to do with it. In 1847 he had reminded the Whigs of Massachusetts that slavery as a political question was separate and distinct from slavery as a moral question, and that "as a legislator, or in any other official capacity," he was bound to "look at it, consider it, and decide it as a matter of political action." While this did not make slavery "less important in a moral point of view," it did leave the moral issue to be settled by private conscience. [57] It also placed the whole question of the existence of slavery outside the province of the federal government, since the Constitution had given it no authority in the matter.

A decade earlier it would hardly have been necessary to mention such distinctions; they were axiomatic in American politics. By 1847, however, the lines were already blurred, and three years later they seemed to have disappeared completely. Slavery and the issues growing from it dominated politics at every level. On both sides positions had acquired the rigidity of absolute principle; everywhere moral commitment and political necessity were inextricably mixed. The result was a total disruption of the normal political processes of the nation. Party alignments became meaningless. It took three weeks to elect a speaker in the House, and even then the ordinary rules of procedure had to be set aside. As 1849 drew to a close and the new year begin, both Houses of Congress seemed paralyzed. Day after day the angry debate ran on — always on the same subject — while nothing was done.

Webster may not have feared an overt act of secession, but he clearly found the situation as it was deplorable. To allow it to continue would have been as damaging to the nation as to his own hopes and ambitions; a remedy of some sort was essential. The remedy he chose followed logically from his analysis of the problem. If "irritation produced by these slavery debates" was the source of all their difficulties, then the surest means of eliminating it was to settle the slavery question as fully and permanently as possible.

On the practical level Webster supported Clay's compromise as the device most likely to achieve that goal. Together Clay's resolutions covered every one of the major issues arising from slavery over which the federal government had jurisdiction. With those issues settled, presumably, discussions of slavery would lose all relevance in national politics and therefore cease. Harmony would be restored, and the business of government could go on as before. This at any rate was Clay's argument. Webster added to it considerably.

What he added, altered to meet the exigencies of the moment, was a statement of his own nationalism. His careful enumeration of grievances, his concessions to the South and the justification he offered for them, his willingness to compromise, his strictures against those who were not, all of these came to the same point: balance. The agitation over slavery had reached the juncture where it threatened — if not the nation itself — the fundamental balance that was at once its essence and finest achievement. A major readjustment had become imperative.

Nor would political readjustment alone resolve the difficulty. With all the instruments of balance to choose from — institutions, culture, and character — Webster in the end put his faith in character. The culture was a constant. Changes could be made through the institutions, but without a corresponding change in men's hearts the issue might still be lost. Better than most men, perhaps because he had suffered more as a result, Webster understood the depth of feeling on the subject of slavery, North and South. Yet in spite of the havoc slavery had caused in his own career, he held out hope that the emotional attachment to the nation that all Americans shared in common remained stronger than anything tending to divide them. If the description of the nation which grew from that hope bore little relation to the actual nation in 1850, it was the nation as he sincerely believed it ought to be, the nation his rhetoric had always celebrated, and the only nation in which Daniel Webster could ever hope to be elected President.

# Six
# The Politics of Compromise

IN THE FIGHT for the Compromise of 1850 Clay's initial proposals and the ensuing Great Debate, of which the Seventh of March Speech was a part, stand as major landmarks. But history might well have counted them moments of little significance had it not been for another, and quite unexpected, event that occurred on July 9, 1850: the death of President Zachary Taylor. Not only did Taylor's death assure the passage of the Compromise, it brought a completely different faction within the Whig party to power and worked a marked change in the fortunes of those Whigs, including Webster, who supported Clay's plan. Indeed in Webster's case the transformation could hardly have been more dramatic.

Yet in those first hectic days following the seventh of March all this lay a good four months in the future. Taylor was still very much alive, and whatever else it accomplished, Webster's great speech had failed utterly to convince the soldier in the White House. He continued to oppose all larger compromise plans and made no secret of his attitude. Meanwhile, too, the storm of protest produced by the speech throughout the North grew steadily. Eloquent letters, signed by dozens of leading businessmen, came from Boston and New York approving Webster's course, but in scores of communities from Maine to Illinois groups of citizens met to condemn him. Even in Massachusetts a good half of the Whig press registered clear dissent.[1]

Taking the direction of the wind from their constituencies and mindful of Taylor's steady hand at the helm, Northern Whig congressmen proved little inclined to follow Webster's lead. "I think they are sent here for little else than to keep up the quarrel on the slavery subject," he commented of his colleagues early in April.[2] Northern Democrats and moderate Southerners of both parties, who tended to approve the speech as they had Clay's original plan, offered more support, but their numbers remained too small to carry the issue in Congress — let alone against a presidential veto.

## II

With the men he needed most to convince all standing against him, it would scarcely have been surprising if Webster began to hedge his bets. And he did; or at least he seemed to. On March 13 in the Senate he declared that "the only course of proceeding efficiently" was to treat California as a separate issue and vote to admit her at once. As for the other issues "under agitation" and the solutions proposed for them: "I see no such hope that such a series of resolutions would pass the two Houses of Congress." In short, Webster now thought it expedient, as he himself stated, "to proceed in that course of legislation which the President has suggested." [3]

Three weeks later, on April 4, he reaffirmed his preference for acting on "California *per se.*" This time, however, he seemed anxious to consider other matters as well. Once California had been admitted he thought it only proper for the Senate "to go and take up the territorial question — the question of a government for the Territories; and I may say upon the whole that I am inclined to think the best way to proceed will be to take up the territorial bills and act upon them." Indeed to do otherwise would be a serious mistake. "I am unwilling to leave any of these questions open, to be the cause of heartburnings, and dissension, and dissatisfaction during the recess." [4]

*

When Webster spoke the second time the principal issue before the Senate was whether or not to refer Clay's Compromise proposals — along with several others that had been put forward — to a special committee. The Committee on Territories had already presented bills admitting California and organizing New Mexico, and Webster was arguing in effect for action on those. In this he sided with Stephen A. Douglas, the vigorous young chairman of the Committee on Territories. Clay, on the other hand, supported the idea of a special committee. Since the administration forces were opposing the plan, it was easy enough for Webster's critics to see his stand as a step backward, if not a complete rejection of Clay's Compromise.

In fact it was neither. In the long run the debate over the special committee was a debate over tactics, not policy. For all the pleasure it gave J. M. Brewer, the Washington correspondent of the proadministration Boston *Atlas,* to find Webster "flitting about like a weather cock," [5] his basic position remained unchanged after the end of March. He was for California, but only as part of a more comprehensive settlement. He opposed the special committee because he thought it a waste of time and because in all probability it would combine the relevant issues in a single bill. Such a bill, he believed, had only the slimmest chance of passing Congress, a judgment that subsequent events amply confirmed. When the resolution creating the Committee of Thirteen passed, he was appointed one of its members but never served, having chosen instead to spend two weeks in Boston. He did give the Committee's proposals his wholehearted support, however, and in those proposals lay the heart of the Compromise of 1850.

It was May 8 before the Committee of Thirteen was ready with its report. Presented by Clay as chairman, it followed all but exactly the lines of his original plan. With a revised fugitive slave law already before the Senate, the Committee proposed two additional pieces of legislation. The first abolished the slave trade in the District of Columbia, and the second — the so-called "omnibus bill" — at a single stroke admitted California, divided the remainder of the Mexican cession into two territories, created governments for each, settled the Texas–New Mexico boundary dispute in favor of New Mexico, and finally, required the federal government to pay the state of Texas $10 million in return for relinquishing its New Mexican claims. In the language of the bill the assemblies of the two new territories were to be prohibited from legislating "in respect of African slavery." Beyond that the subject had been avoided entirely; there was no place in Henry Clay's omnibus bill for a Wilmot Proviso.

Formal debate on the Compromise proposal began on May 13 and a full month went by before Webster declared himself in the Senate. Privately, however, he left no doubt as to where he stood. "I shall of course vote for it, and for all measures, and almost any measure, intended to settle these questions," he wrote Franklin Haven.[6] Before his colleagues, when the time came, he was no less emphatic. Speaking of the provisions of the omnibus bill on June 13 he announced, "I am in favor of each and every one of these subjects, and should be inclined to vote for them, separately or together, as may best suit the convenience or the general judgment of the Senate."[7] Four days later he met the crucial issue of slavery in the territories head on. He was aware that "gentlemen from my own part of the country" disagreed with his view of the subject but he remained convinced. Nature made the Wilmot Proviso unnecessary in New Mexico, and he had "heard no argument calculated in the slightest degree to alter that opinion." If in differing thus with his Northern associates he took upon himself "an uncommon degree of responsibility," he was prepared for the burden. "I know no locality in America; that is my country. My heart, my sentiments, my judgment, demand of me that I shall pursue such a course as shall promote the good, and the harmony, and the union of the whole country. This I shall do, God willing, to the end of the chapter." [8]

Having given the Compromise his unqualified support, Webster watched its progress in Congress anxiously. At first everything seemed to depend on "the number of Southern Senators who may fall off from its support." [9] That was in May, however; a month later the geographical focus of Webster's concern had shifted. "It is certain — quite certain — that if Massachusetts members would cooperate the Compromise Bill *would pass*," he confided to Samuel Lawrence at one point, and a week later: "The Mass. Delegation could settle the whole question, *this day*." [10]

As June wore on the men from Massachusetts proved no more tractable than ever, yet it began to seem as if the Compromise might pass in spite of their opposition. While the omnibus bill's floor managers adroitly fended off amendments, the Nashville convention met and, to the great relief of all but the most extreme Southerners, accomplished little of any consequence. With only nine slave states represented and a group of moderates in control, the Southern "ultimatum" had a soothingly mild ring to it. At the same time the Texas–New Mexico boundary situation had grown worse, which tended to increase the pressure for a general settlement. By the end of the third week in June Webster was writing, "it is certainly now the opinion at the White House, that the bill will pass." [11]

No doubt it was heartening to be able to make such predictions — and receive them — but any hope they inspired was deceptive. The White House might consider the passage of the omnibus bill imminent; what the man in the White House proposed to do about the bill was something else again. Events in Congress and elsewhere had changed Taylor's attitude not a whit. He was still the principal obstacle in the path of Clay's Compromise. If anything, the omnibus bill had sharpened the conflict. In May Alexander C. Bullitt, the editor of the administration-sponsored Washington *Republic*, had been forced to resign because he found it impossible to condemn the Committee of Thirteen's proposals. Within a week his successor, Allen Hall, came out unequivocally for the President's plan against every other alternative.[12]

Whether Taylor would actually have vetoed the omnibus bill remained problematical. Webster, who thought the President entertained "more feeling on the subject than I can well account for," expected no veto,[13] but there were those who did. In any case Taylor's position kept the issue from coming to a final vote in Congress through July 7, and it was on that day the country first learned he was dangerously ill. Two days later Zachary Taylor lay dead of acute gastroenteritis.

### III

Carefully avoiding any mention of the late President's policies, Webster's brief eulogium delivered in the Senate on July 10 concentrated instead on the virtues of the man. "For my part, in all that I have seen of him, I have found much to respect and nothing to condemn." Indeed one could only hope "that in the time that is before us, there may not be wanting to us as wise men, as good men for our counsellors, as he whose funeral we now propose to celebrate." [14]

If this last sounded almost too somber, it was after all what convention required. In private Webster seemed a good deal more sanguine about the future and the men who would shape it. "The President," he wrote Franklin Haven of Taylor's successor, "is a sensible man, and a conservative Whig, and is not likely to be in favor of any 'isms,' such as have votaries at the present day." [15]

Millard Fillmore — the man thus described — would doubtless have been pleased with Webster's evaluation. There was,

too, a sound basis for the hope that evaluation implied. Together chance and the vagaries of New York politics had placed
a man at the head of the government, who, whatever he might
do, was quite unlike Zachary Taylor.[16]

The son of a ne'er-do-well farmer, Fillmore had made his way
in life by dint of hard work, determination, and a healthy measure of caution. Entering politics as a young lawyer in Buffalo,
he had risen steadily — if undramatically — through the ranks:
the state assembly in 1829, a convert to Whiggery in 1834, and
thereafter eight years in the House, which brought him ultimately to the chairmanship of the Ways and Means Committee,
where he played a major role in framing the tariff of 1842. In
1844 the Whigs had nominated him for governor of New York,
but faring no better than the party in general did that year, he
lost.

As successful as he had been up to then, the defeat in 1844
marked a sharp break in Fillmore's career: for the next four
years he got nowhere, though the difficulty had begun even earlier. When Tyler vetoed the second bank bill, Fillmore, an
avowed Clay man, had dutifully followed the Kentuckian's lead
in breaking with the administration. At the time that seemed
the safest course for any Whig to follow, but in Fillmore's case it
turned out otherwise. The balance of power in the New York
Whig organization lay with Seward and Weed, and they stood
by the administration. As for Fillmore, the two never forgave
him. If he managed to win the gubernatorial nomination in
1844, Weed had already decided the Whigs were bound to lose
the state that year. Once the party's position improved, Fillmore became very much an outsider.

To a substantial extent he remained an outsider, even as Vice
President. When Weed and Seward threw their weight behind
Taylor in 1848, Fillmore persisted in backing Clay. His own
nomination at Baltimore had come chiefly as a last-minute at-
tempt to sooth Clay's disappointed supporters. On that basis
Weed was prepared to accept it; moreover, from his standpoint

the arrangement had definite advantages: the vice presidency promised to remove Fillmore from New York, and in all but a few cases in the past it had proved an office of little consequence. Just how inconsequential the second highest elective office in the nation could be Fillmore himself quickly discovered on assuming it. With both Weed and Seward using the full force of their influence against him, he was bested from the start. "Whatever may have been the situation of Vice Presidents heretofore, I do not feel that I have any responsibility as connected with this administration," he wrote Edward Everett in July 1849. "My recommendations for office in my own state and even in my own city have generally been disregarded . . . My advice has neither been sought nor given as to the policy to be pursued." [17]

It was an impossible position, but Fillmore handled it better than many men would have. For all his caution, which sometimes made him seem indecisive to the point of weakness, he had a certain native dignity. He made an impressive presiding officer for the Senate. He also, as time went by, gave signs of increasing independence from the administration that had so little use for him. As a lifelong Clay supporter he was almost certain to find the Compromise proposals attractive. It was less likely that he would do anything concrete about his views, yet by the beginning of July he was threatening just that. In his final interview with Taylor he had announced that if the omnibus bill came to a tie vote in the Senate he intended to use his constitutional prerogative to force its passage.

Here was striking evidence of what the future might hold, but for the moment the stately solemnities of Taylor's funeral claimed the center of the stage. Very soon thereafter, however, a pattern began to emerge.

Mired in a complicated scandal involving the improper use of influence to secure payment of interest by the federal government on a century-old claim first entered against the British colonial government in Georgia, Taylor's Cabinet had been on the verge of dissolution when he died. Two Secretaries, George Crawford of War and William Meredith of the Treasury, as well as Reverdy Johnson, the Attorney General, were directly implicated, but there were rumors that Old Zack planned still further replacements. Even if he had not had John Tyler's unfortunate example to guide him, Fillmore was thus relieved of the burden of having to rely on men chosen by his predecessor; as the existing Cabinet would have been replaced anyway he was free to choose his own. Whom to select was another matter. Taylor would have relied heavily on the advice of Seward. Indeed capital gossip often placed the New Yorker at the head of any reorganized administration. But with Taylor gone and Fillmore in command Seward's chances of becoming Secretary of State had dropped to nothing.

On July 17 — four days after Taylor's funeral — Robert Winthrop had what he later described as "a half hour's private conference" with Fillmore at the new President's temporary headquarters in Willard's Hotel. The interview had been arranged at Winthrop's request. Word had reached him that Fillmore was about to appoint a Secretary of State, that "two gentlemen were pressed upon him . . . both from Massachusetts." Believing he was one of the two men in question, Winthrop wished to settle matters against himself. "I think I have done this conclusively," he wrote John P. Kennedy afterward, adding, "I have great faith that Webster will have the place before the week is out." [18]

Winthrop's prediction proved accurate. Within another four days Webster's appointment as Secretary of State was before the Senate. Precisely when Fillmore made the offer remained unclear, but it may well have been as early as July 16; for all Winthrop's honest concern that the post not be offered him, there was little chance it would have been. From the beginning Webster was the logical choice.

As the only Whig — other than Henry Clay — with any practical experience of the "premiership" he had, perforce, a heavy claim on Fillmore's consideration, and Clay himself was known to favor the appointment, which would have counted for a good deal. Webster had, too, the virtue of coming from Massachusetts, a state Taylor had passed over in making his original Cabinet and one where the Whig party, at the moment, was particularly hard-pressed. Yet if distinguished Bay Staters were wanted, Winthrop, or even Edward Everett, might have done as well — except for one thing: neither man had associated himself with the Compromise, and Fillmore was determined to make some form of comprehensive settlement his first order of business as President. He had come to such a position in part out of reverence for Clay, but only in part. Conservative by nature, he was deeply disturbed by the apparent danger in which the Union stood. Further, with both Seward and Weed — his chief rivals in New York — backing Taylor's plan, it was only natural for Fillmore to move in the opposite direction. A Compromise man as Vice President, he intended to remain one in the White House, and by appointing Webster Secretary of State he not only served notice of the fact, but acquired a valuable ally in the bargain.

For Webster's part the arrangement had everything to recommend it. Freeing him from the Italianate rigors of the Senate, it gave him a broader platform and brought him, in one move, several giant steps nearer his goal for 1852. Fillmore had already given out, according to Edward Curtis, that "under no circumstances" would he stand for reelection.[19] Apart from the added burdens of the office Webster's only other concern was money, and friends in Boston quickly assured him that they stood ready to do "whatever may be required to this end." [20]

Webster delivered his final speech in the Senate on July 17. With his appointment already rumored, his words had special meaning, though he added nothing to what he had said before. Step by step he covered the old ground, returning always to the same point: the great issues that appeared to separate them were in reality abstractions. What would Massachusetts lose if the Compromise passed? Nothing except the Wilmot Proviso. And what was it but "a mere abstraction" — the prohibition of a "naked possibility, upon which no man would act?" To refuse to abandon the Proviso was absurd, and it seemed even more so when one considered the benefits such a step would produce. About the most important of those benefits Webster left no doubt: "the settlement, to an extent of far more than a majority of them all, of the questions connected with slavery which have so long agitated the country." Agitated the country, and brought its government to the verge of paralysis. "Everything is suspended upon this one topic, this one idea, as if there were no object in government, no uses in government, no duties of those who administer government, but to settle one question." In the meantime, Webster reminded his colleagues, they were "the observed of all observers" — the whole world waited to see "whether this great popular government can get through such a crisis." As for himself, he proposed to stay where he was, "to abide by the principles and the purposes I have avowed." This he was prepared to do, moreover, with absolute disregard of personal consequences. "I need no other platform, I shall know but one country." [21]

It was an eloquent and eminently reasonable appeal. Yet for all its eloquence and reasonableness — to say nothing of the added force Webster's appointment gave it — the omnibus bill still hung in the balance. Enough senators remained unconvinced to prolong the debate another two weeks and finally to kill the bill altogether. On the last day in July, with both sides alternately claiming victory and predicting defeat, Clay's omnibus was completely dismantled on the floor of the Senate. One by one, in a series of complicated amendments, its separate provisions were eliminated, leaving in the end only the portion of the bill organizing Utah as a territory. For days beforehand Southern radicals had been caucusing with antislavery, anti-Compromise Northerners. In the final balloting votes fell in utter confusion across every conceivable party and sectional line. Nothing seemed stable or certain, except that the Compromise, as a single, all-embracing piece of legislation, was dead.

To have gained so much in Fillmore's coming to power and still lose the battle was discouraging; that no one who supported the Compromise could deny. Even with Fillmore in office, however, the omnibus bill was at best a dubious proposition. Favoring every one of its provisions individually, Webster had always opposed its inclusiveness. As late as July 25 he was complaining of one "eminent Northern Senator" who had asked what might be done to insure the passage of the bill, saying "he was ready to do anything but to vote for it." There were, Webster supposed, half a dozen other senators "in exactly the same condition." [22] The difficulty had been obvious from the beginning. "There is an unquestionable majority of votes in the Senate, in favor of every one of the propositions contained in the bill, perhaps with some amendments, and yet I have fears that no majority will be found for them together." [23] That was Webster's opinion in May, and the debacle of July 31 more than confirmed it.

Yet if the reason for the failure of the omnibus bill was clear, so too was the corollary: the Compromise might still be achieved — as a series of separate measures. Under Stephen Douglas the Committee on Territories had already drafted bills for California and New Mexico. Like Webster, Douglas had opposed the creation of the Committee of Thirteen and doubted whether the omnibus bill would pass. Now, with all the skill and energy at his disposal — and few men could claim more of either — the "Little Giant" from Illinois took charge. In the weeks that followed he was everywhere, cementing alliances, soothing feelings, pulling votes out of thin air. Clay, in the meantime, had left Washington and was not to return until the end of August. By then the major part of the work had been done.

While Douglas performed his feats of magic, Webster watched with growing hope. The only real stumbling block, he felt, was the New Mexican boundary situation, and when the bill settling that seemed about to fail he lost no time in throwing the entire weight of the administration behind it. Having been asked by Fillmore to draw up a reply to a letter from Governor Peter H. Bell of Texas on the subject, he suggested that the reply might be used as an occasion for a special message to Congress. Fillmore agreed at once. For the next two days Webster worked on a draft of the message and then spent the better part of another day going over it with George Ashmun and Edward Curtis. When the three were satisfied, Ashmun took it around to individual congressmen for approval. On August 6, between five and seven in the morning, Webster was back at work, making last-minute changes. By nine o'clock the message was ready for Fillmore's signature; two hours later it was on its way, from the White House to the Capitol.[24]

The substance of Bell's letter to the President was ominous enough. The legislature of Texas was about to meet for the purpose of extending its authority to the disputed territory — if necessary by force. On that point the message was clear: if Texas resorted to arms the President would have no choice but to meet force with force. His obligation under the Constitution was unavoidable. Having said this, however, the message went on to state Fillmore's earnest hope that such a confrontation would never become necessary, that Congress would find some means of adjusting the difficulty quickly and fairly. Nor was that all. During Fillmore's weeks in office his support of the Compromise had become an established fact, but only through inference. Prior to August 6 he had said nothing, formally, in behalf of a general settlement. Now, in a single paragraph at the end of the message, Webster remedied that situation. There could be no mistaking the President's position, or the strength of his conviction: "I think no event would be hailed with more gratification by the people of the United States than the amicable adjustment of questions of difficulty which have now for a long time agitated the country and occupied, to the exclusion of other subjects, the time and attention of Congress." [25]

The administration had counseled speed, and for a change the Senate seemed inclined to abandon its snail's pace of the past two years. On August 9 — three days after the special message — the boundary bill passed with thirty votes in the affirmative, twenty opposed, and ten abstentions. August 13 saw the California bill through by a slightly higher majority, and two days later the bill organizing New Mexico was approved. On August 23 the senators voted a new fugitive slave bill, thereby completing the Compromise except for the abolition of the slave trade in the District of Columbia. The bill accomplishing that was not passed until September 16.

With the bulk of the Compromise measures through the Senate, the House too snapped into action. The final week in August ended the debate, and by September 6 the first of the Compromise bills — the so-called "little omnibus" combining New Mexico and the boundary settlement — was ready for a last vote. It passed easily. California and Utah followed the next day, and on September 12 and 17, respectively, the House approved the fugitive slave bill and the Senate's abolition of the slave trade in the District. In the meantime Fillmore had been signing the Compromise bills as quickly as they came down from the House. By September 20 the work was finished; the Compromise of 1850 had become law.

The day the California and Utah bills passed the House, Washington broke into a riot of celebration. The end was still two weeks away, but no one could doubt any longer what the result would be. The public buildings were illuminated, and throughout the city impromptu parades, bonfires, dinners, and toasts lasted far into the night. Calling on Webster a group of revelers found him jubilant — if a little the worse for wear. He had to be supported to the door and garbled the first line of his toast, but the crowd loved it anyway. A few days later, summing up the triumph in a more detached mood for Peter Harvey, he said simply, "It is over. My part is acted, and I am satisfied." [26]

## IV

Satisfied — but also exhausted. The strain of the last six months had been enormous. In all that time, Webster remarked to Harvey, he had slept "not more than four hours a night, on an average." [27] As soon as he was able after Congress had adjourned he started north; within four days more he was home — home to rest and to think of the future.

And for a change the future looked tantalizingly bright. A dispassionate observer might have pointed out that Webster's role in passing the Compromise was perhaps less crucial than people supposed. As grand as it had been, the Seventh of March Speech demonstrably changed few, if any, Northern votes. Doubtless it strengthened the hand of Southern moderates, but what after all had any of the thousands upon thousands of words spoken in the Senate accomplished compared with the intrepid, behind-the-scenes maneuvering of a Stephen Douglas? [28] A valid point; yet men at the time were inclined to be less skeptical than historians since have been. The Compromise had passed, and Webster stood in the popular imagination as the person who, more than any other single individual, tipped the scales in favor of Clay's grand design. The next step seemed obvious. "I trust the country will have the discernment & the gratitude to appreciate & recompense the service," wrote Edward Everett,[29] echoing dozens of others.

After a faltering initial response to the Compromise, Everett had become one of its staunchest supporters, and in the flush of victory it was easy to imagine that others — even the most vigorous opponents — had followed a similar route. "The face of everything seems changed," Webster wrote Harvey in September. "You would suppose nobody had ever thought of disunion. All say, they always meant to stand by the Union to the last." [30] And a few weeks later: "Faction, disunion, and the love of mischief are put under, at least for the present, and I hope for a long time." [31] With so much accomplished — and so many people rejoicing at the result — the next step, the ultimate prize, seemed in fact well within Webster's reach.

But what exactly had the Compromise of 1850 accomplished? Webster's own analysis was as simple as it was straightforward, but it also suffered from the defects commonly associated with those virtues. To the end of his life he maintained the Compromise measures represented "a proper, fair, and final adjustment of the questions to which they relate." [32] In the Seventh of March Speech he made clear his desire to see slavery eliminated as an issue in national politics. That, he argued, the Compromise had done. Every aspect of the issue within the proper jurisdiction of the national government had been settled. Henceforth the debate would cease because there was no longer any reason to carry it on. This happy result, moreover, had been achieved through mutual concession. In the crisis both sides had given way for the sake of reestablishing harmony; the Compromise, in other words, was just that — a compromise.

Of all the characteristics Webster came to ascribe, in public, to the five laws Congress passed and Fillmore signed in August and September of 1850, this last — at once the most obvious — also proved the most troublesome. If both sides had given way in the crisis, neither of them, he invariably added, had been forced to sacrifice anything tangible. To argue otherwise might have made the Compromise seem less palatable; everyone was to emerge a gainer — no one the loser. As time passed Webster preferred to speak of the "adjustment" or "settlement." Evidently "compromise" suggested too much. There had indeed been a compromise, with concessions made, but they were concessions of feeling, opinion, not concrete benefits won or lost.

Within the limits Webster set, his point seemed valid enough. Had men voted only on the basis of sentiment, or the immediate interests of their constituencies, the Compromise would have failed. Without a minimum of Southern support California and the abolition of the slave trade in the District could never have passed; without the votes of at least a few Northern congressmen the fugitive slave law would surely have been beaten. Yet here too appearances could be deceptive. The number of congressmen, North or South, who actually voted for the Compromise in toto was very small. The omnibus bill lost. In the Senate when the individual measures came up separately only four men voted yea on all of them. Eight more voted for five out of the six. The rest — better than 80 per cent of the membership — voted no or abstained on at least two of the crucial, final roll calls. Of all the Compromise bills, furthermore, only two — California and the aboliton of the slave trade in the District — received a clear majority of affirmative votes over nays and abstentions in both houses.[33] In the end the Compromise passed less because congressmen voted for it than because they chose not to vote against it. Time and again abstentions provided the margin that insured success. In this context it may still have made sense to think in terms of mutual concession, but the point required careful qualification. It was also important to know — since their character was so ambiguous — precisely who had made the necessary concessions and why. Nor was the answer altogether encouraging from Webster's standpoint.

From first to last the groups in favor of the Compromise had been the Northern Democrats and the Southern Whigs. For all the effort lavished on the task, the Southern portion of the Democracy and the Northern Whigs had never been brought

around. The six final roll calls in the Senate found the Northern Whigs voting in the affirmative only 36 per cent of the time.
Their Southern Whig colleagues, on the other hand, tallied an
impressive 54 per cent for the Compromise, while the corresponding figure for the Northern Democrats rose all the way to
71 per cent.

As a Northern Whig who supported the Compromise Webster was very much in the minority. That had been true in
March and was still true, five months later, in September. The
Compromise had passed — the nation was safe — but the Whig
party remained divided. If concessions had been made for the
sake of preserving the Union, the Northern Whigs had little to
do with making them. For Webster these facts were unavoidable. Having cast his lot with the Southern members of his party
he had earned their gratitude — possibly even their support —
but he had also come perilously close to cutting himself off from
his natural base of support in the North.

Ideally, with the Compromise passed, the breach in the Whig
party could be expected to heal itself, just as Webster now supposed the nation at large would. In both cases the trouble was
the same. Slavery had split the party no less than the nation; the
elimination of the issue promised to benefit each alike. On the
level of specifics, however, the problem was more difficult. Before any lasting accommodation could take place within the
party the Northern Whigs would have to accept the Compromise for what its supporters claimed it was — a fair, final, and
permanent settlement. That, in turn, amounted to a rather
large order. Believing the great majority of Americans approved the Compromise, Webster hoped for the best, but it
never paid to be too optimistic.

Moreover it soon began to appear as if any degree of optimism
about the early return of Whig harmony might be excessive. In
mid-September at the New York state convention in Syracuse a
bitter quarrel broke out between Seward's friends and the pro-
Compromise, proadministration men. Attempting to force the

issue the Sewardites had offered resolutions praising their leader and demanding a firm exclusion of slavery in all new territories. When the resolutions seemed about to pass, the Compromise forces withdrew and drafted a platform of their own, but by then the damage had been done.

Thoroughly annoyed, Webster wrote Peter Harvey in ominous tones about a possible "remodelling of parties." Altogether he devoted three paragraphs to the subject in terms that could not have been more emphatic. "If any considerable body of the Whigs of the North shall act in the spirit of the recent Convention in New York, a new arrangement of parties is unavoidable. There must be a Union party, and an opposing party, under some name, I know not what — very likely the party of Liberty . . . the present administration will not recognize one set of Whig principles for the North and another for the South." [34]

A party of Liberty and a Union party. Eight years earlier Webster had forecast the breakup of the national Whig organization and the emergence of a new party, peculiarly tailored to his own situation.[35] In 1842 the hoped-for "remodelling" had failed to occur. This time there seemed a better chance for it. Together the Compromise Whigs and the Northern Democrats had achieved their ends in Congress; what was to prevent them from extending the alliance indefinitely?

A great deal, perhaps, but in the face of continuing recalcitrance on the part of the Northern Whigs, the Union party idea came to seem increasingly attractive to Webster. If the Whigs could not provide the breadth of support he needed, here was an alternative. Nowhere had the alternative greater relevance, furthermore, than in his own Massachusetts.

## V

"I wish you would go to Worcester & make a speech & *nationalize* the Whig Party," Webster had written Everett shortly before leaving Washington.[36] Whatever Everett thought of the request, Webster himself was under no illusion as to its probable outcome. The speech that could "nationalize" the Massachusetts Whig party was difficult to imagine. Indeed Webster had all but decided his political brethren at home were beyond saving. "They are one half inclined to abolitionism, & when you deduct that, & also what belongs to them of other *isms,* there is very little of true, broad, just & liberal Whig principles left in them." [37]

In the avalanche of protest that greeted the Seventh of March Speech few voices had been louder than those from Massachusetts. For the most part they were the predictable ones: together the Garrisonians, Theodore Parker, and the Free Soilers thundered dissent from one end of the state to the other.[38] But there had also been, from the beginning, a significant portion of the regular Whig organization that joined the hue and cry. In Boston this group found a ready outlet in the *Atlas.* Two years earlier the *Atlas* had backed Taylor for the nomination and was generally conceded to be the Lawrence faction's principal voice in the state. In Congress the redoubtable reformer Horace Mann — serving for a season in John Quincy Adams's old seat — had led the opposition to Webster among the Massachusetts Whigs. As Mann's strictures grew increasingly shrill even so staunch an advocate of Taylor's plan as Robert Winthrop lost patience: "The Whig party will go to pieces, & will deserve its fate, if it listens to such moonstruck ravings." [39] Yet for all Winthrop's disgust, his own position on the Compromise, when the time came, had been a good deal nearer Mann's than Webster's. In the final tally Mann voted only for California and the abolition of the slave trade in the District. Winthrop, having been appointed to Webster's seat in the Senate, had the opportunity to vote separately on the Texas boundary settlement. There, and in the case of the two bills Mann later supported, his vote fell on the affirmative side; at every other point he opposed the Compromise. John Davis in the Senate voted as Winthrop had, and the other Massachusetts Whig representatives by and large

followed Mann's lead. The sole exceptions were George Ashmun, who was absent for most of the voting, and Samuel A.
Eliot, the Representative from Boston. Hand-picked by Webster to fill the vacancy left when Winthrop moved to the Senate,
Eliot voted for all five of the Compromise bills.

At the time the Compromise passed, Webster chose to ignore
the general defection of the Massachusetts delegation in Congress. Instead he concentrated on Eliot, who became "a lion" —
the very "personification of Boston, ever intelligent, ever patriotic, ever glorious Boston." [40] The fact that Eliot had received
the nomination, beaten Charles Sumner in the election, and
then gone on to vote for every one of the "peace measures"
seemed to argue both for the essential soundness of the Massachusetts Whig organization and for the strength of Webster's
control over it. "It was not till Mr. Eliot's election that there
was any confident assurance here that I was not a dead man." [41]

In truth, however, Eliot's election and subsequent stand
proved little. Controlling the local organization was a far cry
from controlling the state party; Boston was not Massachusetts,
as Webster himself well knew. The city's Whigs had always
been more conservative on the slavery issue than their counter-
parts in the country. Most of the federal officeholders in the
state and a good portion of the Whig state central committee
remained more or less openly hostile to both the Compromise
and Webster.

Nor was the difficulty, as it might have been two years earlier,
wholly or even largely traceable to Abbott Lawrence. Many of
the men who now opposed Webster owed their places to Lawrence, but the amount of influence he could bring to bear from
his post in London was slight. Presumably as United States minister to the Court of Saint James's he was above meddling in
domestic politics, and any objections he may have had to the
Compromise — or to Webster's role in it — were effectively
neutralized by Webster's own appointment as Secretary of State.

When word of the appointment reached him, Lawrence hastened to inform George Ticknor that he knew of no man "more competent to discharge the duties of Secretary of State than Mr. Webster . . . whatever difference of opinion may have existed between him and myself upon particular points." [42] Writing Nathan Appleton in a similar vein, he added, "I have nothing to do with party strife at home." [43]

Webster may or may not have been convinced, but he had taken the trouble to speed confirmation of Lawrence's appointment by the Senate — something that had been delayed for over a year.[44] He was also prepared to let Lawrence's followers in Massachusetts keep most of the plums that had come their way on Taylor's victory, though magnanimity here made little difference. In their own view the leaders of the Massachusetts Whig party were fighting for their political lives, and Webster's favor, his ambition, and the Compromise that was irrevocably linked with both could only hinder them in the struggle.

The year before, in 1849, the Whigs had carried the state by a comfortable plurality — but only a plurality. Despite a decline in Free Soil strength, the Democrats and the new third party together received a majority of the popular vote for governor. Under the provision of the Massachusetts constitution that threw any electoral contest not resulting in a clear majority into the legislature, this might well have spelled defeat for the Whigs, but their opponents failed to cooperate with one another. As long as the Free Soilers and Democrats continued to go separate ways the Whigs had nothing to fear; any alliance between them, however, was bound to prove disastrous, and in most states the Free Soilers had already merged with one of the major parties, usually the weaker of the two, which in Massachusetts meant the Democrats. Moreover, in 1849 Free Soil–Democratic cooperation in the state had been kept to a minimum chiefly due to the influence of men like Palfrey and Charles Francis Adams. A year later Palfrey and Adams were no less opposed to a union they felt sacrificed principle to expediency, but the number of Free Soilers who agreed with them had dwindled substantially. At the last minute, plans for a statewide, joint Free Soil–Democratic ticket broke down in 1850, yet the danger remained. Given a majority of votes the two groups could always combine after the election to divide the spoils and indeed were planning just that.[45]

With their opponents moving nearer one another every month, the Whigs prepared to meet the threat as best they could. The party's record on slavery had always been more acceptable in Massachusetts than the Democrats', and Democratic votes in all probability would remain Democratic votes. The wisest strategy, then, seemed to be to go after the antislavery vote. That meant a frank attempt to capitalize on opposition to the Compromise within the state; it meant, too, a head-on collision with Webster. At the state convenion in Worcester resolutions were passed condemning all "unprincipled alliances." The delegates also voted the new fugitive slave law unacceptable without revisions.

Of all the parts of the Compromise, the fugitive slave law was the least popular in the North. Denying the accused fugitive ordinary civil rights — including trial by jury — it required all citizens to aid in returning runaway slaves and imposed heavy penalties for harboring them. From the beginning even moderates on the slavery issue had opposed the bill, and the volume of opposition grew steadily as time passed. In the Senate Webster had proposed a milder version, but when it became clear that his Southern colleagues would insist on their own bill he threw his full weight behind it. Moreover as Secretary of State he was prepared to see it enforced to the limit.[46]

If, as Webster remarked, "the proceedings at Worcester could have been worse," [47] they were still bad enough. By declaring the fugitive slave law unacceptable without revisions, the Massachusetts Whigs had publicly rejected his position on the finality of the Compromise. The issue was joined. As for the source of the trouble, Webster had no doubt where it lay. "Many Whigs are *afraid* to act a manly part, lest they should lose the state government." [48]

Meanwhile, the news from other quarters was more encouraging. Throughout the North and south to Virginia and even Georgia, Union Safety Committees and vast Union rallies were being organized by the dozen. Sponsored as a rule by groups of citizens "without respect to party," they welcomed conservative Whigs and Democrats alike, and more often than not their resolutions abounded in praise for Webster. Each week brought a new invitation to speak from Philadelphia, Westchester, Staunton, Virginia, Bridgeport, Bath, Wilkes-Barre, Boston, or New York City.[49]

In every case Webster declined to attend, but his carefully worded replies made clear the direction his thoughts were taking. The Union Safety Committee in New York had been one of the earliest established and its membership included many of the city's leading businessmen. In refusing its invitation to a meeting in Castle Garden Webster rejoiced that the committee had been created, that its members were "abject slaves to no party," but rather true lovers of the nation. "With you, I declare that I 'range myself under the banners of that party whose principles and practice are most calculated to uphold the Constitution and to perpetuate our glorious Union.'" [50] A few days later, reminding Richard Blatchford, one of the sponsors of the Castle Garden rally, of his earlier prediction "of a decisive split in the Whig party" Webster added, "I now strongly fear that result." [51]

Webster's sympathy for the activities of the Union enthusiasts was not a universally shared emotion. Robert Winthrop, for one, considered the entire affair "nonsense." Such elaborate devices as Committees of Safety, he believed, "ought to be reserved for real dangers. ' 'Tis the eye of childhood fears a painted devil.' " [52]

At the moment the question of just who was painting the devil, and why, was particularly important to Winthrop. Two months after the Compromise he still felt trapped "literally between two fires." On the one hand he had refused to follow Webster in supporting Clay's plan completely, and on the other he had gone far enough to thoroughly arouse the more advanced antislavery opinion in the state. Webster remained cordial, but "his peculiar friends" grew less so every day, according to Winthrop, while the Free Soilers were all but burning him in effigy. To further complicate matters Winthrop was about to stand before the legislature as the Whig candidate for Webster's old seat in the Senate, in which he was serving under an interim appointment. Never sanguine by nature, he held out scant hope for his own success. "I have the strongest presentiment my Senatorial term will not be renewed on the 1st of January." [53]

November brought the Massachusetts elections and the beginning of what ultimately became the confirmation of Winthrop's fears. Once again the Whigs carried the state by a plurality, but only a plurality, while the combined votes of the Free Soilers and the Democrats gave them control of the new legislature and hence — under the state's electoral laws — free rein to distribute, among other things, the governorship, the lieutenant governorship, and a full-term United States Senate seat. According to an agreement worked out beforehand the state offices would go to the Democrats while the Free Soilers were to have the senatorship. The man most often mentioned as the coalition candidate for the seat was Winthrop's old opponent Charles Sumner. [54]

Whatever Webster thought of Sumner as a prospective senator, he had always looked on the Whigs' chances in the election as "very doubtful." When the predicted defeat occurred he laid the blame squarely in one quarter. "I ascribe it," he wrote Fillmore, "entirely to the conduct of the members of Congress from this State, and some of the leading papers, in opposing and denouncing the peace measures of the last session." [55] Together Horace Mann and the Boston *Atlas* stood as the chief architects of the Whig defeat in Massachusetts. Within a month of the election all federal patronage had been withdrawn from the *Atlas*. Mann, however, posed more of a problem. His constituency reelected him by a solid margin. Moreover, of the rest of the Massachusetts delegation in Congress Orin Fowler, Zeno Scudder, and J. Z. Goodrich — though Whigs — were all, according to Winthrop, "open & zealous in their opposition to Webster and his views." [56] The fact that the election coincided with the first abortive attempt to enforce the new fugitive slave act in Boston had done nothing to improve the situation. While Webster and his followers were speaking of the necessity of obedience to law and order, two agents who had come from Georgia to claim a pair of notorious fugitives, parishioners of Theodore Parker's, were being hounded out of the city by angry mobs.

Despite the sorry state of affairs in Massachusetts Webster remained confident. Stopping in New York on his way to Washington at the end of November he found a highly gratifying reception. "You never made a visit here that gained you more friends," one informant remarked. "You have won golden opinions from all sorts of people — Democrats contending with Whigs in your praise." [57] In the South too his stock had never stood higher. "Webster is our great glory everywhere in this latitude," wrote John P. Kennedy to Winthrop. "His noble letter to the New York Union Meeting . . . has made him the main pillar of that great party which is now growing into a consolidated mass from New York to Texas, and will sustain either him or Clay for the Presidency." [58]

If Kennedy was right, Webster's confidence was well founded, though the fact held little comfort for someone in Winthrop's position. In the months since the Compromise, Webster had made it clear that he would tolerate no deviation from the line he had laid down. If the Whigs lost Massachusetts it was unfortunate, but a defeat in Massachusetts was preferable to anything that might sully the party with the taint of abolitionism. If that in turn meant reading the Horace Manns out of the party, or forming a new one without them, then so be it. What it meant for moderates like Winthrop who balked only at the fugitive slave law was less clear, but the outlook was hardly promising. Already, by the end of the year, the signs of Webster's disfavor were becoming unmistakable. Observing them, Winthrop remarked to Everett, "It is quite evident that a desperate struggle for the candidacy is beginning . . . If Webster stands any chance, as I should be glad to believe, he must be less repulsive to his old friends." [59]

# Seven
# The Politics of Union

Eighteen fifty-one was the last full year of Webster's life. It was also the year in which the world at large paused in the midst of its ordinary concerns for the first great international exhibition in London. Born of the fertile imagination of the Prince Consort, Albert, the Great Exhibition was meant to celebrate the fruits of man's peaceful endeavor, and incidentally to advertise before the other nations of the earth the benefits of half a century of British industrial progress. From California and the Isthmus of Panama to the farthest reaches of Imperial Russia, goods and people poured into Joseph Paxton's magnificent Crystal Palace on the banks of the Serpentine in Hyde Park. The competition between nations was stiff, but the United States — despite the fact that its exhibitors had requested more space than they were able to fill — came off surprisingly well. McCormick's reaper and a crude sewing machine, the first ever seen in Europe, created a mild sensation. In the fine arts, too, America won high honors, particularly in sculpture. Hiram Powers' *Greek Slave* became one of the "lions" of the Exhibition, and only slightly less noteworthy were two other American works, a life-sized statute of an Indian and another of Secretary of State Daniel Webster.[1]

When an American capped the season by winning the British regatta at Cowes the pride of his countrymen knew no bounds.

Such triumphs were important to the citizens of a nation barely seventy-five years old. They seemed at once to confirm the genius of American institutions and to foreshadow an ever more brilliant future. They inspired confidence and deepened the wellsprings of national purpose and identity — something Webster himself was more than a little concerned with at the moment.

With the Compromise passed and his own name so closely associated with it, he had staked his future more emphatically than ever on a policy of broad, nationalistic accommodation. On the other hand the Compromise was far from universally popular. For all that had been done to move peoples' hearts and minds in its behalf, the great settlement of the year before remained something at best grudgingly "acquiesced in" over large parts of the country; association with it alone was unlikely to earn any man a following sufficient to elect him President. Part of the problem, then, consisted of finding other themes, different ways of stating the basic principles that underlay the specific policy. Nor would the task be an easy one. Like the flawless contours of Powers' statue those principles may have combined passion and a logic of their own, but the net effect seemed strangely at odds with the sort of hardheaded practicality that produced marvels of innovation like the reaper and the sewing machine. If it was still possible to strike a balance between the two, how did one express that possibility and inspire others with it?

At the same time there was the matter of organization to be dealt with. Webster had pinned his hopes on a drastic revision of the American party system; yet once before he had underestimated the resiliency of existing political divisions. Just how likely was the great new Union party he spoke of so confidently to materialize? And if it did not, what then became of his chances?

All valid questions, perhaps, but the beginning of 1851 also found Webster as optimistic as he had been in years about the future. Though in the end his optimism proved sadly misguided, for the moment everything seemed to further his purposes — even events outside the United States.

## II

In his second term as Secretary of State Webster dealt with a variety of diplomatic problems, but none touched the national imagination more deeply — or cut a wider swath in domestic politics — than the matter of American relations with the Austrian Empire. Three years earlier, in 1848, Europe had undergone a violent attack of civil disorder. For many Americans here was yet another example of the power of the seeds of liberty their own Revolution had nurtured into bloom, and in the case of Austria the connection seemed particularly close. The Hapsburgs' Hungarian possessions had risen to demand their independence — a brave nation fighting to free itself from a repressive, alien regime. There was even, in the person of Lajos Kossuth, an unselfish national leader to rally the people in their struggle.

Under Taylor and Secretary of State John N. Clayton the United States had followed its traditional policy of noninterference with respect to all the Revolutions of 1848, including the Hungarian uprising. The administration did, however, send a special agent — A. Dudley Mann, an old political associate of Webster's — to observe the situation. When it became clear that the Hungarians were not going to make good their bid for independence, Mann informed Clayton, arguing against recognition. Subsequently Mann's instructions were aired in Congress, and at that point the Austrian government, through its minister in Washington, Chevalier J. G. Hülsemann, lodged a formal complaint against what it considered an unwarranted intervention in its internal affairs.[2]

By the time Hülsemann received his instructions from Vienna, Taylor was dead and Clayton out of office, so the duty of answering the complaint fell to Webster. The essential points at issue could have been dismissed in a few paragraphs; from the United States' point of view the attitude of the Imperial government was patently unjustified. Instead of stating the case and letting it go at that, however, Webster chose to expand it considerably. As a result the "Hülsemann Letter" became a hymn of praise to American institutions, achievements, and destiny, coupled with a stirring reiteration of the nation's special mission to cherish and foster by its example the progress of freedom everywhere in the world. The policy of noninterference was studiously reaffirmed, but Webster also went out of his way to make it clear the United States would brook no meddling in its own internal affairs. And lest the Austrians take this as so much bombast, he reminded them that compared to the territory of the young republic, "The possessions of the house of Hapsburg are but as a patch on the earth's surface." [3]

Most Americans were delighted with Webster's Austrian diplomacy, but here and there a dissenting voice arose. One of them came from old friend George Ticknor who evidently thought the Hülsemann Letter overharsh. Noting the criticism, Webster was half inclined to agree yet argued in his own defense, "I wished to write a paper which should touch the national pride, and make a man feel *sheepish* and look *silly* who should speak of disunion." [4]

As it turned out the Hülsemann incident was a splendid example of how diplomacy could be tailored to suit the needs of domestic politics. Pursued indefinitely, however, such a policy could lead to unexpected consequences — as Webster himself discovered before the Hungarian business was over.

When the abortive uprising on the lower Danube finally collapsed, Kossuth fled to Turkey, where the government, at the request of Austria, had agreed to confine him for one year. Later the United States offered him asylum, but by then the Turks — under pressure from both the Austrians and the Russians — seemed prepared to detain him permanently. Early in 1851 Webster sent a dispatch to the American minister at Constantinople instructing him to use every means possible to secure Kossuth's release. There followed a series of elaborate negotiations at the end of which Kossuth and his entourage found themselves — rather to their surprise — aboard the frigate *Mississippi*. They arrived in the United States late in October 1851 — there to live in quiet retirement nourished by the love and affection of a sympathetic nation.[5]

Or so, at any rate, Webster supposed; Kossuth had other plans. Dashingly handsome, with a wonderful flair for rhetoric and gesture, he made a tremendous impression on the American public and promptly set out to capitalize on that impression. His aim was to raise money and if possible to induce the federal government to join in yet another attempt to wrest Hungarian independence from Austria. Within a short time the "Kossuth fever" had reached major proportions: mass meetings abounded, subscriptions totaling tens of thousands of dollars were collected, petitions flooded Congress, and an entire wing of the Democratic party had identified itself with the Hungarian cause and the policy of intervention.[6]

Webster was appalled and so were many of his most ardent supporters — North and South. On the other hand, to appear critical of Kossuth and his mission might have lost countless potential votes. In the end Webster settled the issue by avoiding the huge rallies in the North and waiting to greet the people's hero in Washington. There he presented Kossuth to Fillmore with all the honors appropriate to a visiting head of state and at the great banquet afterward offered a toast that managed to echo the gist of the Hülsemann Letter without once mentioning the principle of noninterference. Meanwhile the President and his

Secretary of State had explained that principle at length to Kossuth in private.[7]

Thus had Webster attempted to steer clear of what he described to Franklin Haven as "both the Scylla and Charybdis" of the affair.[8] The result, as such compromises often do, cost something, but the entire episode was sufficiently short-lived to minimize the damage. By the time the Hungarian party reached Washington the nation's enthusiasm for revolution and revolutionaries had dimmed substantially.

### III

If Kossuth's visit presented Webster with a difficult choice in the diplomatic realm, the dilemmas of domestic politics mounted steadily during 1851. Nor were they all as readily — or successfully — managed.

In point of time the first problem he faced was the senatorial election in Massachusetts. With Robert Winthrop standing for the Whigs and Charles Sumner for the Free Soil–Democratic coalition, there seemed little enough to choose between them. Webster's own candidate was Samuel Eliot, but Eliot's chances proved nil, even after a group of conservative Democrats refused to support Sumner. "Webster's idea, if it be his, of getting Eliot elected is upon a par with the infatuation which has been the 'source of all our woes,' that he can be elected himself to the Presidency," remarked John Clifford to Winthrop.[9]

Chiefly because of the split in the Democracy the balloting in the legislature dragged on from January to mid-April. During most of that time any result seemed possible, yet in the final tally Sumner won the seat from which he later distinguished himself in such singular fashion. There were even a few Whig votes in his column, which cannot have pleased Webster — however little he favored Winthrop's election. Nevertheless, Webster's particular friends in the party were inclined to be philosophical. "If Winthrop is to play *bo-peep*, I prefer Sumner — on the desperate ground of *the worse the better*," wrote Moses Stuart from Andover.[10]

Quite possibly Webster himself had reached a similar conclusion. In the interim, however, another, even more serious problem had arisen. Sumner's election took place on April 23. Nine days earlier the Board of Aldermen of Boston had met and voted to refuse a group of 150 citizens the privilege of holding a meeting in Faneuil Hall at which Webster had agreed to be the guest of honor. By any standard the action was unprecedented, and Webster was furious. "I feel that either I am disgraced or Boston is; & the consciousness of either makes me as unhappy, almost, as that of the other," he wrote Everett.[11]

The origin of the Faneuil Hall incident, if a single cause could have been assigned it, lay in the new fugitive slave law. In the North opposition to the law had already reached major proportions, while Southerners — considering it the acid test of Northern acceptance of the Compromise — were more determined than ever to see it enforced. For Webster the issue was clear. To demand the law's repeal, or suggest changes in some of its harsher provisions, were actions that no free society could prohibit, but, he argued, little good was accomplished thereby and much harm done. The Compromise had removed the slavery question from national politics; opposition to the fugitive slave law could only anger Southerners and reopen the entire debate. As for disobeying the law or interfering with its execution, those were criminal acts just as surely as theft and arson were.[12] In the beginning it had scarcely seemed necessary to make the second point; Webster assumed the law would be obeyed regardless of its unpopularity. As it happened he was wrong, and the proof of his error all too often fell embarrassingly close to home.

Earlier in the year a mob had broken into a United States

district courtroom in Boston, forcibly rescuing an accused fugitive who was being held there overnight. Thoroughly annoyed, Webster lost no time in setting in motion elaborate proceedings to punish those responsible. He was also determined to see that it did not happen again. When a second fugitive — Thomas Simms — was arrested Webster personally supervised arrangements for the trial and return.[13] Successfully blocking a last-minute rescue attempt, federal authorities hustled Simms aboard ship at four in the morning on April 12. Two days later the Board of Aldermen voted to deny Webster's friends the use of Faneuil Hall. If pressed the Board would doubtless have taken issue with some of the more active opponents of the fugitive slave law, but feeling in the city ran high, and between Webster and Theodore Parker, Webster clearly had the worst of it. Even if the mayor had not been, as he was, Abbott Lawrence's brother-in-law, the result would probably have been the same.

In the aftermath of the Board's decision, the Common Council of Boston formally disassociated itself from what it took to be an open insult to Webster, and a group of "Friends of Union without Distinction of Party" in New York City — "in contrast with the recent act of the Mayor and Aldermen of Boston" — invited him to speak there.[14] On April 22, on his way from Marshfield to Washington, he was met by a large, hastily gathered crowd in front of the Revere House in Boston. A temporary platform, made of tables lashed together, had been set up. Mounting it by means of a set of portable steps used to light the lamps in the hotel, he greeted the crowd and said a few gracious words.[15]

According to newspaper accounts the Revere House reception was enthusiastic, but the anger Webster felt at the refusal of Faneuil Hall remained. The incident held, too, an important lesson. To a man the offending aldermen were Whigs. Henceforth Webster would keep to a minimum any contact with the regular party leadership in Massachusetts, and that included not only the Board of Aldermen of Boston but the entire Whig State Central Committee as well. "I am quite resolved not to commit any interest of mine to the management of the Whig State Committee of Massachusetts," he wrote Peter Harvey from Washington early in May. "The leading object of that Committee will be to reestablish a Whig government in Mass., and, if we may judge by the past, we may fear that to effect this object they will be ready to sacrifice high national considerations, and to court, as they have courted, free soilers, and semi-free soilers, abolitionists, and semi-abolitionists." The results of such a policy were obvious. The Massachusetts Whig party had lost the confidence of Whigs everywhere in the country, particularly in the South. "The truth is that sound Whigs and sound Union men in other States very strongly suspect the Whig party of Massachusetts of these tendencies. They are not likely, therefore, to be willing to co-operate with that party in Massachusetts." [16]

All things considered Webster had but one course to suggest to his friends: "call a meeting of Union men of all parties." [17]

The purpose of the meeting in question was to nominate Webster for the presidency. For months his supporters had been discussing the project, debating ways and means. In the opinion of those outside Massachusetts, the first move, logically, ought to come from the Bay State, yet there were a dozen other details to be ironed out. How was the nomination to be made? By whom? Under what auspices? A gathering at the home of S. B. Curtis in Boston that Webster attended in April 1851 made some progress, but it was the beginning of June before anything definite had been decided. [18]

Webster wanted the nomination made at once; his friends favored delay. Arguing that more time was necessary to give the movement the broadest possible base they carried the point. At Everett's suggestion petitions were drawn up to be circulated in every school district in Massachusetts. The letter accompanying the petitions, dated June 5, bore the nineteen names of the specially appointed "Central Committee." Rufus Choate headed the list, followed by Everett and George Ashmun. George T. Curtis, Peter Harvey, and Franklin Haven were also down.[19] Writing Haven from Washington Webster remarked that everything had been done "as well as could be," adding, "The great point, at present, is, to let it be known, in Massachusetts, & *elsewhere,* that the friends of Union in Mass. are determined, & *will not take any backward step, under any circumstances.*" [20]

As compelling as Webster's dictum about backward steps must have seemed, the situation, as it developed, required a good deal of sidestepping — if not a full-scale retreat. Ashmun estimated that the petitions would take three weeks to complete,[21] which left ample time to arrange a movement in Webster's behalf at the Whig state convention in September. Such a movement would give the requisite impression of coming from outside the established party leadership; it would be sufficiently independent to attract at least a measure of Democratic support. The only additional requirement was that the convention do nothing in the course of its other business that ran counter to Webster's views or interests; and right there a problem arose, for the leading contender for the Whig gubernatorial nomination was Robert Winthrop.

Despite repeated protests to the contrary, Winthrop plainly wanted the nomination, and most party leaders were prepared to back him to the limit. His popularity and generally moderate views gave him as good a chance of election as any Whig in the state. In a sense he was a compromise candidate, but for the sake of regaining control of the State House most Whigs were willing to compromise. Webster, however, was not. To be endorsed by the same convention that tendered Winthrop the highest honor in its gift would be a distinct liability — so the argument ran.

Throughout the summer Webster's friends worked to defeat Winthrop. His position on the Compromise was aired at length, and attacked, in the Boston *Courier* — the city's leading

"Union Whig" paper — while half a dozen suggestions were made as to other, better possibilities for the nomination, including Rufus Choate. From Newport, where he was vacationing, Winthrop wrote Everett complaining bitterly of these efforts. "It is a fresh lesson not to put one's trust in princes." [22] A month later, after an interview with George T. Curtis, he was even angrier. At Webster's express request, Curtis had tried to persuade Winthrop to wait a year or two before running on the grounds that his nomination "would *not be satisfactory in Georgia!*" [23]

If the logic of Curtis' appeal failed to convince Winthrop, it fared no better in other quarters. For all Webster's efforts by the beginning of September it was clear that Winthrop had won. At the last minute his supporters tried to smooth matters over by offering Everett the chairmanship of the convention, but Everett declined, and the attempt to create a demonstration in Webster's favor was abandoned. Queried beforehand on the subject, Webster himself was emphatic. "My advice is that you *do not* go to Springfield," he wrote Everett. "A convention which shall nominate me for one high office & Mr. Winthrop for another would be an inconsistent one I think." [24]

The perils of inconsistency in this case were real enough. The alternative, however, imposed burdens of its own. Having given up any chance of a formal nomination or endorsement by the Massachusetts Whigs, Webster was left with no choice but to proceed entirely apart from the regular party organization. That meant a separate convention and raised at once the question of how such a convention should be organized. Again timing was important. On the assumption that the Whigs would lose in November, a date just after the election was chosen. Boston was picked for the site, and smaller conventions were scheduled throughout the state to provide delegates. [25]

All this elaborate machinery took quantities of time, energy, and money to create, but Webster was convinced that only through it could the desired effect be achieved. When Winthrop — true to prediction — was beaten by the coalition, Fletcher Webster hastened to congratulate his father, adding, "I shall never cease to rejoice that your name was not connected with his at Springfield." [26]

## IV

Under the circumstances Winthrop's defeat may have seemed a legitimate cause for celebration, yet the net effect of events in Massachusetts had been to postpone a full five months the convention Webster called for in May. That in turn might have mattered less had the situation outside of Massachusetts developed according to plan. At the end of 1850 Webster had spoken confidently of a sweeping reorganization of parties. Six months later the reorganization had still to occur and there seemed little likelihood it would before another six months went by.

In retrospect it is easy enough to see that the Union party idea was too frail a reed to rely upon. At the time, however, there was a certain amount of solid evidence that could be offered in its support. As Webster conceived the idea it depended on two separate but related assumptions. The first was that the existing parties, each having split over the Compromise, would remain split for the foreseeable future. The second held that the fragmented elements of the two organizations could be made to recombine along radically different lines — specifically to create a party of Liberty and another of Union. If that failed to happen, much in the situation at the end of 1850 seemed to foreshadow a different outcome. The parties were split, and deeply so, and there were definite signs of realignment.

The situation in Georgia was a case in point. Late in 1850

Governor George Washington Towns had issued a call for a convention to consider what action the state should take on the Compromise. Under Howell Cobb and Stephens and Toombs the Union Democrats and Union Whigs had joined forces to protect their common position. It proved a singularly successful venture. Electing a substantial majority of the convention's delegates, the Unionists had gone on to draft an address that committed the state wholeheartedly to the Compromise.[27]

Throughout the following year the Georgia Constitutional Union party remained intact and continued to prosper. In the fall of 1851 Cobb won the governorship by a majority of better than 18,000 votes, while Toombs — with the Unionists firmly in control of the new state legislature — could look forward to a United States Senate seat. Earlier in the year Webster had been concerned about the possible reaction in Georgia to Winthrop's nomination by the Massachusetts Whigs. As matters stood, he had reason to be.

On the other hand the Georgia pattern set few precedents — either side of the Mason-Dixon line. In Mississippi a Unionist coalition, having successfully supported Henry S. Foote for governor, maneuvered a pro-Compromise declaration through the state's special convention on federal relations.[28] Elsewhere in the South party lines held firm. In general the Whigs supported the Compromise; it was the Democrats who found themselves at odds over the issue. Yet despite their continuing quarrel with the radicals, most Union Democrats preferred to remain within the party fold. The force of tradition was strong, and the tangible benefits to be had from offering one's services as a tail for the Whig kite too often seemed vague. Moreover, as time passed the radicals tended to modify their position. A good year for the South's economy and steady pressure from Northern Democratic leaders both helped in this respect.

In the North, meanwhile, the failure of the Southern Democracy to break ranks was matched by an equally persistent strain of Whig unity. With few exceptions Northern Whigs who shared Webster's view of the Compromise chose not to force the issue. In many cases they constituted a minority of the local organization, while in areas where the Whig party itself was weak or in trouble there seemed little to gain from an alliance with the Democrats, who could scarcely be expected to repay support they did not need. Thus in New York, for all the tension between Fillmorites and Sewardites, Compromisers and anti-Compromisers, the elections in 1851 saw the Whigs united again, if only temporarily.

Nor were efforts to isolate those Northern Whigs who objected to the Compromise particularly successful. Having tried this with Winthrop and failed, Webster found that even when he carried the immediate issue — as he did upon occasion — the larger victory eluded him. In Connecticut a handful of Union Whigs in the legislature managed to keep Roger S. Baldwin, the Whig incumbent, from reelection to the Senate. Afterward Baldwin complained that Webster's opposition had been a crucial factor in his defeat.[29] The charge may well have been correct, but Webster still had little enough to show for his labors. A few dissidents did not constitute an organized political force; the traditional party divisions in Connecticut survived unimpaired.

In Pennsylvania a similar situation developed, with similar results. Union Whig forces proved strong enough to write a pro-Compromise plank into the party's platform in 1851, but they failed to prevent the renomination of Whig governor William F. Johnston. An outspoken opponent of the fugitive slave law, Johnston was "no better than a Free Soiler" in Webster's eyes.[30] With the administration working all but openly to defeat him he lost the state, but basic party alignments remained unchanged.

In a few quarters, particularly among Northern business leaders, the Union party idea continued to draw support throughout 1851. For most people, however, Connecticut and Pennsylvania provided a better picture of things to come than Georgia or Mississippi did. The Compromise had indeed split the nation's two major parties, and as a result voters were crossing party lines more often than they had in the past, but the lines themselves seemed to be holding firm — at least for the present.

As the vision of a national Union party began to fade, Webster and those like him who had hoped for a different result were forced to shoulder a substantial burden of uncertainty. If, for example, the existing parties were to remain intact, what would their character become? Which of the two conflicting sides in each would triumph, and by what means? The answers to those questions in turn depended on how one analyzed the basic political situation in the nation in 1851. In effect the Unionists had already settled on a view and one that narrowed considerably the range of alternatives open to them, then and in the future.

"There is but one all-absorbing question and that is the preservation of the Union." [31] Along with his other activities Webster spent more time than he had in years speaking across the country in 1851. In May he traveled the length of the newly opened Erie Railroad from east to west and back again, stopping for addresses and dinners at Buffalo, Rochester, Syracuse, and Albany. The following month he spoke at Capon Springs, Virginia, and on July 4 gave the principal address at the laying of the cornerstone for the addition to the Capitol building in Washington. In September he held forth briefly at the Railroad Jubilee in Boston, then again in October at the New Hampshire State Agricultural Society Fair in Manchester. It was a stiff schedule. Each occasion required a different approach, though with characteristic deftness Webster tailored his message to suit the needs of the moment. The essential features of the message remained the same, however, as did the premise on which it was based: no issue before the nation was as pressing, indeed as critical, as the continued existence of the Union. Everything, finally, must be subordinated to that goal.

Standing packed together in the warm summer sun, Webster's

listeners heard the point made and remade a half-dozen times in a single hour. Before them stood a man long since become a legend, yet old now, his face drawn into cadaverous hollows beneath the great protruding brow. His posture was as erect as ever and his voice still firm, but in other ways he showed his age all too clearly. Many of those who came had never seen him before; only a handful would ever see him again. What they thought of the performance would have been difficult, if not impossible, to tell. As always the man, his words, and the moment transformed each other in a way that blurred their separate values and identity. In the end only the setting remained distinct, and in that setting Webster's appeal struck an oddly dissonant note.

A generation earlier, when he was still congressman, the points Webster reached in his travels in 1851 had been on the fringes of American settlement. Mere frontier villages then, they had grown since into thriving cities. With due regard for local civic pride he never failed to note the transformation. Eloquently, he told the details of Buffalo's progress from a hamlet of 2500 when he first visited it in 1825 to a metropolis of fifty thousand inhabitants — "one of the wonders of the age and of this country." [32] In Albany, Syracuse, and Rochester he had similar histories to tell, and in Capon Springs he spoke of the ever-increasing prosperity of the entire Shenandoah Valley.[33] Stroke upon stroke the picture grew clearer, a vital expanding nation made up of cities, regions, and peoples, themselves alive with growth and the prospect of a boundlessly abundant future.

And then always the swift transition and the difficulty it inevitably produced. What was the cause of all this? What gave life to the wilderness, transforming it into fertile farms and bustling cities? The energies and imagination of a magnificent people, certainly, to say nothing of roads, canals, and that greatest of all material wonders, the railroad; but over and above all those rose another agency, grander and more important by far — if less tangible. That other agency was simply the nation itself, the Union.

If the preservation of the Union was in fact the single most pressing issue facing the American people, then two things about what was to be preserved had to be made clear: first its value and second the magnitude of the danger in which it stood. To demonstrate the value of the Union Webster labored, as he always had, though now more explicitly than ever, to remove it from the realm of abstraction, to associate it with what was concrete and meaningful in the lives of his listeners. The question was whether the effort could have succeeded — however carefully orchestrated the effects — given the material Webster had to work with. There was an immediacy about cities sprung from the wilderness in a generation, about railroads and the changes they brought, about the myriad daily experiences and concerns of Americans in 1851 that belied the kind of translation he was talking about. Some connection there was, surely, between these things and continued national harmony, but to see support of the Union "as a great practical subject involving the prosperity and glory of the whole country, and affecting the prosperity of every individual in it" [34] imposed a rather substantial burden on men who were at the same time vitally concerned with when the next railroad would reach them or what price wheat commanded in Baltimore. Moreover, to see the preservation of the Union as *the* "great practical issue" was even harder, yet that, finally, was what Webster asked of them.

Perhaps the required imaginative leap would have been easier if Webster's second thesis had hit nearer home. Yet was the Union in any real danger of floundering in the summer of 1851, as he argued? To many people the answer seemed obvious: no. A year before, possibly, but not now. To prove his claim Webster pointed to the continuing agitation against the fugitive slave law. This was difficult ground, particularly in western New York, yet he never faltered. Indeed, obedience to the law became the final test of national loyalty, the best and truest means available for Northerners, at least, to cement the bonds of national unity. It was a poor proposition to conclude upon, and in most cases Webster did his best to mask the effect with references to George Washington and the early days of the Republic. The logic stood complete, however, and to one who missed its subtleties it might almost have seemed as if the whole prosperity of Buffalo, and beyond it the state of New York, and beyond it the nation itself depended, in Webster's view, upon the efficient enforcement of the fugitive slave law.

This was bad enough, but the corollary was, if anything, worse. Discussing the fugitive slave law Webster could make the Union appear concrete enough, yet only in terms of the responsibilities it imposed. Whatever benefits it might bestow remained illusive precisely because he had no program to offer beyond simple devotion to the union and obedience to the law. Men who were building cities and railroads had specific needs. In the past Webster had spoken to those needs by expounding upon issues like the tariff and internal improvements. Through such devices the Union manifested itself most tangibly in the lives of people. Now, however, he was barred from talking of traditional issues. To do so would have raised at once the specter of party, narrowed the appeal, and shattered forever the image of disinterested statesmanship. Any one of these would have been serious; the combination of all three could only prove disastrous.

Yet the alternative scarcely seemed more promising. True to the pattern he had set in the Seventh of March Speech Webster directed his appeal time and again to the "hearts" of his audience, but by continuing to argue for the preservation of the Union as the paramount issue before the nation he had backed himself into a corner that offered little if any chance of retreat. Nationalism, even when redefined in emotional terms, had always been, at bottom, a series of abstractions; now there appeared no way of relating those abstractions to the coarser stuff of reality — except, sadly, in the case of the fugitive slave law. From being the paramount issue, the Union had gradually become the only issue and a profitless one at that.

Despite the growing burden of difficulty surrounding his position, Webster's campaign for the nomination was progressing on schedule. Late in November the great convention organized by his Massachusetts supporters assembled in Faneuil Hall. Gathered from every corner of the state, the delegates managed an impressive show of strength and purpose in the setting of so many of their hero's former triumphs. Rufus Choate gave the principal speech, which Webster — in Washington awaiting Kossuth's arrival and the opening of Congress — thought "excellent, most excellent, considering the subject." [35] The Official Address of the Convention was the work of Everett, though Webster himself had determined much of its substance and tone. Cautioned beforehand that "the *Union* idea should be kept up, and strongly put forth," [36] Everett contrived an endorsement of the candidate that rested solely on his character and services to the nation. There was no mention of the Whig party, no attempt to spell out specific programs of action. In the end the delegates stood squarely with Webster — above and apart. "We speak also not as Massachusetts men, but as Americans. We speak for the great cause so highly transcending all local considerations and all merely party objects; the cause around which our hearts and our hopes all cluster; the cause of our common country." [37]

It was a stirring prospect, but apparently it gave at least one of Webster's supporters cause for concern. Having written the address, Everett found it impossible to attend the convention. "In consequence of the continual calls made upon me to attend & address public meetings, I have been obliged, in self-defense, to excuse myself on the score of health." [38] Everett also felt obliged, for whatever reason, to write at length explaining his activities in Webster's behalf to Fillmore. In the course of his explanation he made it clear that he expected traditional party divisions to remain intact and therefore hoped "to keep the basis of the Whig party as broad & solid as possible." This in turn rendered it imperative for the friends of all truly national candidates to cooperate with one another. His basic premise established, Everett hastened to offer the President what assurances he could, which proved to be substantial. "Politically speaking every friend of Mr. Webster must be a friend of yours," Fillmore was informed, while for his part Everett promised to hold himself "in a position to give a cordial support to your nomination, if events should prove that to be the preference of the Whig party & those Unionists who will act with them." [39]

The fact that Everett felt compelled to cover himself with such care spoke volumes, but fortunately for his own peace of mind Webster was unaware of his friend's correspondence with the President. Nor, apparently, did he share any of Everett's obvious misgivings about the venture on which they were embarked. At the end of November he was still predicting a reformation of the two major parties. "I look upon it now as certain that that can be no *entire Whig ticket* nominated for President & Vice President," he wrote Franklin Haven from Washington.[40] In the meantime Haven and Peter Harvey were doing what they could in Boston, while Edward Curtis traveled back and forth from New York almost weekly. In mid-December George Ashmun was in Washington and managed to see Fillmore, reporting afterward, "The coast will be clear, & known to be clear, in due time." [41] This was heartening news. Like everything else it stood subject to revision, however, and no one, least of all Webster, could afford to ignore the fact.

## V

As 1851 drew to a close, Millard Fillmore — whatever he might have confided to George Ashmun — found himself in a state of considerable turmoil. Decisions had always troubled him and he was faced with a particularly difficult one. Ever since his assumption of the presidency, and in a rising crescendo during the last few months, appeals had come imploring him to declare his candidacy for 1852. This he might have done cheerfully, had he been a candidate. But he was not, at least in his own mind. He had tasted the splendors and responsibilities of the presidency; he could claim a number of substantial achievements to his credit, including the Great Compromise. He was satisfied. He was also inclined to accept the standard Whig dictum against more than a single term in office for the Chief Executive, even if those Whigs who continually begged him to run in 1852 were not.

Confronted with their appeals, in fact, Fillmore was at a loss. At first he had stated his position politely, thanking his correspondents for their interest and flattering estimate of his ability and services to the nation. Lately, however, the requests had grown more fervent. There were, too, many more of them, and quite often they came couched in terms that made it difficult, if not impossible, to dismiss the suggestion they contained with mere pleasantries. Week by week the volume of appeals rose, shaping itself finally into a line of argument that seemed as consistent as it was compelling.

In the end Fillmore had no choice — regardless of what he might decide — but to consider that line of argument. Moreover, in it and in his deliberations upon it and the decision he ultimately reached lay the whole burden of what Webster would have to face in the months ahead, during the final phases of his own campaign for the presidency.

At the beginning of 1851 Fillmore and most other Whigs would have conceded that the two leading contenders for the party's presidential nomination — assuming there would be a Whig convention and Whig candidates — were Daniel Webster and General Winfield Scott. Though not himself particularly interested in the subject of slavery, Scott had become the candidate of the Northern, anti-Compromise wing of the party. Webster, on the other hand, was the principal figure in Fillmore's administration and his greatest ally in the recent battle for the Compromise. Should the Secretary of State and the general continue to dominate the field, it was clear where their chief's allegiance would lie.

In addition to Fillmore's support, Webster could count on the backing of those conservative Northern Whigs, particularly along the eastern seaboard, who favored the Compromise. For better than a year they had been signing memorials and staging great Union rallies. The precise degree of their strength within the party had yet to be determined, but the vigor of their activities made it seem prodigious indeed. In any event they would count for something, especially when added to Webster's greatest potential reservoir of support — the Whigs of the South. That his candidacy would have the blessing of most Southern Whigs was something he himself — along with many other people — took all but for granted, at least initially. By the end of 1851 the prospect seemed a great deal less certain, and it was right there that Fillmore's dilemma arose.

For all he had done to win it, the favor Webster enjoyed with his Southern brethren in the Whig party had always been an anomaly. Time proved the anomaly could not be sustained. Searching for an explanation, a practiced observer might have found several, but they all turned finally on a simple mathematical calculation. How would Webster as a presidential candidate fare in the South, not with the politicians, but with the great mass of voters? Asking that question, Southern Whig leaders all too often discovered the answer ran counter to what they, and certainly Webster, had hoped. Attitudes formed over a generation were too deeply embedded; the average man, several steps removed from the center of national political life, could not be made to change his views overnight or even over a year. The author of the Seventh of March Speech had earlier made his fame as the champion of Northern interests no less than as the defender of the Union. Had he really abandoned so much of himself and his past? Most Southerners evidently thought not. Granted Webster had rendered invaluable service in supporting the Compromise and was doing so now by denouncing those Northerners who balked at its terms; how could one forget or forgive all that had gone before?

Meanwhile, the answers to such questions might have mattered less had there been no acceptable alternative to Webster's candidacy. Yet as far as most Southern Whigs were concerned there was an alternative, and a highly promising one. As champion of the cause of national unity Millard Fillmore cut a rather less dashing figure than the Great Defender, but he also stood less intimately associated, at least in the public mind, with Northern interests and the Northern point of view. To those who doubted the validity of sudden conversions in politics he presented a relatively neutral image. He had, too, the added, and very considerable, virtue of being the incumbent. If the horse you had was satisfactory — sure-footed and barely winded — why change him for another in midstream? The logic seemed unassailable, and month by month Fillmore's Southern following grew. As early as April 1851 John P. Kennedy, writing Winthrop from Baltimore of Webster's chances for the nomination, had added, "Fillmore is a great lion with us too.[42] And no one likes to talk of preferences." By August the disinclination to choose had apparently passed, for Kennedy could report, "Fillmore is the favorite of the Whigs in this region for the next Presidency." [43]

Having settled on Fillmore as their candidate the Southern Whigs — together with his Northern friends — turned to the business of securing his cooperation. Patiently they explained the conclusions of their research: Webster's following in the South was too small; he could never carry the section and such Southern backing as he would have at the convention would be inadequate to give him the nomination. That left Scott, unless the President relented. If Fillmore agreed to run, then Scott would be "a dead pigeon." Further, it was still possible that Webster might have the reward he so richly deserved. By offering himself as a candidate Fillmore could draw support, holding it until the convention, at which point he could, if the opportunity arose, transfer it to his Secretary of State.[44]

At the end of 1851, having listened to such arguments for months, Fillmore was still undecided. In a sense he never did make up his mind. Rather he opted for a sort of uneasy compromise between the alternatives open to him. In mid-January Franklin Haven traveled to Washington to discover what the President's intentions might be and left knowing as little as when he arrived.[45] A week later, however, a paragraph appeared in *The Republic,* the unofficial voice of the administration, contradicting a rumor that Fillmore intended to withdraw from the race.[46] As it turned out, this was as much of a declaration as he ever made. Still for his friends it had the desired effect. They could continue to gather support for a candidate, who, if he had not exactly "come out," had at least refused to take his hat from the ring altogether. To Everett, the President wrote that he had as little desire as ever to be a candidate, but could not "for the present" see his way clear to withdrawing. At the same time he felt himself "in a false position" and wished some other were possible. "But yet this sacrifice on my part seems to be demanded by friends whose wishes I am not at liberty to disregard, and I am, therefore, bound to submit to it with as much patience as I can command." [47]

If Fillmore believed his position "false," to Webster it was a blow of the first order. Dining with the Secretary of State the evening of the *Republic* announcement, H. A. Wise, Everett's son-in-law, remarked, "Mr. Webster was not in a very genial mood." [48]

Genial mood or not, however, there was little enough to be done about the situation. Two months before, when he first had reason to suspect such a development, Webster instructed Everett to delete a complimentary reference to the President in the address of the Faneuil Hall convention, but Everett chose to let the passage stand.[49] Now Webster's friends and several of the newspapers supporting him gave out that Fillmore, by refusing to withdraw, had violated a pledge made to Webster when he entered the Cabinet. According to the story the President stated that under no circumstances would he be a candidate in 1852 and further that he would use the full weight of his influence in Webster's behalf.[50] Writing Everett, Fillmore denied flatly that such a pledge had ever been extended. He also made it clear that he was annoyed by the charge, yet when it came to Webster himself he was curiously gentle. Relations between the two were still "most cordial" and the President knew of no reason why that state of things should change.[51]

Fillmore probably was correct about the disputed pledge, and certainly so in the case of his continuing cordial relations with Webster. However odd the arrangement might have seemed, the President and his Secretary of State remained on excellent terms. After the Faneuil Hall convention both men assumed that Webster's position would make it necessary for him to resign,[52] but even that failed to occur. With Kossuth about to descend on Washington and several other fairly serious diplomatic crises breaking early in 1852, the proper moment never arrived. Fillmore needed Webster. He also, by all appearances, preferred Webster's candidacy to his own; he was simply allowing his name to be used for the sake of blocking Scott and holding the party to a policy of sectional peace.

Quite possibly Webster understood this, but he can not have liked the President any better for it. In his own view, Fillmore's supporters were wrong about how matters stood in the South, in the Whig party, everywhere in fact. Moreover, the result of their error had been to jeopardize not only Webster's chances for the nomination but the entire Union cause.

Nor did the events of the next few months in any way improve the situation. In February Webster made what was supposed to have been a triumphant visit to New York City. In the space of a week he saw and was seen by thousands of well-wishers at dinners and receptions, in hotel rooms and great meeting halls. Upon his arrival at the Mercer Street Presbyterian Church in the midst of a sermon on the character of Washington, the entire congregation rose and remained standing for several seconds "in perfect and decorous silence." Later with understandable pleasure — considering the state of his relations with the municipal government of Boston — he joined the mayor of New York in the Governor's Room at City Hall to receive the Common Council and other members of the city administration. The following evening brought a banquet honoring the memory of James Fenimore Cooper, whose works Webster praised as "American throughout and throughout," [53] and the next day, in quite another vein, he held forth on the virtues of African colonization as a final solution to the slavery question. The great event of the visit, however, was the ostensible reason for it: an address to the New York Historical Society. With everything else on his mind, Webster had still lavished quantities of time and energy on the address and the result was in its own way a masterpiece. Bristling with well-chosen allusions it ranged over the entire field of historical literature.[54] From Herodotus to the author of the *Pictorial History of England,* no one was omitted. Observing at the outset that the writing of history arose with the development of free institutions and flourished best under their influence, Webster went on to voice a plea for what later generations would call social history — history written "to illustrate the general progress of society in knowledge and the arts, and the changes of manners and pursuits of men." If there seemed little connection between the two points, what followed, climaxing with the inevitable celebration of American national unity and purpose, was no more tightly knit. At bottom the address remained a series of random reflections, but the overall effect, everyone agreed, was brilliant. On the day of the address, tickets, which had originally been given free to all Historical Society members, were selling for as high as fifty dollars apiece.

All of this should have been most heartening, yet the sequel proved anything but. Within a week of Webster's departure a great convention, similar to the one in Faneuil Hall, assembled in New York for the purpose of promoting his candidacy. Carefully timed to capitalize on the enthusiasm produced by his visit, the convention had all the familiar trappings, including a lengthy address to the people, written this time by William M. Evarts.[55] The speeches were stirring, and Evarts, already well launched on his brilliant legal career, was only one in a long and impressive list of sponsors. Speeches and lists of prominent business and professional men alone were not enough, however, and the sad truth was that the organizers of the New York convention had little else to show for their efforts. The crowd listened attentively, but it gave no sign of having been carried away with fervor for the cause then or afterward. Even allowing for their interest in the verdict, those Fillmore supporters who wrote describing the event as a failure cannot have been far wrong. "It will do no good to Mr. Webster," remarked one, adding, "indications were not wanting as to the feelings of the Whig working man."[56]

Left to thank his New York friends, Webster did so with characteristic grace, but his confidence had begun to slip, and the news from other quarters did nothing to restore it. From Washington Charles W. March wrote that he and George Ashmun were out of funds and needed both men and money if anything were to be accomplished in the South.[57] In Maryland the Whigs had already formally endorsed Fillmore. Farther north in Pennsylvania there seemed more cause for hope, but even there serious problems remained. "There is no regular organization here of Mr. Webster's friends," wrote Robert L. Martin from Philadelphia. "Everything in his favor must be necessarily accomplished by the individual activity of his friends." [58] Then in mid-March came word that Henry Clay had declared himself for Fillmore. Already gravely ill, Clay would be dead in four more months, but that hardly lessened the impact of his announcement or the damage it did to Webster's prospects — particularly in the South.

Altogether it was a depressing season. A new edition of Webster's works, brought out in March by Little, Brown, was selling poorly. By now, too, his health had become a source of constant concern. Ill during much of the fall and winter, late in the spring he suffered a bone-wrenching carriage accident near Marshfield. For ten days he lay in bed, his arms and wrists bandaged, and for weeks afterward could not write or even hold a book.

Whatever he felt during this time, Webster maintained a fair show of calm, at least in public. Privately he spoke more than once of retiring from politics altogether.[59] He toyed with the idea of writing a history of the early years of the Republic and at one point even went so far as to dictate an outline to George Abbot, a clerk in the State Department who served as his secretary, but the project went no further,[60] and if Webster ever seriously considered abandoning politics he decided against it. On one score he did change his thinking, however, and the change was significant. In March, having agreed to do a piece for the *Whig Review* on Webster's candidacy, Everett wrote asking what line he ought to take "on the subject of party organization." Were they to stick to the Union party idea — to continue "to endeavor to give a no-party complexion to the canvas" — or not? [61] Plainly Everett himself thought such a course ill-advised, and Webster, departing completely from his position of the last eighteen months, agreed. His reluctance was obvious, and the words he chose made the situation seem bleak indeed, but on the essential point he was emphatic: "I have to say, that, in my opinion, if we have any good in store for us, it will be through the *Whig Convention*." [62]

## VI

The convention Webster referred to was scheduled to meet in Baltimore at the end of the first week in June. To it would come a goodly portion of all those Whig politicians, major and minor, who made up the hard core of the party's leadership. With picked cadres of enthusiastic "Young Men" they would march in torchlight parades long into the night. The hotels would fill to bursting and over the telegraph — first used eight years earlier at another national political convention in Baltimore — would flash a steady stream of cryptic messages charting the progress of this or that candidate. By now the scene had become familiar; only the actors changed.

And among the changes that year, one of the most striking would be the absence of Thurlow Weed. Late in 1851 Weed had left on an extended trip abroad. Though he pleaded ill health as the reason for his travels and remained suitably vague about when he might return, his timing was deliberate. He had no interest in presiding over a disaster, and that in his view was precisely what the Whig party had arranged for itself at Baltimore.[63]

Of all the people who might have regretted Weed's decision, no one, oddly enough, had greater cause to do so than Webster. The summer before, when Webster was in Albany, Weed had gone out of his way to be cordial.[64] With the two wings of the New York Whig party hard at each other's throats, and Weed associated with one and Webster, through Fillmore, with the

other, that itself seemed surprising. The explanation was relatively simple, however. The passage of time had not changed
Weed; he was as much a realist as ever, and every sign he read
along the political horizon pointed to a Democratic victory in
1852. The best the Whigs could hope to do was keep their own
organization intact and running smoothly. To that end Weed
favored Webster as a candidate or barring him, Fillmore.[65]
Granted either nomination would cost the party something in
Northern antislavery support, with Weed and Seward together
working to pull the element into line the loss need not be great
— assuming, always, that Seward would cooperate.

But when it came to cases Seward chose not to cooperate. Instead he set his sights on winning the nomination for Scott,
whatever the cost in party unity.[66] Nor was there ever any question of Weed's opposing Seward over the issue. In the years he
had been in the Senate Seward's power and prestige had trebled.
Beyond simply quitting the field there was little Weed could
do.

As a result Webster lost a valuable — if unlikely — ally. Had
the hoped-for Union party materialized such a setback would
have mattered less; now he needed every bit of support he could
get from regular Whig sources. Even more disheartening was
the spectacle of Scott's steadily rising prospects. Without Seward behind him, the general would still have been in the race,
but on nowhere near as solid footing. As it was, his forces grew
daily more confident in the final weeks before the convention.
At no point could they count on a majority of delegates on the
first ballot, but neither could Fillmore or Webster.

From the beginning the battle plan of Scott's supporters had
been relatively straightforward. Massachusetts, together with
much of the rest of New England, would go for Webster and the
lower South for Fillmore. That left the North-central states and
the West — areas where Scott was unquestionably the favorite

— and it left the upper South. There Fillmore's position seemed secure, but in fact it was not. To a far greater extent than their brethren further south the Whigs in places like Virginia and Kentucky had resisted the siren call of fusion in the Union excitement of the preceding two years; their organizations were intact and they were anxious to win — all of which made them a prime target for the Scott forces.

But even with the opportunities that existed, wooing support away from Fillmore posed serious problems. One way, certainly, would have been for Scott to make a statement supporting the Compromise, and as the election year opened the pressures on him to do so were mounting. His chief managers, including Seward, were thoroughly opposed to such a move, however. Arguing that if the general were to "come out just a little" the entire North would defect, they managed to keep him silent.[67] At the same time they claimed, as their principal line of appeal, that Scott and only Scott could carry the North for the Whigs. Repeated as often as it was, the claim began to tell and not just in the North. "In Tennessee & Kentucky the [tie?] is not hard to break," wrote Seward at the end of February. "Let us do well in choosing fine, sensible delegates in the North and we shall have not much trouble." [68]

As for Webster, the Scott people never counted him a serious threat. "Let him and his old fogies play it out — it won't hurt," remarked one of them after the New York rally. "Even the tremendous list of names (taken from the tombstones of the city cemeteries or from the directories no doubt) will do him no good." [69] If this seemed to dismiss "Old Daniel" almost too completely, Scott's supporters did rely on him at one crucial juncture in their strategy. He had little chance of winning the nomination, but he could keep Scott from getting it. If enough Webster delegates swung their votes to Fillmore, then nothing could stop the President. Therefore it was imperative that Webster remain in the field and further that he enter the convention with sufficient strength to keep Fillmore from a first-ballot victory. Beyond that point anything might happen.

The net result was that while the Scott forces labored long and hard to weaken Fillmore's position, they left Webster substantially alone. So one-sided was their conduct in this respect that several of Fillmore's supporters became convinced a private arrangement existed between the general's friends and those of the Secretary of State.[70] Yet if there was such an arrangement Webster knew nothing about it. However slim his chances, he still hoped to win.

## VII

Late in May, by unanimous vote of the aldermen and Common Council of Boston, Webster was invited to address his "fellow townsmen" in Faneuil Hall. Considering his treatment at the hands of the aldermen the year before, the invitation itself amounted to something of a moral victory. Expounding on the glories of the place he paused at one point to announce, "This is Faneuil Hall — open." [71] The audience, catching his meaning at once, applauded good-naturedly. For the rest he concentrated primarily on Boston, on his long association with the city, and on the pride he took in that association. Except to announce that he had "no platform but the platform of my life and character," he said nothing at all about politics.

When Webster finished, Mayor Benjamin Seaver proposed that he be given nine cheers. The crowd, many of whom had been in their seats for hours, responded enthusiastically. Rising one after another to the rafters of the old hall, those cheers were a heartening tribute. Without exaggeration Webster could read in them the overwhelming support of his adopted city and beyond it the state. There were gaps of course. The anti-Compromise wing of the Massachusetts Whig party liked his candidacy as little as ever, but the leaders of the group were also astute enough not to waste their energy in a hopeless struggle. "You know the Webster sentiment here is very strong," Phillip Greely, the collector of the Port of Boston, wrote *Atlas* editor William Schouler. "Do not say anything or let anything be said, anywhere, in favor of Scott, but let the old Yankees kill themselves, and then we shall come up as a matter of course." [72] That was in December 1851. Six months later Scott's Massachusetts supporters were still biding their time, and any question Webster may have had about how the state's delegates would perform at Baltimore had vanished. Massachusetts would stand by him; of that he could be sure.

But everything else remained uncertain, which after all seemed ironic. Having directed his appeal to the South and been prepared to sacrifice whatever the effort cost at home, Webster found himself on the eve of yet another Whig convention with no real support outside the Northeast. The Whigs of the South, almost to a man, were committed to Fillmore on the first ballot. If it developed the President could not be nominated, a Southern switch to Webster was always possible, but so were any number of other outcomes. A far smaller shift in vote would give the prize to Scott, and barring him there was still a chance the delegates might try to compromise by choosing somebody else altogether — Crittenden for example.

With so much unsettled Webster's temper wore increasingly thin. "I have had eno' of cheer'g prospects, and sicken'g results," he wrote his son a few days before the Faneuil Hall address. "Nobody does anything on our side." [73]

Doubtless Fletcher Webster knew his father well enough to discount such outbursts, but in this case it would have been a mistake to do so — at least entirely. If Webster was displeased with the progress of his campaign it was clear where the major responsibility lay; the terms of the enterprise — its style and structure — were of his own choosing. As flawed as the basic design was, however, it could have been better executed, and the blame for that failure rested largely with his friends. For all the time, energy, and money they devoted to the cause, their efforts had been from the beginning notably ineffective. Moreover, in light of what was about to happen in Baltimore, it was important to understand why.

In part it came to a matter of age and experience. With few exceptions the men who headed the Webster committees and circulated the petitions in his behalf were the same men who had worked to make him President four, eight, or even twelve years before. They were his contemporaries or at most ten or fifteen years younger. Many of them, too, were interested in politics primarily as an avocation. Only a handful held or were seeking office in 1852. Choate, Everett, Peter Harvey, the Curtises — these were the men Webster relied on, and while they may have served him well enough according to their lights, American politics had changed enormously in a decade.

Of the several errors Webster's friends made, the most serious was their failure to give his campaign the kind of national scope it required. In Boston and New York — cities they were familiar with — they could organize rallies or collect signatures in profusion, but beyond the narrow perimeters of the Northeast their interest and effectiveness fell off sharply. The most they did, in any consistent fashion, to win the West or the South was to have printed and sent out across the country tens of thousands of copies of Webster's recent speeches. The expense was considerable, and the fact that Webster's supporters were willing to bear it bespoke their generosity, yet the entire project cannot have accomplished a fraction of what a few well-chosen associates working in places like Philadelphia, Baltimore, Richmond, New Orleans, and Cincinnati might have. Even in Washington the achievement fell far short of what was needed. As late as the first week in May with delegates already passing through on their way to the convention, one of Webster's supporters complained that there was still no "Webster organization" in the capital. The "Arch Devil Seward" by comparison had had a committee for over a year "working day and night." The conclusion was obvious: "If we are to keep up with the rest we must organize, and that too at once . . . There ought to be money — there ought to be printed matter — and more than all *now*, there ought to be *men, true men*, who will seek out those who come here and exert themselves." [74]

*"Men, true men"* are of course a difficult commodity to come by in any political endeavor, but in this instance they were essential. Given the inherent limitation of Webster's appeal, its tendency to lapse into abstraction and the problems he faced, especially among Southerners, in attempting to broaden the two narrowly regional basis of his following, nothing was more important than personal contact. To read the Seventh of March Speech was one thing; to be told by someone one knew and respected all its author had done to secure a just and lasting foundation for sectional harmony was quite another. Repeated often enough, by the right people under the right circumstances, such a message might have accomplished a good deal, but outside of their own home ground, Webster's friends never organized for the effort.

Indeed so striking was their failure in this respect, that any reasonably skeptical observer might have been moved to question their motives. However out of touch they were, it still seemed incredible that more was not attempted. If, that is, they really wanted to see Webster's cause victorious. Time, energy, and money are no substitute for experience, but they are even less adequate as a replacement for genuine dedication. On the other hand, if Webster's friends did have ends of their own to serve — ends that might be better met by his defeat — it was still too soon to tell what those ends were. For the moment it was enough to try and compensate for their blunders.

Finding things in even poorer condition than he had feared

on his return to Washington June 1, Webster did what he could to remedy the situation. Still suffering from his carriage accident three weeks earlier, he saw as many delegates as would take the time, at all hours of the day and night. The fact remained, however, that no one could do in two weeks work that ought to have been begun eighteen months before. The basic moves in the contest, to say nothing of the relative strengths of the opposing sides, had long since been set. The most to be hoped for was some unlikely — and unlooked for — break in the pattern.

# Eight
# Baltimore, June 1852

Such another collection of very respectable, out of place gentlemen was never seen." [1] An old hand at Whig party politics and national conventions, Francis Granger had been Postmaster General under Harrison and Tyler. His opinion of Webster's supporters at Baltimore in 1852, confided shortly afterward in a letter to Fillmore, was stinging but accurate. They had acted, "Choate included," for all the world "like a parcel of school boys waiting for the sky to fall, that they might catch larks." Such behavior had a certain comic charm, but its results were deplorable, and in some cases quite premeditatedly so. More than a few of the Webster group, Granger felt, "were Scott men at heart." [2]

Webster's own evaluation was more charitable. "Our friends, one and all, did their best," he wrote Richard Blatchford, having observed of the convention in general that it showed "a great deal of folly and a great deal of infidelity." [3]

Under the circumstances Webster's efforts to relieve his friends of the onus for what happened at Baltimore were commendable, but even he cannot have been much persuaded by the result. From first to last the convention was a disaster, and though those "very respectable" Webster men might never have secured his nomination, they had ample opportunity to arrange a better outcome than one that left Scott victorious and the Whig party on the verge of dissolution.

Nor could it have been argued in their defense that the time was too short or the pace of events too rapid to admit of any other result. Altogether it took four days and fifty-four separate ballots to nominate Scott. Moreover, in all that time the essential character of the deadlock remained the same: no one of the candidates alone had a majority, but any two of them together did.

## II

Without a chance of winning on the first ballot, Scott's supporters had based their hopes and strategy on just such an impasse. Their greatest fear always was that the Fillmore and Webster forces would find some means of accommodation, either before the opening of the convention or in its early stages.

On the face of it no fear could have been better justified. The proceedings in Baltimore got underway on Thursday, June 18, and for the next two days the Webster and Fillmore camps worked together in near perfect harmony. While the faithful listened to speeches imploring the party to unite in the face of adversity, representatives of the two candidates — in complete agreement ideologically — were moving with deft efficiency to organize the convention. Contest after contest saw delegates committed to the President or Secretary of State seated over the conflicting claims of Scott supporters. In the case of one particularly crucial seat in the New York delegation the Webster-Fillmore majority ran as high as forty-seven votes — a healthy margin by any standard. When the delegates turned to the task of drafting a platform, the same pattern predominated. A Southern demand that the party go on record with its statement of principle before choosing candidates was quickly acceded to. On the difficult question of voting in the platform committee, the "kinkhead," Northern anti-Compromise, bloc proposed assigning individual states a numerical strength proportionate to

their representation in the electoral college, only to find the proposal roundly defeated, and George Ashmun — as much a Webster man as ever — made chairman of a committee drawn on a
strict one-state, one-vote basis.

None of these proceedings was accomplished without a good
deal of rancor on both sides. For two days the volume of threats,
accusations, and ultimatums rose steadily until at times it
seemed as if the convention would degenerate into anarchy before ever getting to the business of choosing candidates.
Throughout the entire sequence, however, the lines of cooperation between the Webster and Fillmore camps remained firm.
From the standpoint of Scott's supporters, that in itself must
have seemed alarming, but even more so were certain widely
circulated rumors about the instructions Fillmore's chief lieutenants carried with them to Baltimore.

The rumors were accurate. In the end the President chose to
stand by the shaky, half-year-old compromise he had permitted
between his supporters and his own inclination to retire. He
would allow his name to be used, but he had no desire to run;
his personal preference for the nomination lay as always with
the Secretary of State. Accordingly Fillmore had asked his managers at the convention to make every effort to cooperate with
the Webster people, to do nothing that might interfere with
their chances of winning, and finally, if and when the proper
moment arose, to withdraw his own name and engineer the
transfer of his votes to Webster.[4]

Considering that the President was bound to receive a plurality on the first ballot, it was no mean gift he offered. Frankly
appalled, his friends did what they could to change his mind,
but he remained adamant. For their part, Webster's supporters
were overjoyed. Entering the convention in a flurry of renewed
confidence they made no secret, during those first few days, of
the great good fortune that was about to befall them. "Very
noisy & unyielding" was the impression they gave one observer,

and there were other, less flattering descriptions.[5] In the general euphoria such somber notes as were occasionally sounded went unnoticed except by a few pessimists. "The story here is that we are sold to Southern ingratitude & injustice," wrote one of Webster's friends from New York with obvious concern.[6] But who on the spot in Baltimore could be expected to credit such a tale?

The most obvious form for "Southern ingratitude and injustice" to take, as Webster's managers saw it, was for the South to "come in" for Scott, which they simply did not believe would happen. Moreover, two days of the bitterest sort of wrangling on the convention floor seemed to confirm that view. In their enthusiasm, however, the Webster men missed the full range of possibilities the situation contained. As matters stood, a handful of Southern delegates who had a mind to could virtually insure Scott's victory without ever casting so much as a single vote in his favor. Here too, with keener vision, the Scott forces had seen and appreciated what eluded their opponents.

The first hint came even before the balloting started. By late Friday afternoon, having taken less than a day to do its work, Ashmun's committee was ready with a draft platform. The tension in the hall was terrific. For two years this moment had loomed before the Whigs — a confrontation which threatened to shatter forever the fragile ties that bound the party together, yet one too which no amount of negotiation or rhetoric could longer postpone. The great issue before the delegates, of course, was the Compromise, and the line Ashmun's committee would take there had been clear from the start. The Southern wing of the party wanted the Compromise in all of its provisions — including the fugitive slave law — declared a "finality"; the proposed platform did just that, adding, "We insist upon their strict enforcement . . . and we deprecate all further agitation of the questions thus settled." [7]

In the general confusion that followed Ashmun's reading, it was Rufus Choate who reached the platform first to speak. Proclaiming that the history of the Republic offered no finer example of high and disinterested statesmanship than the Compromise acts, he went on to "thank God for the civil courage which, at the hazard of all things dearest in life, dared to pass and defend them, and 'has taken no step backward.' " [8] A marvel of the sort of extravagant eloquence that was Choate's specialty, the speech was followed by two others in much the same vein, and then abruptly the third speaker, John M. Botts, moved the question. At that point the convention broke into complete pandemonium. In every part of the hall delegates were on their feet demanding that the debate be allowed to continue. Asked to withdraw his motion, Botts refused, but the clamor made it impossible to record the vote for fully another fifteen minutes. When the chairman finally did manage to gavel down the chorus of boos and hisses, the pro-Compromise forces — to no one's surprise — scored an easy victory. Only then could the roll of states on the platform itself begin.

And it was there the break occurred. Thus far divisions in the convention had all fallen along similar lines. The combined Webster-Fillmore totals consistently amounted to between 54 and 57 per cent of the whole, which left the Scott forces with somewhere in the neighborhood of 125 votes out of a possible 296. In the case of the platform the basic pattern did not change, but the relative strengths of the opposing sides did, and dramatically. When the last state had recorded its vote the tally showed only sixty-six delegates — or just over half the normal Scott strength — on the negative side of the issue. The other half of Scott's supporters had joined the majority in approving the platform by a resounding 227 votes.

Why they did so was a question to which any one of several answers were possible. Certainly a desire to preserve the appearance of Whig unity was a factor. Since the platform was bound to pass whatever Scott's supporters did, a heavy vote against it would merely have emphasized the split in the party. Voting with the majority had the value, too, perhaps, of conciliating some of its members. Yet what exactly could the Scott people have hoped to gain thereby? In votes for their candidate, the platform's most vigorous backing came from Southern delegates already committed to Fillmore. Were they now to shift their allegiance as part of an intraparty, cross-sectional bargain? In fact, such a charge was made, and a good deal of superficial evidence seemed to support it — everything indeed except what actually took place, for Scott never did receive a significant number of Southern votes. On the other hand, that hardly proved there had been no bargain at all; only that its terms were not the obvious ones. When Henry Raymond, editor of the *New York Times,* telegraphed his paper the day before the platform fight that the Northern wing of the party would have every reason to "charge breach of faith on the South" if Scott were not nominated,[9] he was simply giving public notice to what had been a matter of private speculation for days in Baltimore.

In Raymond's view the Southern delegations that leaned most heavily toward Scott were Kentucky, Tennessee, and Virginia. Writing Fillmore from Baltimore on June 17, the day after the convention opened, John Barney had mentioned Kentucky, Virginia, and North Carolina. The following day he added Tennessee to the list.[10]

Barney had gone to the convention as one of Fillmore's chief lieutenants. An admirer of Webster, and well aware of the President's preference for the Secretary of State, he nevertheless considered it " 'res adjudicata' " that Webster's friends should, in the end, throw their support to Fillmore.[11] Any other arrangement would have been unjust and also, Barney quickly concluded on his arrival in Baltimore, disastrous.

He first learned of the problem, which lay in the same four

Southern delegations he listed for Fillmore, in a conversation with the governor of Virginia. Its basic outline was simple: the least suggestion that Fillmore's name was being withdrawn or his votes transferred to Webster would immediately cause just enough delegates from the four states to shift their support to Scott to nominate him. In plain truth the President could not insure Webster's victory; even to try would have the worst possible consequences. To Barney that left only one solution: "Prudence requires Mr. Webster's phalanx to join your Legion." [12] Moreover, if Fillmore doubted his friend's analysis, the mail from Baltimore during the next two days amply confirmed it.[13]


### III

Forced by custom to remain in Washington, Fillmore had no choice but to let others play out the game for him — however little he might like the stakes or the result. What made it doubly difficult was that, as he well knew, for Scott's managers the situation Barney described marked the successful culmination of eighteen months of planning and effort. In the opening moments of the convention it almost seemed as if they had failed, but already, with the vote on the platform, the tide was turning.

The reasoning behind the strategy began with the fact that whoever won the nomination — barring some previous settlement — would have to have his majority forged for him on the floor of the Convention Hall. In Scott's case that meant adding to his initial total such votes as could be coaxed or pried loose from the ranks of his opponents. Logically, too, those votes would be Northern votes. For the average Southern delegate, casting his lot openly with the kinkheads promised to have consequences far too serious to make the option seem anything but unattractive. All of which might have settled the issue except for one circumstance — thanks to the skill and energy of Scott's managers there were at least a few Southerners in Baltimore who felt that the general, as a candidate, had considerable appeal. They could ill afford to vote for him, but they were anxious to do whatever else they could to see him nominated, provided their needs were taken account of in other ways — the platform for example. As it turned out the only favor asked of them was that they sit tight.

To achieve their objective, what the Scott people needed above all was time, and ultimately the time they needed came as the gift of their Southern friends. Delegates had to be seen, cajoled, and persuaded one by one, and there were only so many people to do the job. Meanwhile, at any moment the Webster and Fillmore camps might reach an agreement and with their combined votes carry the day. Merely by making that impossible those few Southern delegates who stood apart from their fellows rendered Scott a service of inestimable worth. Whether they would actually have voted for the general if Fillmore's votes were transferred to Webster, as they threatened, is an interesting question, but one for which the record contains no answer because their bluff — if bluff it was — worked.

By the time the platform passed, it was seven-thirty in the evening, Friday, June 18. The balloting for nominations began an hour later. Altogether there were six separate ballots recorded between that time and the point when the delegates voted to adjourn until the following morning. With no one predicting a quick victory the fact that six ballots failed to settle the issue was not particularly surprising. Nor was the distribution of the vote. Both Scott and Fillmore did less well than their supporters claimed they would, but the President, with 133 votes on the first ballot as opposed to Scott's 131, at least started off in the lead.[14] By the fourth ballot, Fillmore's total had fallen to 130 while Scott's rose to 134. However, the next time the margin shifted back the other way and then on the sixth ballot reversed itself again to leave Scott with 133 votes to Fillmore's 131. So far the impasse was complete. Both men, even at their maximum strength, needed fully another fifteen votes to win. As frustrating as such a situation might have appeared for the time being everyone could extract some comfort from it.

And did, though ironically it was Webster's friends, not the supporters of either of the two leading candidates, who seemed most pleased at the evening's outcome. With the exception of the fifth ballot, where his total rose by one vote, Webster had stayed consistently at the level of twenty-seven. It was a miserable showing; even Barney had expected a figure a good ten votes higher.[15] Yet if Webster's managers were disappointed they gave no sign of it. The great thing was that Scott's drive had been checked. Together the President and the Secretary of State still commanded a majority of the vote; the time had come to put that majority to work.

Meanwhile Webster himself waited in Washington with such faith and patience as he could muster. The day the convention opened he had written the Reverend Dr. Putnam of Roxbury that he would meet the result, "whatever it may be, with a composed mind." [16] It was an admirable goal, but one that proved utterly impossible to achieve in practice. Appalled at the initial result of the balloting, Webster noted grimly that not a single Southern delegate had chosen to support the author of the Seventh of March Speech. His friends, of course, argued that this was purely a temporary situation, that if he stood firm now he would soon find gathered beneath his banner the entire Fillmore party — including the South. If such were the case, well and good; but what if Webster's friends were wrong — what if Choate, Ashmun, and the others in Baltimore had misjudged the matter completely? Theirs were by no means the only voices reaching the capital, and most of the others told a very different tale.

Writing Fillmore shortly before the start of the balloting Barney noted that he had informed Webster of how matters stood and would travel to Washington early the following day for a personal interview with the Secretary of State if no decision had been reached by then.[17] Arriving at 6:30 Saturday morning, Barney was back in Baltimore by noon. The meeting, as he described it later to Fillmore, was a difficult one. Webster seemed "overwhelmed by the humiliating posture in which he stood before the world." All he asked was a "decent vote" so he might "retire without disgrace." When Barney advised that further delay would almost certainly result in Scott's nominaton, Webster answered that "none of his friends advised him to act forthwith," to which Barney replied, "you have no other friends" and left his host "deeply wounded and offended." [18]

Throughout the day Webster continued to receive appeals like Barney's, but he responded to none of them. The weakness in the Southern delegations, the impossibility of transferring Fillmore's strength without sacrificing votes, the fact that the only way to stop Scott now seemed to be for Webster to throw his weight behind the President — however stated, the argument fell for the moment on deaf ears. "Hold on, Mr. Webster recommends no wavering. He is firm as a rock — fixed & immovable" was George Abbot's only message to Baltimore on Saturday.[19]

As shortsighted as such advice seemed, at least the deliberations of the convention that day left Barney's direst predictions unconfirmed. Scott was not nominated — nobody was. Through a total of forty separate ballots the three candidates traded votes within roughly the same range as the evening before. Toward the close of the session Webster's count appeared to be increasing, but in the end it never rose above the level of thirty-two. Once again the hoped-for union between the two "national" camps had failed to materialize. Moreover, while Scott may have been stopped, his share of the total vote had definitely grown. On the thirtieth ballot of the day it reached 135 — scarcely more than ten votes away from victory. Thereafter it fell back to 132 only to rise again by the time the convention recessed to 134, as opposed to 127 for Fillmore, and 31 for Webster.

Nearer the end perhaps, but one could still work toward whatever outcome one wished. Which was precisely what the delegates did, virtually without a break, for the next thirty-six hours. Considering the rigors of the day's proceedings and the fact that the convention would not be in session again until Monday, it might have seemed as if everyone involved deserved a respite Saturday evening. But groups of delegates began meeting almost immediately, over dinner at first, and then back in hotel rooms long into the night. Already exhausted, the men who attended those meetings did their best to check frayed tempers and preserve what little accord remained among competing factions. In the eyes of many of them the fate of the Whig party hung in the balance. Yet they were all faced, too, with the inexorable mathematics of normal democratic procedure.

For Webster's managers that confrontation proved particularly acute. Having expected every moment for two days to find themselves made a majority through a transfer of Fillmore's votes, they now began to negotiate in earnest for what they had assumed would come as a matter of course. The results were not encouraging. Meeting with a group of Southern delegates early in the evening, the Webster forces — including Rufus Choate, who had risen from a sickbed to attend — were told they could have Fillmore's entire vote the moment the Secretary arrived "at the Maryland line" with a count of forty votes. In other words, if eight more Northern votes could be found for Webster the Southerners would guarantee his nomination. If not they asked — as a simple quid pro quo — that his delegate strength be transferred to Fillmore. Whatever Webster's managers

thought of their chances of picking up the extra votes they refused outright to accept the second part of the proposition, and
the meeting came to an abrupt end.[20]

Another meeting, held early Sunday morning, fared little
better. This time a "Webster committee" headed by William
Hayden of Massachusetts carried on the negotiations. Asked
whether they had indicated to Scott's people that if more were
not done for Webster his votes would be turned over to Fillmore, the members of the committee replied they had. Would
they, then, consider a "final & last proposition" — namely to
cast on each consecutive ballot Monday four additional Webster
votes for Fillmore up to the point where the President's count
reached 145? By then the Scott forces should be sufficiently
frightened to begin throwing votes to Webster. If Webster
could in that fashion build his total to seventy-five the South
would then — voting in order after the North — provide another seventy-five safely transferable votes to give him the victory. If, on the other hand, he failed to receive the initial
seventy-five, would his supporters agree "in good faith" to unite
behind Fillmore? To most of the Webster committee this
seemed a reasonable arrangement. Not to Hayden, however.
He could never, he said, "go home telling his people the South
had abandoned Mr. Webster & nominated Mr. Fillmore."
Could he "with much more propriety" let it be known that
Scott had been nominated because of the refusal of Webster's
friends to cooperate with those of the President? Or did the
Webster people after all prefer Scott to Fillmore? Indeed not,
Hayden replied. But on the fundamental point he never wav-
ered, and the meeting broke up in confusion.[21]

## IV

By Sunday afternoon every conceivable avenue to a Webster-
Fillmore alliance had been explored and each in turn had
proven a dead end. For all their desire to see the President nom-

inated, his managers had honestly tried to carry out the instructions they were given. When it became clear no simple transfer of Fillmore's vote was possible, they labored long and hard to find some other means of accommodation. Yet always the response was the same: Webster's supporters would accept nothing that committed them to backing the President at any point. Whatever happened they intended to stand by their candidate. When Hayden's committee was told "if *shame* & *disgrace* ATTACHED TO ANY ONE'S *SKIRTS* FOR OUR DEFEAT & the election of Scott, it would be theirs . . ." its members were visibly shaken but still broke off negotiations.[22]

And there matters stood throughout the rest of the day — at least in Baltimore. In Washington the contest went on, minus the pressure and confusion of the convention milieu, yet every bit as intensely. Notified by telegraph of the results of each ballot, Webster knew with painful accuracy all there was to know about his own position. On Saturday his instructions to his supporters had been to hold fast. Now, a day later, the rationale behind those instructions appeared to be stretching thinner by the hour. But what others could he send? His determination to see it through, without retreat or compromise, had been based on the information friends on the spot in Baltimore gave him. If they were wrong — as seemed more and more likely — what alternatives were left to him?

The point Barney and others continued to make could hardly have been clearer on that score. The fact that they had erred in assuming the end would come Saturday altered nothing. The choice was still Webster's: he could either persist and see Scott nominated or he could throw his support to Fillmore thereby assuring the President's victory. If in following the second of those two courses he gave up all hope of winning himself, the other way promised no better result. At least, too, the cause of national peace and harmony would have triumphed.

Which, after all, ran the argument time and again, was the real issue at stake. Having sacrificed so much in that cause was

Webster suddenly prepared to find it abandoned by his own party? Granted the Whigs of the South owed him a debt that they now seemed unwilling to repay, he owed it to himself — to everything he had been and done — not to desert his principles out of pique or disappointment. For the author of the Seventh of March Speech to permit the nomination of "Higher Law" Seward's candidate, when a single word might have prevented the disaster, was something history would never forgive.

Perhaps, but the prospective judgment of history is a difficult incentive to keep sight of at such times. All Sunday Webster waited, debating with himself and those around him what to do. His son Fletcher had arrived in Washington the morning before with William Paige, Webster's brother-in-law. Recording snatches of their conversation George Abbot left a vivid picture of the day's mood. With open bitterness Webster denounced Fillmore and his supporters. The President was a misguided fool who had allowed himself and his office to be used by a group of selfish, unprincipled schemers. If the Union cause stood in jeopardy the fault was theirs; let them rescue it! As for the Southern delegations in general, the annals of politics held nothing to match their treachery and ingratitude. Any fate that befell them, they richly deserved.[23]

For the time being such invective was a soothing remedy. Ultimately, however, it could only postpone the moment of decision. On Monday the convention would be in session again and nothing Webster could say would obviate the need for some sign from him by then. When Sunday evening passed without any change in the situation he must have known what he would do, but still he delayed sending word to Baltimore. Tomorrow would be soon enough.

"Mr. Bell, Mr. Paige & Fletcher will go down at 7 o'clock & arrive probably before much is done." [24] Whatever this cryptic message — sent by telegraph early Monday morning — conveyed to Edward Curtis and George Ashmun, Webster's mind was made up. Having alerted Curtis and Ashmun, he gave final instructions to the group going to Baltimore, sent them on their way, and then sat down to write Fillmore. The resulting note, barely three sentences long, wasted nothing on aimless courtesies. "I have sent a communication to Baltimore, this morning, to have an end put to the pending controversy. I think it most probable you will be nominated before 1 o'clock. But this is opinion merely." [25]

For better than two decades Webster had dreamed of being President; now he knew he never would be. Somehow the great prize had eluded him, leaving in the end only the Union cause and his place in history to weigh in the balance against what might have been. On the other hand in choosing between two evils he had at least chosen the lesser one. Men would say that Daniel Webster had lost, but not that he had deserted his principles or destroyed his party out of spite — provided, of course, that everything in Baltimore went as he supposed it would. The fact that it did not clouded the issue considerably.

Carefully recording the hour and date he received Webster's note — "9½ A.M. June 21" — Fillmore wrote back saying that he too had made arrangements to have his name withdrawn. He presumed his supporters would do so promptly "unless the knowledge of your communication shall prevent it." [26]

With representatives of both the President and Webster arriving in Baltimore at roughly the same time, and the convention due to reconvene at any moment, the conditions under which the two camps had to labor were less than ideal. Still Webster's instructions were sufficiently simple — the immediate transfer of his entire delegate strength to Fillmore — to require a minimum of negotiation. He asked nothing in return, not even the "courtesy vote" the President's managers had earlier offered to arrange. But Webster's instructions were one thing, and what his supporters would perform quite another. If in those hectic minutes before the chairman gavelled open the final session of the convention, Fillmore's victory seemed almost certain, the balloting very quickly indicated a different result. Moreover, the crucial margin — the votes that might have put the President over the top had they ever been forthcoming — remained Webster's.

Not until the sixth ballot of the morning, with Scott only seven votes away from victory, did Webster's total fall below 28. On the next ballot it dropped to 21, but a break in the Pennsylvania delegation had already ended the struggle; with 159 votes — after better than fifty separate ballots — Winfield Scott had become the Whig party's nominee for the presidency of the United States. His victory was plainly a Northern triumph, yet it could never have been achieved without the tacit cooperation of at least a few Southern delegates. It would also never have been achieved if Webster's supporters had followed his instructions.

## V

In Baltimore alone the week of the convention, the men who were backing Webster spent over $4000.[27] It would have been foolish to doubt their sincerity or question the depth of their devotion to the cause, but inevitably the result itself seemed to raise a challenge on that score, however reluctant one was to face hard issues at such a juncture. With fewer qualms than most men, Webster's old enemy Abbott Lawrence, writing from his post in London, put the question bluntly enough: "If the Boston Whigs did not desire to have General Scott as the candidate, why did they not throw their votes for Mr. Fillmore?" [28]

Why indeed? For some of Webster's supporters, doubtless — men like Choate, whose attachment was personal as well as political — the prospect of abandoning a friend already "betrayed" by so many others may simply have been more than conscience could bear. But what of the rest? Writing Fillmore during the convention, B. M. Edney, one of his managers, thought he understood what lay behind the obstinacy of Webster's "friends." The fact was that by supporting him on the Compromise, and particularly the fugitive slave law, they had placed themselves in a highly awkward position at home. "They are tired of this fight & now want an excuse to get back into harness, & occupy their original position." Thus, knowing full well that Webster could never win they stuck by him because that way the prize would go to Scott, and they could "then go home & say the South refused to stand by Mr. Webster on the slave question, & now let them take care of themselves." The profitless association with the Southern cause would be ended and those "former good relations" that bound the Massachusetts Whig party to its counterpart in other Northern states reestablished.[29]

If Edney's analysis seemed hard on Webster's supporters, there was more evidence in its favor than simply the outcome of the convention. From first to last the entire effort in his behalf had been remarkably ineffective. The same group that refused to follow his instructions at Baltimore had also failed in all the months before the convention to give his campaign the kind of national scope and organization it so badly needed. Here at least was a plausible explanation for the whole dreary sequence.

Nor in the end could one say much worse of such men than that they were merely being realistic. In backing Webster they had assumed of necessity the burden of upholding his position. And it was a burden. However popular the man himself may have been within his own region, the stand he had taken in March 1850 and held to since remained anything but popular over large parts of New England and the North generally. Under the circumstances the prospect of supporting that position indefinitely would have been enough to dampen anybody's enthusiasm.

Even less appealing, by the same token, was the prospect of having to support the position without the man — which Fillmore's victory would have entailed. Loyalty has its limits after all; up to a point a practiced politician like George Ashmun would honor his commitments, but with the Free Soil–Democratic coalition still to be beaten in Massachusetts he was not about to sacrifice his own political future for either the fugitive slave law or Millard Fillmore — whoever asked the favor.

All of which may or may not have been clear to Webster, but nothing about the entire debacle in Baltimore threw into sharper focus the full extent of his own failure. It was as if for two long years he had been speaking and acting in a vacuum, unheard and unheeded by anyone. At the beginning of the period, in the midst of the great sectional crisis, he had undertaken to eliminate from American politics what he took to be the source of that crisis — the issue of slavery. Yet slavery and the divisions it produced continued to dominate national politics as every moment of the convention proved. For his own part too, having made the effort, Webster had failed utterly to convince the men he most wanted to — the Whigs of the South — of his sincerity. Or if they were convinced, apparently they counted the favor an inconsequential one, for painfully few had seen fit to repay it in the only coin that mattered, their support. And finally, when he counted on those representatives of the sort of moderate Northern opinion he had always rallied in the past to salvage what little remained to be salvaged in the situation by standing fast on the platform he had chosen, they balked — balked because according to their own calculations the real support for Webster's position at home was too thin to justify the risk.

Altogether it was a thoroughly depressing ending, and if Webster — struggling to accept "an evil now without a remedy" [30] — found the task at times almost overwhelming, the brief, sorry sequel proved even harder to face. A product of the same tensions and currents that had eddied through Convention Hall in Baltimore, it both confirmed and magnified them. The only difference was that this time Webster was to be spared the denouement.

# Nine
## Silence

In the aftermath of the convention, men made all the kind and consoling gestures one would have expected. A group of returning delegates serenaded Webster at his house, and Rufus Choate stopped on his way back through Washington for tea, a sad affair reminding him "of the first meal after the return from the grave, when the full force of the bereavement seems to be realized." [1]

With more practical effect, perhaps, John Barney labored to get up a list of 106 Fillmore delegates who would have voted for Webster had the right moment ever come,[2] and several congressmen planned a dinner honoring the Secretary of State, to be attended by various members of the House and Senate.[3] Fillmore too did his best. Supposing that Webster might prefer to be somewhere other than Washington for the present he offered the legation in London, which Abbott Lawrence would soon be leaving.[4] The offer was declined, however, and though capital gossip had Webster's resignation in the President's hands, neither man made any immediate plans for a change. Then, early in July, Webster went north for a month of rest.

His ultimate destination was New Hampshire, but his route there lay through Boston, and inevitably a public reception had been planned that, in the weeks beforehand, had grown to awesome proportions. Not since Lafayette visited the city in 1823 had there been anything like it — the crowds, the procession, or the cheering. All businesses were closed for the day, and a larger collection of troops than had ever before assembled in New England on a purely voluntary service sweltered under the blazing sun. Everywhere Webster's barouche passed flags decked the doorways and windows — flags, and a really incredible number of statues, busts, and portraits of the "Great Defender" himself.[5]

By the time the procession made its way through the city's jammed streets to the Common, it was after seven in the evening, but Webster had planned only a few brief remarks. Thanking those who had taken part, he expressed his delight at finding that he had not been "disowned" in a place where "I have lived for so many years, and which for so many years I have endeavored to serve to the best of my ability." [6] He felt doubly rewarded, too, because the place in question was not just any spot on the map but Massachusetts — "the great and ancient and glorious State of Massachusetts." Expanding upon the theme, he observed that prior to his going to Congress from Boston in 1823 the state's political history — which he had ever taken to be "a sort of *beau ideal*" — could be divided into two distinct epochs, both equally brilliant: the revolutionary period when "Massachusetts struck for the liberty of a Continent" and the later, constitutional period. In many respects the two were quite different, but a common theme linked them irrevocably: throughout all those years the people of Massachusetts had put loyalty to the nation above everything else. Such was the state's character when Webster entered its service, and such was the character he had dedicated himself to maintaining ever since, "with all the devotion of my heart." The value of his efforts they could decide for themselves; he was not likely to change course now. "What I have been," he announced at the end, "I propose to be."

## II

Standing on the Boston Common in the fading light of a hot summer's evening in 1852, it was perhaps possible to dismiss the specter of the Hartford convention as Webster in effect did, but there were other, more recent events that resisted such treatment. He had lost, and all the Roman splendors of his reception could not alter that fact. For a season the citizenry of Boston might prefer to pretend otherwise. Webster himself might even perform the role assigned to him to near perfection, as indeed he did, rising like some venerable tribune in the midst of laying down the burdens of office to summon the people back to a contemplation of their origins. But the moment came and went, turning theater back into politics and leaving the problems of defeat to be dealt with in the harsher light of day.

In 1848 Webster had waited until September to endorse Zachary Taylor and thus perform the act required of him by the unwritten canons of American party politics. What now would he do about Scott? If, being Webster, he could pick his own time, custom left him no alternative on the basic issue, and already, by the end of the first week in July, the pressures on him were growing.

And would continue to grow throughout the summer. For a while those pressures could be ignored, but not indefinitely. Yet what if Webster chose to try — to forge the alternative custom denied him? In the days immediately following the convention, he struck out in letters and conversation as bitterly as he ever had at those he felt had betrayed him. "I shall soon be in New York," he remarked at one point, "and think it is about time to shake hands with some of those gentlemen and part, and with some of them we can part without shaking hands." [7] As the weeks passed the sheer weight of disappointment and bitterness subsided though never entirely. By now, too, Webster's health had begun to deteriorate at a really alarming rate. Listless, with little or no appetite, he still suffered the effects of last year's carriage accident. In September his annual catarrh was due, promising — if it followed the pattern set in the past — to disable him for at least a month.

As ill and dispirited as he was, Webster said nothing in public during his brief stay in Boston about the current state of politics. Or so it seemed. For those who listened carefully to his remarks on the Common there may have been in his final assurance the barest hint of a warning. Four years earlier, he had set aside his principles to endorse the victorious Whig nominee; perhaps he was announcing that this time there would be no such retreat. "What I have been, I propose to be." But that was all. If he had intended a warning, his subsequent departure for New Hampshire left it dangling and nothing there was likely to force him to clarify his meaning.

Having several years before purchased his family's farm in Franklin, Webster used it at just such times as this. The house at Marshfield, in the decade since he had made it his principal residence, had grown very grand indeed. With its lofty gothic library and every table, shelf, and corner filled with Mrs. Webster's huge collection of knickknacks, it may even have been too grand for some purposes.[8] In any case, Webster gloried in his interludes at Elms Farm in Franklin and wrote movingly of the place. "Railroad cars run across it three or four times a day, and that is all the motion which is seen or heard. There is no manufacturing; no coach, wagon, or cart going along the highway except very infrequently. The fields are quite green, shaded with beautiful elms and maples, with high ranges of hills on both sides of the river."[9] If he neglected to add that one of the further virtues of Franklin was the relief it offered from the political pressures of Boston or Washington, he scarcely needed to.

Such soothing isolation was at best temporary, however. By

the end of July, Webster was back at Marshfield for yet another great homecoming celebration, and ten days later he left for Washington. In the interim he had reached a number of important conclusions.

The first concerned his position in the Cabinet. Between the sorry state of his health and the constant "vexation, and humiliation, growing out of the events connected with the convention," he had about decided by midsummer to leave office, or if he stayed to do so only under certain clearly understood conditions.[10] Pointing out to Fillmore that he could in no way consider "passing the ensuing hot months at the table of a department in Washington," Webster doubted whether Congress would tolerate so long an absence on his part.[11] Carefully worded, the letter left the final decision to the President, however, and Fillmore apparently preferred risking congressional displeasure to doing without the services of his Secretary of State. Webster could stay as long as he liked, on whatever basis he chose.

Fillmore's attitude was a help in that it solved one of Webster's problems, but the far more pressing question of what to do about the Baltimore nominations remained. Privately, he made no secret of the fact that he considered Scott unfit for the presidency and his chances of election nil. Nor was the certainty of losing in November the only misfortune the Whigs had brought upon themselves. In the act of choosing Scott they had sounded the party's death knell in America. Ever "a puppet in [Seward's] hands," the general was a purely sectional candidate; with his nomination Whiggery had "withdrawn into the North" and no party "which did not extend throughout the entire Union" could ever hope to administer the government in Washington, let alone win a national election.[12]

What might have seemed simply "another dose of availability" — and a personal tragedy for Webster — then, promised to become something fully as disastrous for the Whig party as a whole. But that was a private opinion. As a defeated candidate for the nomination Scott had won, Webster was still expected to endorse the general in public. The fact that even Scott's managers feared his campaign was floundering only sharpened the issue. Throughout the South, loyal Whigs were quietly refusing to support the party ticket, and in many of the larger cities of the North contributions had fallen off markedly; a word from Webster would have helped in both quarters.

Yet the weeks passed and he said nothing. In 1848 it was at Marshfield that he had finally spoken out for Taylor. Now, given a similar opportunity at the great homecoming reception planned by his neighbors, he announced himself under "a well-understood covenant" to utter "not a word about law or politics." [13] And if he did allow the covenant to lapse, only the most perceptive of observers would have noticed. Referring at one point to "recent occurrences," he remarked, "it may not be fitting in me to say one word now. The time has not yet come." Having gone that far, however, he went on to add that he was not entirely unknown at home or abroad and then, in a single, neat thrust, pushed the argument one step farther — "And, I say, . . . if I have anything good or valuable, I hold it in my own keeping, and will not trust it to the waywardness of others."

Another warning? Possibly, but the entire passage was ambiguous — so ambiguous that it might have alluded to almost anything. The long-standing Anglo-American quarrel over fishing rights off the coast of Canada had just entered a new and highly critical phase. Since most of the rest of what Webster had to say that day was devoted explicitly to a discussion of "our fisheries . . . the very nurseries of our navy," his final words may well have referred to the same subject. Considering, too, that many of his listeners were themselves fishermen, such an explanation made sense.

But if Webster had intended no warning, it was not, this time, out of a sense of doubt or uncertainty. By the time he arrived at

Marshfield he had made up his mind. Perhaps it was the spectacle of the Whig party — cut loose from the nationalistic moorings he had labored so hard to provide for it — dissolving before his eyes, or the knowledge that his own time on earth had about run out, or perhaps in the end it was simple pique; but whatever lay behind the decision, he had "come out" as far as he ever would. The men who had arranged things so smoothly at Baltimore could face the American people without the benefit of his endorsement. He did not propose to attack Scott, but neither would he utter a single syllable in the general's behalf.

Silence. As a settled policy it had the virtue of any essentially negative approach — it required a minimum of effort. It could also — in the unlikely event the situation changed — be broken at any point. And both features were important to Webster. Quite apart from everything else, he had little energy to spend fighting battles, old or new. Without some sign from him, of course, the appeals would continue to come. Friends could handle those, however, and eventually he would be taken at his word and left in peace.

But peace — the kind of peace Webster wanted — proved a very illusive quantity. Had nothing changed after the middle of July, this might not have been the case. By then both of the major parties had chosen their candidates. For those Whigs who could not accept Scott, there was always the option of staying home or voting for the Democratic nominee, Franklin Pierce of New Hampshire. An old friend and neighbor of Webster's, Pierce was standing firm behind his party's pro-Compromise platform, and Webster — convinced the former senator and Mexican War general would win in November — frankly advised his closest associates to cast their ballots for the Democratic ticket.[14] No doubt many of them would. To at least a few, however, voting for Pierce, or any of the other available alternatives, seemed inadequate. Whether out of personal loyalty to Webster or simple political opportunism, they were quite unprepared to give up the struggle that most people — including Webster — thought had ended in Baltimore. In the final weeks of July, their efforts were just beginning to take shape, but within a very short while thereafter, they had managed to change the entire complexion of the campaign, and Webster, having lost his party's nomination barely a month before, found himself once again a candidate for the presidency.

III

"I fear, I greatly fear, that Webster's friends are bent on mutiny." [15] Since losing the Massachusetts gubernatorial race the year before, Robert Winthrop had come to consider himself more of an observer of the state's political battles than a participant in them. Surprisingly, he bore Webster only a modest grudge and seemed genuinely sorry the delegates at Baltimore had given his old mentor and friend so little cause for comfort. Surely a more impressive showing ought to have been arranged — out of courtesy, if nothing else. But personal feeling was one thing and party loyalty another. Winthrop was still a good Whig and had in due course attended the great meeting held in Faneuil Hall to "ratify" Scott's nomination. The possibility that Webster's friends might be planning to bolt the party, therefore, was most disturbing. Writing John P. Kennedy to alert him of the danger, Winthrop added that he sincerely hoped that the administration in Washington — of which Kennedy, recently appointed Secretary of the Navy, was a member — would not give "any aid or comfort" to the rebels.[16]

When Winthrop wrote, it was still only the middle of July and to date the formal aspects of the "mutiny" had been confined to a single meeting in Faneuil Hall called for the purpose of protesting the Baltimore nominations. A second meeting, held July 14, developed the theme further and urged the presentation of Webster to the people as an independent candidate. In both cases there was a good deal of impassioned rhetoric and the level of enthusiasm ran high. On the other hand, for those who wished to find them, there were signs enough that the entire enterprise had been rather hastily knocked together. At neither meeting, for example, was anything done about establishing a permanent organization, and from the proceedings of both it was clear that the sponsors of the movement saw it primarily as a local affair, with no real connections beyond Massachusetts. Finally there was the matter of the sponsors themselves. Wholly missing from the list were the names of those who had heretofore rallied the state behind Webster — men like Choate, Ashmun, and Everett. Whether they had been asked to participate and refused would have been difficult to determine, but their absence was striking.

As long as the drive for an independent Webster electoral ticket failed to attract any of his more powerful backers and remained so exclusively local and, at best, half organized, there was little to fear from it. Winthrop might have saved himself the trouble of worrying. As it happened, however, the situation had already begun to change by the date of his letter to Kennedy.

Ironically the source of the change was one of those Southern Whig organizations Webster had once looked to with such high hopes only to find that, when push came to shove at Baltimore, its votes were pledged to Fillmore. For two years the Georgia Union Whigs under the leadership of Toombs and Stephens had maneuvered through the complexities of Southern politics with singular skill, but now their alliance with the Democratic Unionists was breaking down. One simple solution would have been a return to Whig regularity, yet any ticket with Scott at its head was almost certain to lose in Georgia. When, therefore, the general neglected to mention the Compromise in his letter accepting the nomination, Toombs and Stephens hurried into print with formal resolutions of rejection. That much accomplished, they had only to find a suitable replacement.[17]

Both men, no doubt, would have preferred Fillmore. They had backed the President before Baltimore, and his following in the South remained large. The fact that he was a Northerner, too, could be counted a distinct advantage. To have chosen a Southern standard bearer would have branded the movement as purely sectional in character — a connotation its leaders were most anxious to avoid. They were bound to lose nationally, but so too, they felt, was Scott, and properly exploited his defeat could be used to reconstruct the Whig party, purging it forever of Seward's disastrous influence. Meanwhile they would have preserved their position at home and done so in such a fashion as to make clear their commitment to all truly national forms of political organization.

As compelling as this line of reasoning might have seemed, it presented one substantial difficulty. Fillmore had already emphatically refused to bolt the party.[18] Having once allowed his name to be used against his better judgment, with regrettable consequences, he had no intention of duplicating the error. Which left several other possibilities, the most logical of them, obviously, Webster.

By the third week in July, plans were well underway for an "Independent Whig" convention at Macon. The date set was August 18. In the interim Webster — still resting at Marshfield — received the first, unmistakable signs of what was in store for him. Would he allow his name to be used? Would he accept a nomination if one were tendered? "We desire to know this before the meeting of that convention because should you refuse to accept the nomination it will embarrass our movement by placing us under the necessity of calling another convention," ran one letter dated August 3.[19]

In keeping with his general policy, Webster handled all such appeals by simply not answering them. From the standpoint of the Georgia group this was inconvenient, but not tremendously so. They could always consult his friends, and did — a bit of circumnavigation that, as it turned out, was amply rewarded.

Among those queried, and by Stephens himself, was George T. Curtis. He responded on August 13 — five days before the Macon convention was due to assemble. Explaining that Webster's friends were at the moment quite concerned that "his personal honor, dignity, comfort and reputation . . . be most carefully guarded," Curtis still managed to approve wholeheartedly the idea of an independent Webster electoral ticket in Georgia. Nothing was said about Webster's own views on the subject, but Stephens could at least be satisfied that if he and his colleagues went ahead they would not be acting alone. Curtis made that quite clear. Webster's supporters in Massachusetts had "hung back" to date because they did not want it to seem that he was "dictating a nomination in Massachusetts through his personal friends, which other Whigs of other States are not willing to follow." They were more than ready to move, however, and would "as soon as your or any other state will take the lead." Furthermore, their chances for success seemed excellent. "It is the opinion of many of our best politicians, that Mr. Webster can carry the electoral vote of the state if he is run in other states." In short, urged Curtis, "If you will only strike a good blow, now, we will follow it up, with good will." [20]

Such assurances may not have been all Stephens and his colleagues wanted, but at least Curtis had not said Webster opposed the independent ticket idea, and that in turn could be construed as speaking volumes. In any case, by the time their convention met, the Georgia group apparently felt they had enough to go on, for — with Union and the Compromise as his platform and Charles J. Jenkins of Georgia as his running mate — Webster was duly nominated by the delegates at Macon.

Meanwhile Curtis had ends of his own to serve. His reply, as

Stephens doubtless supposed, had been drawn from the most unimpeachable of sources, but it was also something less than wholly candid. On August 4 Curtis had visited Webster at Marshfield and discussed the current political situation with him in detail. On the subject of all "movements designed to make him an independent candidate for the presidency," Webster declared that he would neither "invite or encourage" such activity, nor would he "interfere to prevent any portion of the people from casting their votes for him, if they should see fit to do so." Whatever others undertook, his own role would remain completely passive. He did add, however — or at least Curtis noted the fact later in his biography — that "he wished his friends in Massachusetts not to undertake any movement for making him a candidate in the election." [21]

Precisely what could be put down to strategy and what to a simple failure of memory on Curtis' part would have been a nice point to debate. Yet for the moment the question remained academic, at least as far as his own activities were concerned. In his relations with Stephens and the rest of the Georgia group, Curtis proved as good as his word. On August 16 — a full two days before the convention met in Macon — a public assembly of the "Friends of Webster" was held at the Tremont House in Boston. Having passing resolutions stating that the interests of the country still required Webster's election as President, those who attended went on to form a "committee of Seven." The task set for the committee was to call a convention for the purpose of nominating a separate electoral ticket. Among the men slated to serve was G. T. Curtis. [22]

Fully organized in two states, the Webster movement had become — by the third week in August — a source of more than mild concern in some quarters. Winthrop wrote Kennedy a second time wondering, "How are Fillmore and his Cabinet to stand?" [23] And from Washington, Seward asked the editor of the Boston *Atlas* for his views. "Is there any responsibility anywhere for these convention efforts of Mr. Webster's friends in Boston? Or are they merely the dying throes of a proud and defeated faction?" What had happened in Georgia Seward tended to dismiss as unimportant, but Boston left him thoroughly puzzled. "George Ashmun is here and he has no sympathy with disorganization." [24] Who then was behind it all?

Nor were those closest to Webster any clearer on the essential issues involved. Writing his father on August 25, Fletcher Webster observed that the "Webster meetings" seemed to be gathering a momentum "which will carry them along a good distance." A good distance, perhaps, but in which direction? Even Fletcher refused to hazard a guess on that score. "I don't know to what point exactly, but they gain on it." [25]

As for Webster himself, if he knew the answers to his son's questions, or Winthrop's or Seward's, he was more determined than ever to keep his own council. His reply to Fletcher's letter simply restated — in blunter terms — what he had already said. "I am a little provoked that my friends will not believe what I have so often declared and I now once more repeat, that on the subject about which you write, I have not one word to say." If there were those who wished to bring his name forward, then so be it; barring unforeseen circumstances he did not propose to interfere in any way. "I have no advice to give my friends, either to act, or not to act. I shall disavow nothing unless it be something that implicates me personally, or purports to express my wishes. Let this suffice." [26]

Having returned to Washington, Webster had to rely on his son to clarify his position and preserve what peace he could at home. The task was becoming more difficult each day, however. As long as it was simply a question of endorsing Scott, Webster could with some reason expect to be left alone. The events in Macon and Boston changed all that. Virtually overnight the pressures on him trebled, reaching a point finally where no statement, nothing he could have said — short of demanding publicly that his name be withdrawn — would have reversed the trend. Fully as troublesome and significant as the fact of the pressures, too, was the direction from which they came. For the moment those responsible for the Webster movement were content to have him remain silent. Rather it was the regular party leadership that pressed the issue. And no portion of that larger group worked harder to get Webster to speak out — to undo what had been done in Georgia and Massachusetts — than the men who had managed his campaign prior to Baltimore.

The truth was that Seward's remark about Ashmun and his lack of sympathy with "disorganization" could as easily have been applied to Choate, or Everett, or Peter Harvey, or Edward Curtis of New York, or any one of a dozen others. Against all odds and at considerable expense to themselves they had tried to win the regular Whig nomination for Webster, but failing that, they had no intention of carrying the contest further. Their names remained conspicuously absent from the Webster lists that now began to circulate; they took no part in any of the various committee meetings or conventions held to further the cause.

The sole exception was George T. Curtis, whom Everett would soon describe as without a doubt "the most disliked man in the community." [27] Like the others, Everett would also, before long, take steps to dissociate himself in more pertinent ways from Curtis and his associates. A cordial letter to Scott, expressing unqualified support for the regular Whig nominations, may or may not have helped in this respect, but it at least drew an equally cordial reply from the general. [28]

In the meantime, from his post in London, Abbott Lawrence watched the rising furor with mixed emotions. For those Whigs "who proposed not to be bound by the Baltimore Convention" he had nothing but contempt, yet their actions simply confirmed what he had long felt about "the man worship which has been practiced by a certain few in our state." He himself had left the country "under the displeasure of the man worshippers" and he supposed he would return "under the same shade" — which did not really bother him. Rather what he objected to more than anything else was the fact that his brother, Samuel, had joined the dissidents. "I shall charge brother Sam with want of discretion when I get home." [29]

To someone nearer the situation the relative calm with which Abbott Lawrence greeted the activities of Webster's supporters might have seemed misguided, but Lawrence was, after all, an observer of no mean insight. If he knew that "brother Sam" was laboring on behalf of an independent ticket, he must have known too something of the movement's other Massachusetts sponsors. Of the large Lawrence clan, Samuel had always been the least involved politically. And for all his ability — and friendship with Webster — George T. Curtis was young and inexperienced. "He has not the slightest political weight" was Everett's judgment, offered at the same time he noted Curtis' unpopularity.[30] For the rest, the men who attended the Webster meetings, signed the petitions, and served on the State Executive Committee tended to fall into the same category. Well-intentioned businessmen, younger politicians, or older ones whose careers had gotten sidetracked, they were not an especially formidable group.

Even when the movement began to show signs — as it had by the end of August — of spreading to areas outside Massachusetts and Georgia, the pattern remained the same. In both Pennsylvania and New Jersey, there was talk of a Webster ticket, and in New York City a particularly active drive was underway. Yet of all Webster's perennial New York backers — including his old friends Edward Curtis and Richard Blatchford — only Hiram Ketchum lent any support. The others, assuming the same posture as Everett, Choate, and Ashmun in Massachusetts, remained aloof and privately condemned the whole affair.

In New York and elsewhere in the North disaffection over the apparent victory of "Sewardism" within the Whig party provided the strongest shove for those who were, of a sudden, rushing to embrace Webster's cause. On the other hand precisely what "Sewardism" meant to such men would have been difficult to determine. For many, personal considerations must have been paramount. With no great standing in the party, they had little to gain — and possibly much to lose — from any triumph it might enjoy at that particular moment. If Edward Everett could treat directly with Winfield Scott, George T. Curtis was scarcely in a position to do so. There remained, too, of course, the cause of Union and sectional peace. However much the general's managers might now try to counter the point, Scott's nomination at Baltimore had marked a defeat for the pro-Compromise moderates, one that left many of them bitter and a few bound and determined to oppose the regular party nominations in any way they could.

Nor, on the level of issues, was Union the only cause those involved might have hoped to further by backing a separate Webster electoral ticket. Although its full development lay in the future, already, by 1852, nativism was breaking down old political barriers and alliances. Beginning in the mid-1840s a marked increase in immigration to the United States had produced widespread opposition to foreigners, especially Catholic foreigners. Growing year by year, that opposition, together with the immigrants themselves, would end by transforming the entire American party system. For the moment, except in a few places, the lines were still too loosely drawn to make precise calculations possible, but the signs were there for those who cared to read them. Gravitating to the ranks of the Democrats, the Irish — the largest group of immigrants — tended to confirm the Whig party's traditional character as the preeminent home of Americans of "native" stock. However, a few enterprising Whigs — and among them William H. Seward — had tried to reverse that trend in various ways, with the result that party members who entertained particularly strong nativist sentiments came to look askance at Seward and his works, including the Baltimore nominations. Their hostility grew when Scott — accused by the Democrats of anti-Catholic prejudice — undertook to refute the charge in a number of forthright statements.

Webster's own position on the "foreign" and Catholic issues was far from clear; indeed, he seems to have consciously avoided committing himself. Yet precisely for that reason he was ideal for the nativists' purpose. Unable to cast their ballots for either of the major party candidates they could join the movement for an independent electoral ticket — and not a few of them apparently did. By thus drawing votes away from Scott they were, of course, aiding the Democrats; but only in the short run. Like the Georgia Unionists, the antiforeign, anti-Catholic elements in the Whig party — having lost their point at Baltimore — were willing, even anxious, to see Scott beaten. Their sights were all set on the period after November 1852 and on the sweeping changes within the organization defeat would bring.

Such logic, on the other hand, was likely to appeal only to the very dedicated or, again, to those whose stake in things as they were remained relatively minor. And this, in turn, went far toward explaining the odd clutch of political nonentities, novices, and ne'er-do-wells who made up the core of the latest Webster movement. Well might Abbott Lawrence scoff at such a motley crew and its doings.

But if Lawrence — safe in England and protected by his longstanding feud with Webster, to say nothing of his excellent relations with the Seward wing of the party — could scoff, Webster's pre-Baltimore supporters could ill afford to do so. The connection was too close, too easily misread; the specter of guilt by association haunted them all. To George Abbot, Everett was to make the point abundantly clear. If the Whig party were to suffer disaster because of Webster's refusal to disown the efforts made in his behalf, what would become of "his good name"? — and then the real heart of the matter: "I do not ask in what condition it will leave his friends, young enough to still be useful (of whom I am not one)." [31]

Feeling as they did, Everett and the others took every opportunity to press their case, especially after Webster's return from Washington early in September. Nor did the fact — which gradually became apparent — that he had at last come home to die in the least dissuade them. It simply rendered the issue, from their standpoint, more critical.

## IV

But more than ever now Webster wanted — and needed — that calm he had sought since Baltimore, and for a while longer he managed by sheer force of will to impose it on those around him. In mid-September Richard Blatchford visited Marshfield. "We talked of everything but law and politics," Webster wrote Fillmore.[32] Later the same week, C. C. Felton of the Harvard faculty spent an afternoon driving over the estate with its owner. Their conversation touched on an amazing variety of "moral, literary, religious topics . . . but politics not at all." [33] The following week it was George Ticknor, his daughter, and George T. Curtis who came, this time for a visit of several days. Ticknor had never been to Marshfield before and found the place charming, the meals well served "in the style of a handsome country establishment," and the Webster family cherished as "a peculiar and favorite people" by their humble neighbors, who expressed "an anxiety about Mr. Webster's health," which was at once "very great and sincere." To Ticknor the great man seemed ill, but by no means mortally so. "I had no misgivings that it was the last time I should see him." In conversation Webster was as agreeable as ever, though "it was some effort to him to be so," Ticknor felt, and like those who had come before, he discovered that certain topics were simply not mentioned. "The political campaign, which ended in the election of President Pierce, was then at the height of its violence, and no conversation, that approached the subject, occurred while I was at Marshfield." [34]

And so the time passed. According to George Abbot, who went north with Webster and would remain until the end, leaving a telling picture in hastily scribbled letters and notes of the last month of his chief's life, Webster "read no newspapers," [35] a fact that he himself confided to Fillmore, describing it as "one advantage of my condition." [36] Avoiding the newspapers, however, and carefully choosing guests from among his nonpolitical acquaintances could guarantee Webster only so much protection. There were still the mails — as he found to his discomfort.

Most of the letters — a veritable flood to which, in Abbot's words, there seemed "no end" — that poured in imploring Webster to "come out" could be ignored. They came "from sources that it was not absolutely necessary to heed." [37] But there were exceptions and, as it turned out, one in particular. Signed by seven of his most influential New York "friends," including Moses Grinnell, W. M. Evarts, J. Watson Webb, and Charles Stetson, it put the case in no uncertain terms. Feeling fully "as much sorrow and chagrin" as any of Webster's other supporters at his "ill success" in Baltimore, the seven still viewed "with much solicitude" the efforts currently being made in his behalf. Such activity was bound to produce unfortunate consequences. "We can anticipate no result . . . at all suitable to your dignity" — only "a most false record of the state of feeling in the Country towards you," disaster for the Whig party and for the nation itself. The entire proceeding, too, violated established practice in American politics in a way that the seven could never support. "We do not find any warrant to disregard the observance of that good faith towards the successful competitor, which in a different result we should, rightfully, have claimed from his friends." Would Webster himself, therefore, consider offering some sort of "public disclaimer"? His friends most earnestly hoped so.[38]

Dated September 24, the letter was not finally sent to Webster until October 9. Attached to it was a short note from Grinnell, who expressed himself "full of interest and solicitude for your happiness." [39] Even before the letter and Grinnell's note arrived, however, the group at Marshfield had been told what to expect, probably by Peter Harvey, who was there for a short stay beginning October 2. Other than to advise his old friend to vote for Pierce and remark, in passing, that he thought the attempt of "some persons friendly to me" to get up a separate electoral ticket "a very foolish movement," Webster said little about politics and nothing at all about the possibility of a public disclaimer.[40] Later the same evening discussing the subject with Abbot, Harvey was openly bitter about Webster's attitude. Painstakingly, he went over the details of all that had been done before the convention, of the thousands spent "in the purchase of newspapers and the employment of agents." But they had lost — and that, Harvey felt, ought to have been that.[41] Yet if he managed to convince Abbot, he had failed with Webster, which did not augur well for whatever response might great subsequent appeals, including the one from New York.

Even more discouraging in that respect was the state of Webster's health. Quite clearly time was running out. At the beginning of October he was still able to leave his room, but Harvey found him failing "perceptibly from day to day" and the whole tenor of his conversation suggested he did not expect to live longer than a few months.[42] What Harvey probably did not know — though the rest of the circle at Marshfield did — was that even that estimate was too generous.

Within a week of Webster's return it had become obvious that something more than the salt air of his old retreat would be required to restore his health. On September 20 he traveled to Boston to be examined by John Jeffries, his physician there. Jeffries did what he could to relieve the symptoms — the intestinal disorders and the painful swelling in the arms and legs — but a week later "a violent attack of constipation in my stomach and bowels, and much swelling of the parts" [43] left Webster utterly spent. That night Jeffries was sent for and Fletcher Webster acknowledged for the first time that his father would never recover.[44] In the days that followed there were occasional moments of hope and an elaborate consultation with at least one other doctor from Boston, but the hope always proved misplaced, and when the doctors prescribed a change in diet from lime water and gruel to "plain nutritious food," their patient found himself with insufficient appetite to follow the suggestion.[45] Instead the attacks continued, mounting in severity, and Webster grew steadily weaker.

Weaker, but no less determined to keep any knowledge of his condition from the public at large. Fillmore was told, but no one else. "To all others, I give the general answer, that it is the season for my catarrh, but that the disease is light." [46] When Harvey was at Marshfield, Webster even went so far as to sit at his desk and write a letter in his friend's presence, so that Harvey if asked about Webster's health could repeat what he had seen. "It will be an answer," Webster remarked, "and save me from annoyance." [47] Later, when rumors of the melancholy state of affairs at Marshfield began to appear in the newspapers, they were strenuously denied, and those few people who knew the truth were cautioned repeatedly not to say anything.

This was where things stood on October 11, when the letter from Webster's former New York supporters finally reached him. Warned beforehand that it was coming, he had still to decide what answer to give. As a result, the next few days saw a sharp break in the rigidly enforced regime of calm at Marshfield.

Edward Curtis arrived from New York to put the case in person, and George Abbot, feeling, as he later asserted, that Curtis was acting only to further his own "miserable political interests," wrote Everett asking for advice.[48]

Like Curtis, Abbot believed that Webster should make some sort of statement disassociating himself from the independents. The issue was one of motive and style, and on both counts Abbot trusted Everett where he did not trust Curtis. He trusted Everett sufficiently, also, to reveal to him the full particulars of Webster's condition, which in turn came as a complete surprise to Everett, who had known nothing of the imminent danger in which his friend stood or "of the state of mental abstraction" it produced. Neither, he added, did the world at large. On the contrary, it supposed Webster "to be wide awake to the entire movement of things at home and abroad and it cannot be doubted that his supposed sanction to the independent nomination is a source of great discouragement in the Whig ranks." [49] Abbot had asked Everett to draft a reply to the New York letter. By the evening of October 14 the draft had reached Marshfield, explicitly disavowing any interest in independent action and calling on Webster's friends to support the regular Whig nominee.[50]

In the meantime two other drafts had been prepared, one dictated by Edward Curtis, the other by Webster himself. The shorter of the two, Curtis' simply referred Grinnell and the others to Webster's published Works "and more especially to my speeches in Faneuil Hall, and at Marshfield, on the 20th of September 1842, and the 1st of September 1848 respectively." Though a trifle oblique, the point was still clear enough: on those earlier occasions Webster had, when the issue seemed in doubt, freely declared himself a loyal Whig; by implication he did so now. He accepted defeat; he would support the Baltimore nominations.[51]

But if that was Curtis' view of what the situation required,

Webster's own was very different. His reply, which as Abbot observed covered the ground "fully," was emphatic. He would do "almost anything" to please the gentlemen from New York—anything, in fact, but what they asked, for to do so "would gratify not only you and your friends, but that great body of implacable enemies, who have prevented me from being elected President of the United States." He could never endorse Scott, would never endorse Scott. "If I were to do such act [sic], I should feel my cheeks already scorched with shame by the reproaches of posterity." As for the proceedings of his friends, "I encourage nothing, I discourage nothing." They were "entirely free" to do as they chose, but Webster did offer, in closing, a possible explanation for their behavior. "Probably they think they see indications that within a fortnight, the Whig party in the United States will have become merely Historical." [52]

No, in thunder — complete with pronouncements about the impending demise of the Whig party. Instead of the public disclaimer Curtis, Grinnell, and the others wanted, Webster was all but openly encouraging the independents. With every ounce of reason he could muster, Curtis argued against sending such a letter. His own draft, in fact, had all the earmarks of a desperate compromise, but even that Webster seemed reluctant to sign. On October 15, Abbot wrote Everett that only "the shortest and most general letter" was likely to be sent — if that.[53] Two days later, the odds had definitely shifted away from all drafts, however composed. "I think on the whole," wrote Abbot, "that Mr. Webster has decided not to write a note of the character I mentioned." [54] Nor did the following day bring any change. "I adhere to the opinion that no letter of the kind I spoke of will be sent." [55]

The spectacle of a man hounded on his deathbed by friends to do something that violated his every instinct was not a pleasant one. Abbot, who initially thought it advisable for Webster to answer the New York letter, very soon lost all taste for the enterprise and later wrote of the "ineffable disgust" he felt witnessing those sorry attempts "to extort from the expiring statesman the written expression of reluctant acquiescence." Why was Webster "so persecuted"? Abbot thought he knew. Why else, if not for money — "for a bribe of 'twenty' pieces of silver, each weighing $1,000." [56] Whether the money had already been paid on some previous occasion, or was to be if Webster agreed to cooperate, Abbot neglected to say. Neither did he mention from what source the money had or would come. The charge was not lightly made, however, and it served to darken an already grim picture.

Yet for all its dreary aspects, the scene at Marshfield could at least be understood on the level of normal political debt trading. Webster owed his friends a great deal; their political futures were at stake. He quite clearly had none to worry about. If they chose to press their case at the worst possible moment and, in terms that were less than delicate, from their standpoint, the circumstances justified it. The attempt to build a national political movement around the cause of Union had failed. Recognizing this, the same men at Baltimore had ignored Webster's explicit instructions in order to extricate themselves from what had become an untenable position. There was little to suggest that in the interim they had become more punctilious, or their estimate of his debt any the less substantial.

But for once Webster had nothing to gain by placating the gentlemen from New York, or Boston, or anywhere else, though the effort to say so cost him dearly. Reluctant to see Edward Curtis alone, he generally contrived to have a witness present as he entered the room "with slow and feeble steps," looking, Abbot recalled later, "sick, dejected, brokenhearted." What followed might last only a few minutes but invariably left Webster exhausted and weak.[57] On Saturday, October 15, he suffered an attack that, as he wrote Fillmore, "cost Dr. Jeffries, with his oil, morphine, and squills, two hours to subdue." [58]  The next day he was confined to his bed, and Ticknor wrote Abbot that George T. Curtis was on his way to Marshfield to help prepare Webster's will. Curtis was "a lawyer, familiar with the political state of things, and a true and safe friend"; he would be, Ticknor remarked pointedly, *"nothing but help."* [59]

Arriving early Monday, Curtis found Webster "excessively emaciated and weak" and the rest of the group at Marshfield still wrestling with the problem of what to do about the New York letter. Curtis himself, Fletcher Webster, and Webster's brother-in-law William Paige were all of the opinion that no "political manifesto of any kind" should be sent. The only dissenting voice belonged to Edward Curtis, and even he "after a time," as George T. Curtis put it later, changed his mind [60] — but not before a final interview with Webster.

The occasion of the interview was the arrival Wednesday, October 20, of a second letter from New York "begging that the first one, in relation to the support of General Scott's nomination, might be answered." [61]  One by one Edward Curtis went over the familiar arguments. He wanted to see Webster "place himself on a proper footing"; there was his "character" to think of — his "future fame." "I have no future on earth," Webster cried out in answer to this, "my past is my future." He would send, or sign, nothing.[62] At the time he seemed quite upset, yet later he managed to joke with George Curtis about the matter. More than ever opposed to any sort of disclaimer, the younger Curtis had read him a letter from a friend in Boston urging that Webster "remain firm." "Tell him to look over toward Charlestown, and see if Bunker Hill monument is still standing," came back the reply.[63]

To a point the image was apt, but stone and mortar are after all sturdier than flesh and blood. If Webster's resolve held, the physical structure that contained it had by Wednesday evening reached the point of utter collapse. The following day he began

to vomit blood; the end could now be only a matter of days —
or hours — away.

With quiet efficiency those around him did what they could to
ease his passing. Though there was little left but to administer
morphine in ever larger doses, the doctors made their patient as
comfortable as possible. Peter Harvey came down from Boston,
and George Curtis, having arranged to have Webster's annuity
paid to his wife during her lifetime, put the finishing touches to
his will. In a brief note Abbot informed Fillmore of how things
stood. "You will be deeply pained to learn that within the last
few hours the disease under which the Secretary of State is laboring has taken an unfavorable turn, and that no hopes are entertained for his recovery." [64]

The world at large, too, could now be told; with the end so
near there was no longer any reason not to do so. Late Friday
the first authoritative reports began appearing in Boston. By
Saturday morning the news was already well on its way across
the nation. Before notifying the press, however, the group at
Marshfield had taken one last step. On Thursday, October 21,
George Curtis wrote the secretary of the Webster Executive
Committee. Using almost the same language Abbot had in his
note to Fillmore, he explained Webster's condition and then requested, on behalf of the family, "that all political action in reference to Mr. Webster be now discontinued." [65] This was not
precisely the disclaimer Webster's former supporters wanted,
but under the circumstances it served well enough. Within
twenty-four hours the Committee had voted to suspend all activity "for the present." [66]

Sinking by degrees, his mind clouded with drugs, Webster
probably knew nothing of the letter to the Executive Committee. If there was a final clash between the two Curtises over the
issue, it almost certainly did not take place in his presence,
though it would scarcely have mattered if it had. The truth was

he simply did not care anymore. According to the tradition of the time, he had made his peace with God; the rancors of this world were now at last quite unimportant. Besides, after Baltimore, everything had mattered a great deal less. The growing confusion in the Whig party, his own silence, the entreaties of his friends were all, perhaps, full of import for those who would have to cope with their consequences; the fate of the party to say nothing of a dozen or so personal political careers might hang in the balance. But for Webster the great game had already been played and lost. Nothing that he could say would alter the result. Only death could supersede it in significance, and that came quietly in the early morning hours of Sunday, October 24.

In Marshfield and Boston and on beyond across New England tolling bells and minute guns announced the event. Awakened in the midst of a dream about "the great secretary," Robert Winthrop reflected on their long association. In spite of the differences between them, he counted his services to Webster above those of many of his more "forward" friends, including that group which had lately been "making capital out of his infirmities, and stealing notoriety from his very deathbed." For the rest, Winthrop felt it unjust to talk only of what might have been — to forget what a man Webster was. With all his faults "the impress of greatness was upon him all over in larger characters than have appeared anywhere within our region and within our day." [67]

It was a generous epitaph and a fair one, however much it left unsaid.

# Notes

# Notes

The following abbreviations have been used throughout in the notes:

DWLC   Daniel Webster MSS., Library of Congress.
DWDC   Daniel Webster MSS., Dartmouth College.
DWW   *The Writings and Speeches of Daniel Webster,*
       National Edition, 18 vols. (Boston, 1903).

*Chapter One*

1. *Mr. Webster's Address at Bunker Hill, June 17, 1775; (From the Original Manuscript)* (Boston, 1843) contains a vivid account of the dedication and the procession.
2. See George Ticknor Curtis: *Life of Daniel Webster* (New York, 1870), II, 222–223, and Henry Cabot Lodge: *Daniel Webster* (Boston, 1883), 127–128. Even Curtis, the most worshipful of all Webster biographers, devotes only a paragraph to the Second Bunker Hill Address. Lodge calls it "perceptibly inferior" to the first.
3. Webster, Speech of June 17, 1825, DWW, I, 235–254.
4. Webster, Speech of Jan. 26–27, 1830, *ibid.*, VI, 3–75.
5. Webster, Speech of June 17, 1843, *ibid.*, I, 259–283.
6. Ralph Waldo Emerson: "The Fugitive Slave Law," *Selected Writings,* Brooks Atkinson, ed. (New York, 1950), 863.
7. George Santayana: *Character and Opinion in the United States* (Garden City, 1956), 2.
8. John Quincy Adams: *Memoirs,* C. F. Adams, ed. (Philadelphia, 1874), XI, 383–385.
9. David H. Fischer in his *The Revolution of American Conservatism* (New York, 1965) offers a wealth of insight into the motives and methods of the "Young Federalists." The same group is treated in detail within the context of New Hampshire politics by Mark D. Kaplanoff in "From Colony to State: New Hampshire, 1800–1815," an unpublished Yale College Scholar of the House Essay (New Haven, 1970).

10. George Ticknor: *Remarks on the Life and Writings of Daniel Webster of Massachusetts* (Philadelphia, 1831), 1.
11. Norman D. Brown's *Daniel Webster and the Politics of Availability* (Athens, Ga., 1969) contains an excellent account of Webster's activities as a presidential candidate during the 1830s.

*Chapter Two*

1. Webster to Citizens of Worcester County, Jan. 23, 1844, DWW, XVI, 418–424.
2. Webster to Hiram Ketchum, July 17, 1841, *ibid.*, XVI, 348–351.
3. Webster, "Memorandum Respecting the Bank Bills & the Vetoes," MS. in DWLC.
4. J. Q. Adams: *Memoirs*, XI, 13–14.
5. John Tyler, Jr., to Lyon G. Tyler, Jan. 29, 1883, in Lyon G. Tyler: *Letters and Times of the Tylers* (Richmond, 1884–96), II, 121–122, note.
6. Oliver P. Chitwood in his *John Tyler, Champion of the Old South* (New York, 1939), 279–280, offers convincing evidence that Tyler had considered dismissing Webster with the rest of the Cabinet before the second veto and offering Louis McLane the chief post in a new Cabinet.
7. Webster to Messrs. Gales and Seaton, Sept. 13, 1841, DWW, XVI, 358–359.
8. Webster to Ketchum, Sept. 11, 1841, DWLC.
9. John Tyler to Webster, Oct. 11, 1841, *ibid.*
10. Webster, Speech of Feb. 21, 1837, DWW, II, 193–230.
11. Albert Fearing to Webster, Sept. 25, 1841, DWLC.
12. William H. Seward to Webster, Sept. 28, 1841, *ibid.;* Thurlow Weed to Webster, Dec. 18, 1841, *ibid.;* Glyndon G. Van Deusen: *Thurlow Weed: Wizard of the Lobby* (Boston, 1947), 123–124.
13. John McLean to Webster, March 29, 1842, DWLC; A. Dudley Mann to Webster, May 6, 24, 25, and June 28, 1842, *ibid.* Traveling through Ohio and Kentucky late in the spring of 1842, Mann evidently spent a considerable amount of time sounding out local Whig politicians on their attitude toward Webster and the administration. His reports were encouraging. Subsequently he was appointed United States consul at Bremen.
14. Robert C. Winthrop to John H. Clifford, Feb. 12, 1842, Winthrop MSS.; Webster to Edward Everett, Aug. 25, 1842, Everett MSS.
15. Waddy Thompson to Webster and to Tyler, April 29, 1842, quoted in Chitwood: *Tyler*, 336–337.
16. Webster to Waddy Thompson, June 27, 1842, DWW, XIV, 611–612.
17. Clyde A. Duniway: "Daniel Webster," *The American Secretaries of State and Their Diplomacy*, Samuel F. Bemis, ed. (New York, 1928), V, 29–53; Claude M. Fuess: *Daniel Webster* (Boston, 1930), II, 105–116; Curtis: *Webster*, IV, 94–125.
18. Everett to Webster, Oct. 1, 1842, Everett MSS.
19. Everett to Webster, Oct. 17, 1842, *ibid.*
20. Everett to Webster, Aug. 31, 1842, *ibid.*

21. Webster to Everett, Aug. 25, 1842, *ibid.*
22. *Ibid.*
23. Webster to Everett, Nov. 28, 1842, *ibid.* In December Webster received word that he had been made an honorary member of the Democratic Tyler Club of New Orleans. (James Graham to Webster, Dec. 12, 1842, DWLC.)
24. Everett to Webster, Sept. 16, 1842, Everett MSS.
25. Everett to Caleb Cushing, Oct. 10, 1842, *ibid.*
26. Webster to Everett, Nov. 28, 1842, *ibid.*
27. Webster to Thompson, Jan. 17, 1843, DWW, XII, 134; Webster to General Don J. N. Almonte, Jan. 21 and 30, 1843, *ibid.*, 134–135.
28. *Congressional Globe,* 27th Cong., 3rd Sess., 61–62, 99.
29. *Ibid.,* 74.
30. *Ibid.,* 297.
31. Tyler, Message of Dec. 23, 1842, *Messages and Papers of the Presidents,* James D. Richardson, ed. (New York, 1897), V, 2063–2064.
32. Duniway: "Webster," *American Secretaries of State,* V, 27–28.
33. Everett to Webster, Oct. 17, 1842, Everett MSS.
34. Webster to Everett, Jan. 29, 1843, *ibid.*
35. Tyler to Webster, three letters, n.d. but Jan., L. G. Tyler, *The Tylers,* 261.
36. Everett to Webster, Jan. 2, 1843, Everett MSS.; Lord Ashburton to Webster, Jan. 2, 1843, DWW, XVIII, 162–164.
37. Webster to Everett, Jan. 29, 1843, Everett MSS.
38. J. Q. Adams: *Memoirs,* XI, 329.
39. *Ibid.,* 327.
40. H. Shaw to Webster, Feb. 28, 1843, DWLC.
41. Winthrop to Clifford, Feb. 19, 1843, Winthrop MSS.
42. J. Q. Adams: *Memoirs,* XI, 355.
43. *Ibid.,* 335.
44. Webster to Everett, March 10, 1843, Everett MSS.
45. Everett to Tyler, April 18, 1843, *ibid.*
46. Webster to Everett, May 12, 1843, *ibid.*
47. Tyler's biographer, Robert Seager, in his *And Tyler Too* (New York, 1936), 210–236, rejects the idea that Tyler was ever a serious candidate to succeed himself. Cf. Chitwood: *Tyler,* 369–383, and Robert J. Morgan: *A Whig Embattled, The Presidency under John Tyler* (Lincoln, Nebraska, 1954), 169–172.
48. Tyler to Webster, Oct. 11, 1841, DWLC.
49. Webster, Speech of March 15, 1837, DWW, II, 193–230.
50. *Ibid.*

*Chapter Three*

1. The fullest treatment of Lawrence's life remains Hamilton Andrews Hill's *Memoir of Abbott Lawrence* (Boston, 1883). Hill discusses the Webster-Lawrence feud only briefly (73–79). For other treatments see: James Schouler: "The Whig Party in Massachusetts," *Massachusetts*

*Historical Society Proceedings* (1916–17), 39–53; Arthur B. Darling: *Political Changes in Massachusetts, 1818–1848* (New Haven, 1925), 325–326; David Donald: *Charles Sumner and the Coming of the Civil War* (New York, 1960), 156–158; Martin B. Duberman: *Charles Francis Adams* (Boston, 1961), 123–124. All of these authors date the quarrel from Webster's decision to remain in Tyler's Cabinet. The evidence suggests, however, that the difficulties between Webster and Lawrence began at least three years earlier and were due throughout primarily to a conflict of ambitions.

2. Winthrop, Speech of Aug. 20, 1855, *Addresses and Speeches* (Boston, 1867), II, 210–212.
3. Amos A. Lawrence, diary, Jan. 24, 1842, A. A. Lawrence MSS.
4. Lawrence to Webster, Jan. 5, 1835, Curtis: *Webster*, I, 503–504.
5. J. Q. Adams: *Memoirs*, X, 43.
6. Winthrop to John Clifford, Feb. 12, 1838, Winthrop MSS.
7. Everett to Winthrop, May 21, 1838, *ibid.*
8. J. Q. Adams: *Memoirs*, X, 43.
9. Henry Clay to Harrison Gray Otis, July 7, Sept. 24, Dec. 13, 1838, and March 22, 1839, Otis MSS.
10. Cf. Robert G. Gunderson: *The Log-Cabin Campaign* (Nashville, 1957), 42–43. The author misreads Everett's role. The articles in the Boston *Atlas* referred to were in all probability written with Webster's knowledge and approval.
11. Everett to Winthrop, June 8, 1838, Winthrop MSS.
12. Winthrop to Clifford, Sept. 22, 1838, Winthrop MSS.
13. Clay to Otis, Dec. 13, 1838, Otis MSS.
14. J. Q. Adams: *Memoirs*, X, 43.
15. "Boston Dec. 11, 1838. — The following Amts. paid over to Hon. Dan. Webster," Ward MSS.
16. Abbott Lawrence to Thomas W. Ward, April 26, 1839, *ibid.*
17. Ward to Baring Brothers, April 29, 1839, *ibid.*
18. Webster to John P. Healey, June 12, 1839, DWW, XVI, 311.
19. Gunderson: *Log-Cabin Campaign*, 43.
20. Webster to Everett, June 12, 1839, DWW, XVIII, 50; Webster to I. P. Davis, June 24 and July 31, 1839, *ibid.*, 50–52, 61.
21. The decisive issues in the election were purely local, the major one being a law passed the year before and signed by Everett making it illegal to purchase liquor in quantities of less than fifteen gallons. The law was highly unpopular and the Whigs bore the onus for it (Darling: *Political Changes*, 236–250).
22. J. Q. Adams: *Memoirs*, X, 437–438; Nathan Appleton to George Ticknor, Feb. 9, 1853, Appleton MSS.; Van Deusen, *Weed*, 119–120.
23. Winthrop to Everett, Dec. 30, 1840, Everett MSS.; Clifford to Winthrop, Jan. 20, Feb. 21, and March 31, 1841, Winthrop MSS.
24. Lawrence to Leverett Saltonstall, Aug. 2, 1841, Saltonstall MSS.; Appleton to Thomas Appleton, July 31, Aug. 15, and Sept. 16, 1841, Appleton MSS.

25. J. Q. Adams: *Memoirs,* XI, 28.
26. Clifford to Winthrop, Feb. 21, March 31, and Aug. 6, 1841, Winthrop MSS.
27. Lawrence to Webster, July 30, 1842, Curtis: *Webster,* II, 131.
28. Winthrop to Saltonstall, July 7, 1842, Saltonstall MSS.; Clifford to Winthrop, Sept. 4, 1842, Winthrop MSS.
29. Boston *Atlas,* Sept. 18, 1842; Hill: *Lawrence,* 73–75. For the resolutions of the convention see Curtis: *Webster,* II, 141, note.
30. Webster to Charles P. Curtis, Sept. 17, 1842, DWLC.
31. Harrison Gray Otis, et al., to Webster, Sept. 8, 1842, DWW, III, 111–112; Webster to Otis et al., Sept. 9, 1842, *ibid.,* 112.
32. Webster to C. P. Curtis, Sept. 15, 1842, DWLC.
33. Webster, Speech of Sept. 30, 1842, DWW, III, 117–140.
34. Charles Sumner to Lord Morpeth, Oct. 1, 1842, Hill: *Lawrence,* 74–75.
35. Winthrop to Clifford, Oct. 17, 1842, Winthrop MSS.
36. J. Q. Adams: *Memoirs,* XI, 255–256.
37. Tyler to S. W. Tazewell, Oct. 24, 1842, Tyler MSS.; John P. Kennedy to Saltonstall, Nov. 11, 1842, Saltonstall MSS.
38. Winthrop to Everett, Oct. 15, 1842, Everett MSS.
39. Webster's son, Fletcher, was appointed secretary to the China mission at a salary of $5000 (Peter C. Brooks to Everett, April 30, 1843, Everett MSS.).
40. Winthrop to Everett, July 12, 1843, Everett MSS.
41. Webster to Everett, Dec. 29, 1842, *ibid.* "If Mr. Davis had run *without carrying weight,*" remarked Webster obviously referring to the Clay endorsement, "he would have come in by 10,000."
42. C. P. Curtis to Webster, March 23, 1843, DWLC.
43. Charles Francis Adams, diary, June 5, 1843, Adams MSS.
44. *Ibid.,* June 6, 7, and 8, 1843; A. A. Lawrence, diary, June 8, 1843, A. A. Lawrence MSS.; J. Q. Adams: *Memoirs,* XI, 380–381; Boston *Atlas,* June 7 and 8, 1843.
45. Winthrop to Clifford, Feb. 19, 1843, Winthrop MSS.
46. Winthrop to Everett, July 12, 1843, Everett MSS.
47. *Ibid.*
48. A. A. Lawrence, diary, June 10, 1843, A. A. Lawrence MSS.
49. Thurlow Weed to Alvah Hunt, May 24, 1843, Knollenberg MSS.
50. Ward to Baring Brothers, April 29, 1839, DWDC; Ward to Joshua Bates, April 15, 1839, and Feb. 27, 1843, Ward MSS.
51. Bates to Ward, Dec. 3, 1843, *ibid.*
52. Ward to Bates, April 22 and July 2, 1842, Feb. 27 and April 29, 1843, *ibid.*
53. Bates to Ward, May 29, 1843, *ibid.*
54. Ward to Bates, Nov. 1, 1843, *ibid.*
55. Webster, Speech of Nov. 9, 1843, DWW, III, 159–185.
56. J. P. Kennedy to L. Saltonstall, Nov. 11, 1842, Saltonstall MSS.
57. Winthrop to Everett, May 16, 1843, Everett MSS.
58. J. Q. Adams: *Memoirs,* XI, 387–388.

59. Lawrence to Appleton, Aug. 16, 1843, MS. in Houghton Library, Harvard University.
60. For an analysis of the Whig origins of the Liberty party vote in Massachusetts see: Darling: *Political Changes,* 290–291, note.
61. William Appleton, diary, Dec. 19, 1843, W. Appleton MSS.
62. Webster to Everett, Nov. 30, 1843, Everett MSS.
63. *Massachusetts House Documents,* 1843, Nos. 41, 48, and 49.
64. For two excellent accounts of "Young Whig" motives and activities that nonetheless ignore Webster's early connection with the movement see: Donald: *Sumner,* chs. vi and vii; Duberman: *Adams,* chs. ix, x, xi, and xii.
65. Webster to Ketchum, Dec. 2, 1843, DWDC.
66. Webster to John Warren and others, Jan. 3, 1844, Curtis: *Webster,* II, 236–238.
67. Tyler, Message of December 1843, Richardson, ed.: *Messages and Papers,* V, 2110–2125.
68. Webster to Charles Allen, Dec. 3, 1843, DWW, XVI, 417.
69. Webster to Citizens of Worcester County, Jan. 23, 1844, *ibid.,* 418–424.
70. Webster to Allen, March 13, 1844, *ibid.,* 417.
71. Winthrop to Everett, Dec. 12, 1843, Everett MSS.
72. Winthrop to Everett, Jan. 29, 1844, *ibid.*
73. Ticknor's account is quoted in full in Curtis: *Webster,* II, 230–235.
74. *Ibid.;* J. Q. Adams: *Memoirs,* XI, 531; C. F. Adams, diary, March 17, 1844, Adams MSS.; Winthrop to Clifford, March 19, 1844, Winthrop MSS.
75. C. F. Adams, diary, Feb. 16, 1844, Adams MSS.; Winthrop to Clifford, March 19, 1844, Winthrop MSS.
76. C. F. Adams, diary, March 17, 1844, Adams MSS.
77. *Ibid.,* March 20, 1844.
78. *Ibid.,* March 21, 1844.
79. Ticknor in Curtis: *Webster,* II, 230–235.
80. C. F. Adams, diary, April 26, 1844, Adams MSS.
81. Lawrence to A. A. Lawrence, May 12, 1844, A. A. Lawrence MSS.
82. Clifford to Winthrop, April 24, 1844, Winthrop MSS.
83. A. A. Lawrence, diary, May 13, 1844, A. A. Lawrence MSS.; Webster, Speeches of May 2 and 9, 1844, DWW, XIII, 196–211.
84. Winthrop to Everett, May 11, 1844, Everett MSS.
85. Weed to Hunt, May 11, 1844, Knollenberg MSS.
86. Bates to Ward, Nov. 4, 1844, Ward MSS.
87. C. F. Adams, diary, Aug. 1844, Adams MSS.
88. Webster, Speech of Oct. 1, 1844, DWW, III, 253–273.
89. Webster to Everett, Dec. 15, 1844, Everett MSS.
90. Darling: *Political Changes,* 319, note, gives the Massachusetts election returns for 1844.
91. Webster to Winthrop, Dec. 13, 29–30, 1844, and Jan. 11, 1845, Winthrop MSS.
92. C. F. Adams, diary, Jan. 9, 1845, Adams MSS.
93. Webster to Allen, Jan. 20, 1845, DWW, XVI, 429.

94. C. F. Adams, diary, Jan. 7, 9, and 11, 1845, Adams MSS.
95. *Ibid.,* Jan. 29, 1845. The address is reprinted in DWW, XV, 192–212.
96. J. Q. Adams: *Memoirs,* XII, 163.
97. C. F. Adams, diary, Jan. 29, 1845, Adams MSS.
98. *Ibid.,* Jan. 25, 1845.
99. *Massachusetts Senate Documents,* 1845, No. 31.

*Chapter Four*

1. Charles Dickens: *American Notes for General Circulation, and Pictures from Italy* (London, 1910), 136–137.
2. Webster, Speech of March 17, 1845, DWW, XIV, 286–290.
3. Lawrence to Everett, March 31, 1845, Everett MSS.
4. Webster to David Sears, Feb. 5, 1844, DWW, XVIII, 182–183; Webster to Jeremiah Mason, Feb. 6, 1844, *ibid.,* XVI, 424–425.
5. Ward to Bates, Jan. 30, 1845, Ward MSS.; C. F. Adams, diary, Jan. 17, 1845, Adams MSS. Upon hearing of the fund Adams decided to withhold his vote from Webster in the Massachusetts legislature, but he half regretted having to do so. "Had it not been for this," he wrote referring to the fund, "his political course during the summer has so far reconciled me that I should have contributed my mite to place him in the Senate."
6. H. G. Otis to George Harrison, Feb. 7, 1845, Otis MSS.
7. Ward to Bates, Jan. 16, 1846, Ward MSS.
8. Appleton to Webster, Aug. 4, 1845, Appleton MSS.
9. Webster to Appleton, Aug. 8 and Sept. 11, 1845, Appleton MSS.; Webster to Appleton, Aug. 8, 1845, DWW, XVI; Appleton to Webster, Sept. 11, 1845, *ibid.,* note.
10. J. Q. Adams: *Memoirs,* XII, 213–214. "All Webster's political systems are interwoven with the exploration of a gold-mine for himself, and all his confidential intimacies with Lawrence have been devices to screw from him, or, by his agency, from others, money by the fifty or hundred thousand dollars at a time," remarked Adams in disgust.
11. Lawrence in the meantime had arranged for a large gift to Clay and offered Calhoun a loan of $30,000. Calhoun refused the loan because the interest was too high. Clay accepted the gift gratefully (Clay to Lawrence, March 20, 1845, MS. in Houghton Library, Harvard; Calhoun to Lawrence, April 9 and May 13, 1845, *ibid.;* Lawrence to Calhoun, April 30, 1845, *ibid.*).
12. David Sears to Webster, March 21, 1846, DWW, XVI, 445–446; Webster to Sears, March 26, 1846, *ibid.,* 446–447.
13. The circular of the Anti-Texas Committee, June 25, 1845, copy in the Massachusetts Historical Society.
14. C. F. Adams, diary, Oct. 21, 22, and Nov. 4, 1845, Adams MSS.
15. Appleton to C. F. Adams, John G. Palfrey, and Charles Sumner, Nov. 10, 1845, Appleton MSS.; C. F. Adams, diary, Nov. 17, 1845, Adams MSS.
16. Duberman: *Adams,* 105.

17. Webster, Speech of Nov. 7, 1845, DWW, XIII, 310–324.
18. Webster, Speech of Dec. 22, 1845, *ibid.*, IX, 55–59.
19. Polk, Message of Dec. 2, 1845, Richardson, ed.: *Messages and Papers,* V, 2235–2266.
20. Webster to Appleton, Jan. 20, 1846, DWW, XVI, 440–441.
21. Webster to David Sears, Jan. 17, 1846, *ibid.,* XVIII, 215; Webster to Franklin Haven, Feb. 2, 1846, *ibid.,* 216.
22. Webster, Speeches of Dec. 15, 1845, Feb. 26, and March 30, 1846, *ibid.,* IX, 60–77; May 26 and June 1, 1846, *ibid.,* XIV, 301–306.
23. Curtis: *Webster,* II, 261–288; Fuess: *Webster,* II, 390–391.
24. Webster to Appleton, Jan. 29, 1846, DWW, XVI, 441.
25. *Cong. Globe,* 29th Cong., 1st Sess., 1053.
26. Webster to Appleton, July 8, 1846, DWW, XVI, 456–457.
27. Webster to James K. Mills, July 19, 1846, *ibid.,* 458–459.
28. Mills to Webster, July 23, 1846, DWLC; E. H. Robbins to Webster, July 27, 1846, *ibid.;* Webster to Fletcher Webster, July 29, 1846, DWW, XVI, 459–464. Abbott Lawrence, however, thought that if there was going to be a compromise it should be presented by a Democrat (Lawrence to John J. Crittenden, July 24, 1846, Crittenden MSS.).
29. Webster to Mills, July 21, 1846, DWW, XVI, 457.
30. Webster to Fletcher Webster, July 27, 1846, *ibid.,* XVIII, 231–232; Webster to Fletcher Webster, July 29, 1846, *ibid.,* XVI, 459–464.
31. Webster to Mills, July 21, 1846, *ibid.,* 457–458.
32. Webster, Speech of July 25–27, 1846, *ibid.,* IX, 161–235.
33. Polk: *The Diary of a President,* Allan Nevins, ed. (London, 1952), 124–125, 128–131.
34. *Cong. Globe,* 29th Cong., 1st Sess., 1144.
35. *Ibid.,* 1158; Polk: *Diary,* 132–133.
36. Webster to Fletcher Webster, July 29, 1846, DWW, XVI, 459–464.
37. *Ibid.*
38. *National Intelligencer,* Jan. 18, 1844, reprinted in DWW, XV, 189–191.
39. Winthrop to Clifford, May 15, 1846, Winthrop MSS.
40. Boston *Whig,* July 16, 1846.
41. *Ibid.,* July 22, 1846.
42. Donald: *Sumner,* chs. ii–vi.
43. Sumner to Winthrop, Aug. 5, 1846, Winthrop MSS.
44. Winthrop to Sumner, Aug. 7, 1846, copy in Winthrop MSS.
45. Boston *Whig,* Aug. 13, 1846.
46. Winthrop to Sumner, Aug. 17, 1846, copy in Winthrop MSS.
47. Winthrop to Clifford, Sept. 9, 1846, Winthrop MSS.
48. Charles Sumner: *Works* (Boston, 1870–83), I, 304–316.
49. C. F. Adams, diary, Sept. 23, 1846, Adams MSS.; Boston *Whig,* Sept. 24, 1846; Boston *Courier,* Sept. 24, 1846.
50. Webster, Speech of Sept. 23, 1846, DWW, XIII, 327–329.
51. C. F. Adams, diary, Sept. 23, 1846, Adams MSS.
52. Sumner to Webster, Sept. 25, 1846, DWLC.
53. Webster to Sumner, Oct. 5, 1846, DWW, XVI, 464.
54. J. Q. Adams: *Memoirs,* XII, 214.

55. Charles Buxton Going: *David Wilmot, Free Soiler* (New York, 1924), chs. vii–ix; Richard R. Stenberg: "The Motivation of the Wilmot Proviso," *Mississippi Valley Historical Review*, XVIII (1932), 535–541.
56. Van Deusen: *Weed*, 156–157.
57. Webster, Speech of Dec. 2, 1846, DWW, IV, 7–56. In November Winthrop wrote John P. Kennedy urging him to attend the Philadelphia dinner. At the same time he remarked, "You and I probably think alike as to Webster's chances for the Presidency, but I think it every way important to keep him in good heart. He will do us good service now & always, if we will let him. New England will prefer him as President, but New England is never uncompromising" (Winthrop to Kennedy, Nov. 11, 1846, Winthrop MSS.).
58. *Cong. Globe*, 29th Cong., 2nd Sess., 422.
59. *Ibid.*, 308–309.
60. *Ibid.*, 453–455.
61. *Ibid.*, 545, 555–556.
62. Webster, Speech of March 1, 1847, DWW, IX, 253–261.
63. *Cong. Globe*, 29th Cong., 2nd Sess., 556.
64. Webster, Speech of May 12, 1847, DWW, IV, 87–92.
65. Webster, Speech of May 8, 1847, *ibid.*, 73–75.
66. Webster, Speech of May 26, 1847, *ibid.*, 99–103.
67. Webster, Speech of May 8, 1847, *ibid.*, 79–81.
68. Webster to Fletcher Webster, May 5 and 12, 1847, *ibid.*, XVIII, 242–243, 249; Webster to Edward Curtis, May 6, 1847, *ibid.*, 243; Webster to Mrs. James William Paige, May 9, 13, and 15, 1847, *ibid.*, 244–245, 249–254; Webster to Seth Weston, May 10, 1847, *ibid.*, 246–249.
69. Webster to Fletcher Webster, May 23, 1847, *ibid.*, 254.
70. *Ibid.*
71. Kennedy to Winthrop, May 23, 1847, Winthrop MSS.
72. John M. Berrien to Webster, n.d. but June 1847, DWLC.
73. Webster to William W. Seaton, June 21, 1847, DWW, XVI, 486–487.
74. Webster to Mrs. James William Paige, Aug. 21, 1847, MS. in Houghton Library, Harvard.
75. Boston *Whig*, July 29 and Aug. 4, 1847.
76. C. F. Adams, diary, Sept. 29, 1847, Adams MSS.
77. Webster, Speech of Sept. 29, 1847, DWW, XIII, 345–365.
78. *The Liberator*, Oct. 8, 1847.
79. C. F. Adams, diary, Sept. 29, 1847, Adams MSS.; Boston *Whig*, Oct. 1, 2, 6, and 16, 1847.
80. Duberman: *Adams*, 127–130; Donald: *Sumner*, 159.
81. Frank Otto Gatell: "Palfrey's Vote, the Conscience Whigs, and the Election of Speaker Winthrop," *New England Quarterly*, XXXI (1958), 218–231.
82. Webster to Richard M. Blatchford, Jan. 30, 1848, DWW, XVI, 491–492.
83. Hiram Ketchum to Peter Harvey, n.d., DWLC; Ketchum to Fletcher Webster, n.d., *ibid.*; Clifford to Winthrop, Jan. 14, 1848, Winthrop MSS.; Winthrop to Clifford, Jan. 17, 1848, *ibid.*

84. Van Deusen: *Weed,* 160–161.
85. Lawrence to Appleton, April 18, 1848, MS. in Houghton Library, Harvard.
86. Hugh Maxwell, M. H. Grinnell, J. D. Hall, and S. Draper to Appleton and Charles H. Warren, May 16, 1848, Appleton MSS.
87. Polk: *Diary,* 312–313.
88. *Ibid.,* 314.
89. *Ibid.,* 314–315.
90. Webster, Speech of March 17, 1848, DWW, IX, 262–270.
91. Webster, Speech of March 23, 1848, *ibid.,* X, 3–33.
92. The complete figures for all four ballots can be found in Curtis: *Webster,* II, 339, note.
93. Charles Allen, quoted in Holman Hamilton: *Zachary Taylor, Soldier in the White House* (Indianapolis, 1951), 95.
94. Webster to Blatchford, June 10, 1848, Appleton MSS.
95. Blatchford to Appleton, June 12, 1848, *ibid.*
96. Webster to Fletcher Webster, June 16, 1848, DWW, XVI, 495–496.
97. Webster to Fletcher Webster, June 19, 1848, *ibid.,* 496–497.
98. Everett to Webster, June 26, 1848, Everett MSS.
99. Webster to Fletcher Webster, n.d. but "Thursday," June 1848, DWW, XVI, 497.
100. Duberman: *Adams,* 139–157; Donald: *Sumner,* 165–169.
101. Henry Wilson to Webster, May 31, 1848, DWDC.
102. Webster to Fletcher Webster, n.d. but "Thursday," June 1848, DWW, XVI, 497.
103. Webster to E. Rockwood Hoar, Aug. 23, 1848, *ibid.,* 498–499.
104. Webster, Speech of Sept. 1, 1848, *ibid.,* IV, 123–144.
105. Winthrop to Kennedy, Sept. 19, 1848, Winthrop MSS.
106. Berrien to Webster, June 16, 1848, DWLC.

*Chapter Five*

1. For a sampling of historical opinion on the Seventh of March Speech and Webster's role in 1850 generally see: James Parton: "Daniel Webster," *North American Review,* CIV (1867), 65–121; Curtis: *Webster,* II, 381–436; Lodge: *Webster,* 297–332; Herman E. Von Holst: *Constitutional and Political History of the United States* (Chicago, 1876–92), III, 501–506; James Ford Rhodes: *History of the United States from the Compromise of 1850 to the Final Restoration of Home Rule at the South in 1877* (New York, 1910), I, 135–162; Herbert D. Foster: "Webster's Seventh of March Speech and the Secession Movement, 1850," *American Historical Review,* XXVII (1922), 255–264; Albert S. Beveridge: *Abraham Lincoln* (Boston, 1928), III, 127–131; Fuess: *Webster,* II, 198–246; Vernon Parrington, *Main Currents in American Thought,* I, *The Romantic Revolution in America* (New York, 1930), 304–316; Allan Nevins: *Ordeal of the Union* (New York, 1947), I, 286–345; John

F. Kennedy, *Profiles in Courage* (New York, 1955), 55–80; Hamilton: *Taylor*, 302–315 and 372–385; Hamilton: *Prologue to Conflict* (Lexington, Ky., 1964).

2. Peter Harvey gave a full account of the incident in his *Reminiscences and Anecdotes of Daniel Webster* (Boston, 1877), 170–176. See also: Hill: *Lawrence*, 75, note.

3. Harvey: *Reminiscences*, 174–176.

4. Blatchford to Crittenden, Nov. 20, 1848, Crittenden MSS.; Appleton to Crittenden, Dec. 4, 1848, *ibid.;* Alexander H. Stephens to Crittenden, Dec. 6, 1848, *ibid.;* John M. Clayton to Crittenden, Dec. 13, 1848, *ibid.;* Winthrop to Clifford, Dec. 12, 1848, Winthrop MSS.; John Davis to Crittenden, Jan. 19, 1849, Crittenden MSS.; Webster to Blatchford, Feb. 25 and 27, 1849, DWLC; Edward Curtis to Samuel B. Ruggles, Feb. 28, 1849, Curtis MSS.; J. O. Charles to Millard Fillmore, July 30, 1850, Fillmore MSS.; Sam Adams to Fillmore, Sept. 6, 1850, *ibid.*

5. Lawrence's appointment drew unfavorable comment from several quarters. Winthrop was especially critical, though his remarks may have been tinged with disappointment at not receiving the post himself. "As to Lawrence's fitness . . . & that of his family, for doing the elegancies of such a station, you & I should probably not differ, nor, indeed, as to his claims to monopolize all that may be thought due to New England. He will be poorly off with John Davis's son as Secretary" (Winthrop to Kennedy, June 30, 1849, Winthrop MSS.).

6. Webster to A. F. Perry, Feb. 22, 1849, DWW, XVIII, 302.

7. Webster to Blatchford, Feb. 16, 1849, *ibid.*, XVI, 505–506.

8. Webster to Blatchford, Jan. 16, 1849, *ibid.*, 504.

9. Webster to C. B. Haddock, March 9, 1849, *ibid.*, XVIII, 304–305.

10. Webster to Fletcher Webster, March 26 and 27, 1849, *ibid.*, XVI, 515–516.

11. *Ibid.;* Webster to Fletcher Webster, March 29 and April 12, 1849, *ibid.*, 516–518; Webster to Thomas Ewing, May 1, 1849, *ibid.*, 519–520.

12. Webster to Harvey, Jan. 27 and Feb. 22, 1850, *ibid.*, XVIII, 352–353, 356.

13. Harvey: *Reminiscences*, 176–178.

14. Polk, Message of Dec. 5, 1848, Richardson, ed., *Messages and Papers,* VI, 2479–2520.

15. Webster, Speech of Feb. 24, 1849, DWW, XIV, 317–322.

16. Polk: *Diary*, 381–387; Webster's exchange with Calhoun is reprinted in full in DWW, XIV, 323–335.

17. Robert Toombs to Crittenden, Dec. 3, 1848, Jan. 9 and 22, 1849, Crittenden MSS.

18. Webster to Blatchford, Feb. 25, 1849, DWLC.

19. Taylor, Address of March 4, 1849, Richardson, ed., *Messages and Papers*, VI, 2542–2544.

20. Taylor quoted in Hamilton: *Taylor*, 225.

21. Robert Toombs to Crittenden, April 23, 1850, Crittenden MSS.

22. Webster to Haven, Dec. 25, 1849, DWW, XVI, 527.

23. Taylor, Message of Dec. 24, 1849, Richardson, ed., *Messages and Papers*, VI, 2547–2562.
24. *Ibid.*, 2564–2568.
25. Robert Toombs to Crittenden, Dec. 3, 1848, Crittenden MSS.; Reverdy Johnson to Crittenden, Dec. 12, 1848, *ibid.;* William L. Dayton to Crittenden, Dec. 14, 1848, *ibid.;* Crittenden to John M. Clayton, Jan. 7 and 30, 1849, *ibid.*
26. *Cong. Globe,* 31st Cong., 1st Sess., 244–252, and Appendix, 115–127.
27. Curtis: *Webster,* II, 397–398. The anonymous gentleman was undoubtedly Curtis himself.
28. *Cong. Globe,* 31st Cong., 1st Sess., Appendix, 149–153.
29. *Cong. Globe,* 31st Cong., 1st Sess., 451–455.
30. Winthrop to Clifford, March 4, 1852, Winthrop MSS.
31. Winthrop to Everett, March 3, 1850, Everett MSS.
32. William Plumer, journal entry, copied in a letter from Plumer to G. T. Curtis, April 2, 1853, DWLC.
33. Webster to Haven, Jan. 13, 1850, DWW, XVI, 529–530.
34. Webster to Harvey, Feb. 13, 1850, *ibid.,* 532.
35. Webster to Harvey, Feb. 14, 1850, *ibid.,* 533.
36. Webster to Everett, Feb. 18, 1850, Everett MSS.
37. Webster to Harvey, Feb. 14, 1850, DWW, XVI, 533.
38. Webster to Harvey, Feb. 22, 1850, *ibid.,* XVIII, 356.
39. Webster to Fletcher Webster, Feb. 24, 1850, *ibid.,* XVI, 533–534.
40. Thurlow Weed: *Autobiography* (Boston, 1883–84), I, 176–178.
41. Webster to Charles Henry Warren, March 1, 1850, DWW, XVI, 534–535.
42. Charlotte Everett to Everett, March 5, 1850, Everett MSS.
43. Webster to Harvey, April 7, 1850, DWLC.
44. Winthrop to Clifford, March 4, 1852, Winthrop MSS.
45. Charlotte Everett to Everett, March 8, 1850, Everett MSS. In spite of her discomfort, Everett's daughter enjoyed the speech. "You know Mr. W.'s style of address. He does not charm you by a constant steady flow of beautiful language as you do dear Papa, but he tries you for a long time with his slow deliberate enumeration, & then repays you . . . by a burst of eloquence."
46. Harvey: *Reminiscences,* 218.
47. Webster, Speech of March 7, 1850, DWW, X, 57–99.
48. See above: 77–79.
49. See above: 209–211.
50. Webster to Everett, Sept. 27, 1851, Everett MSS.
51. Winthrop to Everett, March 17, 1850, *ibid.*
52. See above: 199–203.
53. Winthrop to Clifford, March 10, 1850, Winthrop MSS.
54. Parker's speech is reprinted in his *The Slave Power* (Boston, 1907), 218–247.
55. Webster to Haven, Jan. 13, 1850, DWW, XVI, 529–530.
56. Webster to Haven, May 18, 1850, *ibid.,* XVIII, 369–370.
57. See above: 209–211.

*Chapter Six*

1. Samuel T. Armstrong to Webster, March 12, 1850, DWW, XVIII, 357; Charles L. Vose and others to Webster, March 28, 1850, *ibid.*, 361; C. P. Curtis to Webster, April 5, 1850, DWLC; Winthrop to Everett, April 7, 1850, Everett MSS.; Everett to Winthrop, April 10, 1850, Winthrop MSS.; Curtis: *Webster*, II, 429–433.
2. Webster to Harvey, April 7, 1850, DWLC.
3. *Cong. Globe*, 31st Cong., 1st Sess., 517. Whether because of their brevity or the obvious conflict with the position Webster had taken on March 7, his remarks in the Senate on March 13 were never included in any edition of his published works.
4. Webster, Speech of April 4, 1850, DWW, XIV, 348–352.
5. J. M. Brewer to William Schouler, n.d., Schouler MSS. Brewer was by no means the only member of the press who took this view. James S. Pike, the Washington correspondent of the Boston *Courier*, a paper that strongly supported Webster, wrote in much the same vein. As a result the *Courier* refused to print Pike's letters (Pike to Schouler, April 21 and May 3, 1850, *ibid.*; Brewer to Schouler, April 26, 1850, *ibid.*).
6. Webster to Haven, May 18, 1850, DWW, XVIII, 369–370.
7. Webster, Speech of June 13, 1850, *ibid.*, X, 107–108.
8. Webster, Speech of June 17, 1850, *ibid.*, 113–117.
9. Webster, to Haven, May 18, 1850, *ibid.*, XVIII 369–370.
10. Webster to Samuel Lawrence, June 10 and 18, 1850, *ibid.*, XVI, 548.
11. Webster to Haven, June 19, 1850, *ibid.*, XVIII, 374.
12. Nevins: *Ordeal*, I, 319–320.
13. Webster to Haven, July 4, 1850, DWW, XVI, 549.
14. Webster, Speech of July 10, 1850, *ibid.*, X, 140–143. Some people found Webster's public expression of grief at Taylor's death more convincing than others. "In view of all that has happened, it is a little amusing to see Webster seizing every opportunity to associate himself with popular sympathy for Taylor," wrote Winthrop, "announcing his illness in the Senate on Tuesday, eulogizing him on Wednesday, desiring to be Chairman of the Committee of Arrangements, etc. Today he asked Clarke, who preached a funeral sermon at the Capitol, for a copy of it" (Winthrop to Clifford, July 14, 1850, Winthrop MSS.).
15. Webster to Haven, July 11, 1850, DWW, XVIII, 376. Webster had not always held such a high opinion of Fillmore. At the time of the Cabinet resignations in 1842, Fillmore had supported Clay and joined in the attacks on Webster. For several years thereafter relations between Webster and Fillmore had been quite strained, but a cordial exchange of notes between the two in May 1848 had resolved the difficulty (Fillmore to Webster, May 2, 1848, *ibid.*, XVI, 552, note).
16. The best general treatment of Fillmore's career is Robert J. Rayback: *Millard Fillmore: Biography of a President* (Buffalo, 1959).
17. Fillmore to Everett, July 11, 1849, Everett MSS.

18. Winthrop to Kennedy, July 17, 1850, Winthrop MSS. See also: Winthrop to Clifford, July 17, 1850, *ibid.;* Winthrop to Everett, July 19, 1850, Everett MSS.; Winthrop, "A Chapter of Autobiography," MS., n.d., Winthrop MSS. Fillmore, meanwhile, was receiving a steady stream of letters urging him to appoint Webster (D. D. Barnard to Fillmore, July 10, 1850, Fillmore MSS.; Lewis Allen to Fillmore, July 11, 1850, *ibid.;* Sam Houston to Fillmore, July 11, 1850, *ibid.;* Samuel Lawrence to Fillmore, July 11, 1850, *ibid.;* C. T. Reyburn to Fillmore, July 12, 1850, *ibid.;* Alexander Mann to Fillmore, July 12, 1850, *ibid.;* Arthur Pickering to Fillmore, July 12, 1850, *ibid.;* Edward Curtis to Fillmore, July 13, 1850, *ibid.*).

19. Edward Curtis to Samuel L. Ruggles, July 20, 1850, Curtis MSS.

20. J. K. Mills to Webster, July 17, 1850, DWLC. Webster's arrangement with his benefactors later produced an extended public controversy from which George T. Curtis was only partially successful in rescuing him (Curtis: *Webster,* II, 464–465. See also: Winthrop to Kennedy, April 23, 1851, Winthrop MSS.). As usual the older Lawrence brothers refused to contribute (T. B. Curtis to A. A. Lawrence, Aug. 13, 1850, A. A. Lawrence MSS.).

21. Webster, Speech of July 17, 1850, DWW, X, 144–170.

22. Webster to Haven, July 25, 1850, *ibid.,* XVIII, 379–380.

23. Webster to Haven, May 18, 1850, *ibid.,* 369–370.

24. Webster to Fillmore, July 30 and Aug. 6, 1850, *ibid.,* XVI, 554–555; Webster to Haven, Aug. 10, 1850, *ibid.,* 558–559.

25. Fillmore, Message of Aug. 6, 1850, Richardson, ed., *Messages and Papers,* VI, 2603–2609.

26. Webster to Harvey, Sept. 10, 1850, *ibid.,* XVIII, 385.

27. *Ibid.*

28. For a compelling analysis of the importance of the role played by Douglas in the passage of the Compromise see: Hamilton: *Prologue,* 133–150.

29. Everett to Webster, Sept. 13, 1850, Everett MSS.

30. Webster to Harvey, Sept. 10, 1850, DWW, XVIII, 385.

31. Webster to Harvey, Oct. 2, 1850, *ibid.,* XVI, 568.

32. Webster to G. A. Tavenner, April 10, 1852, *ibid.,* 652–654.

33. For an analysis of the vote in both the Senate and the House on the final Compromise bills as well as a breakdown of the votes of individual senators and representatives see: Hamilton: *Prologue,* 133–165 and 191–200.

34. Webster to Harvey, Oct. 2, 1950, DWW, XVI, 568–569.

35. See above: Ch. II.

36. Webster to Everett, Sept. 26, 1850, Everett MSS.

37. *Ibid.*

38. For a concise sampling of attacks on Webster by his fellow Bay Staters, including a stanza from John Greenleaf Whittier's "Ichabod," see: Nevins: *Ordeal,* I, 291–293. Even some of Webster's staunchest regular backers had taken issue with his stand, at least initially. Asked to de-

fend the Seventh of March Speech in Faneuil Hall, Everett demurred, and later, when the "Address of Thanks and Congratulations" was circulated for signatures by "Citizens of Boston," he refused to add his name to the list (Webster to Everett, March 10, 1850, Everett MSS.; Everett to Winthrop, March 21 and April 10, 1850, Winthrop MSS.). Everett's position probably cost him the opportunity to go to the Senate when Webster was appointed Secretary of State, a circumstance Everett regretted a good deal (Everett to Caleb Cushing, July 31 and Aug. 10, 1850, Everett MSS.).

39. Winthrop to Everett, May 12, 1850, *ibid.*
40. Webster to Haven, Sept. 12, 1850, DWW, XVIII, 388.
41. *Ibid.*
42. Lawrence to Ticknor, Aug. 20, 1850, Ticknor MSS.
43. Lawrence to Appleton, Aug. 16, 1850, MS., Houghton Library. Lawrence also wrote Everett on the subject, adding on that occasion, "Mr. Webster's appointment is highly satisfactory to the British people" (Lawrence to Everett, Aug. 16, 1850, Everett MSS.).
44. Winthrop to Everett, June 25, 1850, Everett MSS. The delay in Lawrence's confirmation had more than once been blamed on Webster. Despite several denials the charge was probably accurate (see: Webster to Samuel A. Eliot, June 14, 1850, DWDC; Eliot to Webster June 18, 1850, DWLC; Edward Curtis to Harvey, July 7, 1850, *ibid.*; C. W. Cutler to Webster, Sept. 27, 1850, *ibid.*).
45. Donald: *Sumner*, 183–204.
46. Webster to Harvey, June 4, 1850, DWW, XVI, 546–547; Webster to Fillmore, Oct. 19, and Nov. 15, 1850, *ibid.*, 569–571 and 576–577.
47. Webster to Everett, Oct. 8, 1850, Everett MSS.
48. Webster to Fillmore, Oct. 24, 1850, DWW, XVI, 573.
49. A representative selection of such invitations can be found in the Abbot MSS. For Webster's replies see: DWW, XII, 251–260.
50. Webster to F. S. Lathrop and others, Oct. 28, 1850, *ibid.*, 251–253.
51. Webster to Blatchford, Nov. 2, 1850, *ibid.*, XVIII, 399.
52. Winthrop to Kennedy, Nov. 12, 1850, Winthrop MSS.
53. Winthrop to Kennedy, Oct. 18, 1850, *ibid.*
54. Donald: *Sumner*, 183–204.
55. Webster to Fillmore, Nov. 5, 1850, DWW, XVIII, 401. Webster often went to considerable lengths to explain to Fillmore the details of Massachusetts politics and particularly stressed the role of the *Atlas* (see for example: Webster to Fillmore, Oct. 24, 1850, *ibid.*, XVI, 573). On the subject of the *Atlas* he apparently managed to convince Fillmore, for the President posed no objection when the paper's federal patronage was withdrawn (Webster to Thomas Corwin, n.d., *ibid.*, 582–583).
56. Winthrop to Kennedy, Nov. 12, 1850, Winthrop MSS.
57. Charles W. March to Webster, Nov. 21, 1850, DWLC.
58. Kennedy to Winthrop, Nov. 10, 1850, Winthrop MSS.
59. Winthrop to Everett, Dec. 31, 1850, Everett MSS.

*Chapter Seven*

1. For a discussion of the Great Exhibition and America's role in it see: the author: *American Participation in the Great Exhibition of 1851* (Amherst, 1960).
2. Chevalier J. G. Hülsemann to the Secretary of State, Sept. 30, 1850, DWW, XII, 162–164.
3. The Secretary of State to Mr. Hülsemann, Dec. 21, 1850, *ibid.*, 165–178.
4. Webster to Ticknor, Jan. 16, 1851, *ibid.*, XVI, 586.
5. For a statement of the official United States position with respect to Kossuth and his party as well as a view of what Webster supposed their life in America would be see: Webster to George P. Marsh, Feb. 28, 1851, *ibid.*, XII, 265–268.
6. Nevins: *Ordeal*, I, 547–548.
7. Webster to Haven, Dec. 23, 1851, DWW, XVIII, 497; Webster to Blatchford, Dec. 30 and 31, 1851, and Jan. 11, 1852, *ibid.*, 501–502 and 504; Webster to Fillmore, Jan. 7, 1852, *ibid.*, 503; Webster to Charles J. McCurdy, Jan. 18, 1852, *ibid.*, XVI, 588–591.
8. Webster to Haven, Dec. 23, 1851, *ibid.*, XVIII, 497.
9. Clifford to Winthrop, Jan 3, 1851, Winthrop MSS. Winthrop, meanwhile, saw a good deal of irony in the situation. Writing Kennedy he commented, "If my friends see fit to drop me at any stage of the canvas, upon them shall be the responsibility. I shall stand in my lot. Or rather, I shall stand in Webster's lot, for it is as true as it is funny, that I am to have a vicarious punishment and take the fall which was arranged for him, and from which he could not have escaped, had Taylor lived and he [Webster] remained in the Senate" (Winthrop to Kennedy, Jan. 5, 1851, *ibid.*).
10. Moses Stuart to Webster, April 18, 1851, DWDC.
11. Webster to Everett, April 23, 1851, Everett MSS.
12. Webster to J. A. Hamilton and others, Jan. 27, 1851, DWW, XII, 256–260.
13. Webster to Fillmore, April 4, 6, 9, and 13, 1851, *ibid.*, XVI, 603–606; Webster to George Lunt, April 4, 1851, *ibid.*, 603.
14. Webster replied at length to both groups. Webster to Francis Brinley, April 19, 1851, *ibid.*, 609–610; Webster to George Griswold, May 9, 1851, *ibid.*, XII, 269.
15. Webster, Speech of April 22, *ibid.*, XIII, 405–407.
16. Webster to Harvey, May 4, 1851, *ibid.*, XVI, 611.
17. *Ibid.*
18. William W. Evarts to William W. Greenough, May 11, 1851, DWDC; Webster to Fletcher Webster, May 5, 1851, DWW, XVI, 612; Webster to Harvey, June 3, 1851, *ibid.*, 613; Ashmun to Webster, n.d. but "Thursday night," DWLC; Everett to Webster, June 3, 1851, Everett MSS.
19. A copy of the "Central Committee's" letter was enclosed in a letter

written by Phillip Greely, the Collector of the Port of Boston, to Fillmore. Greely had refused to sign the petition (Greely to Fillmore, July 19, 1851, Fillmore MSS.).

20. Webster to Haven, June 11, 1851, DWW, XVI, 617.
21. Ashmun to Webster, n.d. but "Thursday night," DWLC.
22. Winthrop to Everett, July 9, 1851, Everett MSS.
23. Winthrop to Clifford, Aug. 11, 1851, Winthrop MSS.
24. Webster to Everett, Sept. 3, 1851, Everett MSS. The following day Webster had second thoughts on the subject, but Everett, acting on his own initiative, had already refused the invitation (Webster to Everett, Sept. 4, 1851, *ibid.;* Everett to Webster, Sept. 3, 1851, *ibid.*).
25. Copies of the "calls" for several of these smaller conventions can be found in the Abbot MSS.
26. Fletcher Webster to Webster, Nov. 17, 1851, DWLC. At the same time Winthrop received considerable sympathy for his defeat, and not a few of those expressing such feelings laid the blame squarely at Webster's door (see for example: Lawrence to Winthrop, Nov. 5, 1851, Winthrop MSS.).
27. Nevins: *Ordeal,* I, 355–356 and 374.
28. *Ibid.,* 365–366.
29. Roger S. Baldwin to Winthrop, July 7, 1851, Winthrop MSS.; Winthrop to Baldwin, July 11, 1851, Baldwin MSS.
30. Webster to Hiram Ketchum, June 27, 1851, DWDC. Webster's subsequent attempt to defeat Johnston aroused a good deal of antipathy among the Whigs of Pennsylvania (see: James E. Harvey to Fillmore, Oct. 19, 1851, Fillmore MSS.).
31. Webster, Speech of May 21, 1851, DWW, IV, 231–241.
32. *Ibid.*
33. Webster, Speeches of May, 1851 (2), Speech of May 28, 1851, and Speech of June 28, 1851, *ibid.,* XIII, 404–428, *ibid.,* IV, 263–290, and *ibid.,* XIII, 429–441.
34. *Ibid.*
35. Webster to Harvey, Nov. 27, 1851, *ibid.,* XVIII, 490–491.
36. Webster to Haven, Nov. 21, 1851, *ibid.,* XVI, 629–630.
37. "Address to the People of the United States," Nov. 25, 1851, quoted in Curtis: *Webster,* II, 579–581.
38. Everett to Fillmore, Nov. 26, 1851, Fillmore MSS.
39. *Ibid.*
40. Webster to Haven, Nov. 30, 1851, DWW, XVI, 629–630.
41. Webster to Haven, Dec. 14, 1851, *ibid.,* 630.
42. Kennedy to Winthrop, April 3, 1851, Winthrop MSS.
43. Kennedy to Winthrop, Aug. 19, 1851, *ibid.*
44. The Fillmore MSS. contain dozens of letters urging him to run. See for example: Daniel Lee to Fillmore, Dec. 4, 1851, Fillmore MSS.; H. H. Hilliard to Fillmore, Dec. 9, 1851, *ibid.*
45. H. A. Wise to Everett, Jan. 18, 1852, Everett MSS.
46. Wise to Everett, Jan. 24, 1852, *ibid.*

47. Fillmore to Everett, Feb. 16, 1852, *ibid.*

48. Wise to Everett, Jan. 24, 1851, *ibid.*

49. Everett to Webster, Nov. 25, 1851, DWDC.

50. Edward Curtis to Samuel L. Ruggles, July 20, 1850, Curtis MSS.; Wise to Everett, Jan. 24, 1852, Everett MSS.; S. P. Lyman to Henry J. Raymond, Jan. 24, 1852, Raymond MSS.

51. Fillmore to Everett, Feb. 16, 1852, Everett MSS.

52. Fillmore to Everett, Nov. 28, 1851, *ibid.;* Webster to Haven, Dec. 13, 1851, DWW, XVI, 632.

53. Webster, Speech of Feb. 25, 1852, DWW, XIII, 501–504.

54. Webster, Speech of Feb. 23, 1852, *ibid.,* 463–497.

55. "Address to the People of the United States," March 5, 1851, quoted in Curtis: *Webster,* II, 582–584. Evarts' address differed from that adopted by the Faneuil Hall convention the preceding November in one significant respect: in this instance Webster was nominated for the presidency with the express provision that the nomination was "subject to the approval of a Whig National Convention."

56. H. Maxwell to Fillmore, March 6, 1852, Fillmore MSS. See also: J. P. Phoenix to Fillmore, March 6 and 10, 1852, *ibid.*

57. Charles W. March to Webster, Feb. 24, 1851, MS. Houghton Library.

58. Robert L. Martin to J. W. Webb, March 12, 1852, Webb MSS.

59. Abbot to Everett, April 12, 1857, Abbot MSS.

60. *Ibid.*

61. Everett to Webster, March 8, 1852, Everett MSS.

62. Webster to Everett, March 13, 1852, *ibid.*

63. Van Deusen: *Weed,* 186–192.

64. Weed to Webster, May 24, 1851, DWLC. In inviting Webster to dinner Weed remarked that though his relations with "the general administration" were "hostile," he had only "a high respect for *your* character and services and cherish a grateful remembrance of your many kindnesses" (emphasis Weed's).

65. James B. Taylor to Fillmore, Oct. 11, 1851, Fillmore MSS.

66. Glyndon G. Van Deusen in *William Henry Seward* (New York, 1967), 141–142, suggests that Seward was essentially lukewarm toward Scott's candidacy. My own research, on the other hand, indicates that at least from the beginning of 1852 on Seward worked quite hard to promote Scott.

67. Nevins: *Ordeal,* II, 26–28.

68. Seward to Schouler, Feb. 27, 1852, Schouler MSS.

69. L. D. Campbell to Schouler, March 5, 1852, *ibid.*

70. J. O. Choules to Fillmore, May 8, 1852, Fillmore MSS.; James E. Harvey to Webb, May 9, 1852, Webb MSS.

71. Webster, Speech of May 22, 1852, DWW, XIII, 510–522.

72. Phillip Greely to Schouler, Dec. 4, 1851, Schouler MSS.

73. Webster to Fletcher Webster, n.d., DWW, XVI, 643.

74. Alexander H. Lawrence to Abbot, May 5, 1852, Abbot MSS.

*Chapter Eight*

1. Francis Granger to Fillmore, June 30, 1852, Fillmore MSS.
2. *Ibid.*
3. Webster to Blatchford, June 22, 1852, DWW, XVI, 657.
4. Fillmore to George Babcock, June 12, 1852, Frank H. Severance, ed., *Millard Fillmore Papers* (Buffalo, 1907), II, 329–330; John Barney to Fillmore, June 12, 1852, Fillmore MSS.; Granger to Fillmore, June 30, 1852, *ibid.*; Fillmore to Everett, June 25, 1852, Everett MSS. Rayback in his generally excellent account of the Convention asserts that Fillmore's delegates arrived in Baltimore "uninstructed" but then goes on to cite the President's letter to Babcock explicitly requesting the withdrawal of his name if the right moment ever came (Rayback: *Fillmore,* 355–358).
5. S. G. Haven to Fillmore, June 18, 1852, Fillmore MSS.
6. J. H. Williams to Webb, June 15, 1852, Webb MSS.
7. Platform quoted in Curtis: *Webster,* II, 624, note.
8. Choate quoted in Rhodes: *History,* I, 254.
9. Raymond quoted in von Holst: *History,* IV, 193, note.
10. John Barney to Fillmore, June 17 and 18, 1852, Fillmore MSS.
11. Barney to Fillmore, June 12, 1852, *ibid.*
12. Barney to Fillmore, June 17, 1852, *ibid.*
13. S. G. Haven to Fillmore, June 18, 1852, *ibid.;* B. M. Edney to Fillmore, June 20, 1852, *ibid.*
14. For a complete list of the results of the balloting in the Convention see: Curtis: *Webster,* II, 621, note.
15. Barney to Fillmore, June 18, 1852, Fillmore MSS.
16. Webster to Putnam, June 16, 1852, DWW, XVIII, 534.
17. Barney to Fillmore, June 18, 1852, Fillmore MSS.
18. Barney to Fillmore, n.d. but "Thursday," *ibid.*
19. Abbot to [?], June 19, 1852, Webb MSS.
20. Joseph Cobb to Fillmore, June 28, 1852, Fillmore MSS.
21. B. M. Edney to Fillmore, June 19, 1852, *ibid.*
22. *Ibid.*
23. Abbot, notes of a conversation, MS., n.d., Abbot MSS.
24. Webster to Curtis and Ashmun, June 21, 1852, copy of a telegram, Webb MSS.
25. Webster to Fillmore, June 21, 1852, Fillmore MSS. Endorsed "Rec'd & ans'd at 9½ A.M. June 21."
26. Fillmore to Webster, June 21, 1852, *ibid.* Endorsed "Not sent but seen — M.F."
27. Abbot to Ann Abbot, Oct. 2, 1852, Abbot MSS.
28. Lawrence to Winthrop, July 8, 1852, Winthrop MSS.
29. B. M. Edney to Fillmore, June 20, 1852, Fillmore MSS.
30. Webster to Abbot, June 24, 1852, Abbot MSS.

*Chapter Nine*

1. Choate quoted in Harvey: *Reminiscences*, 195–196.
2. Barney to Fillmore, n.d. but "Saturday," Fillmore MSS.
3. The invitation, dated June 28, 1852, was reprinted in the Boston *Courier*, July 2, 1852.
4. Webster to Everett, Aug. 14, 1852, Everett MSS.
5. The procession is described at length in Curtis: *Webster*, II, 628–631.
6. Webster, Speech of July 9, 1852, DWW, XIII, 532–538.
7. Webster quoted in Abbot, "A Record of the Last Days of Daniel Webster," MS., n.d., Abbot MSS.
8. Describing the house at Marshfield to his wife, Abbot particularly stressed this aspect of it. "I was never in a house so full in all its parts with all sorts of knickknacks — cups and saucers, statuetts, busts — large and small — china and porcellen ware, shells, toys, etc. I think there are too many for perfect good taste, though I may not be correct" (Abbot to Ann Abbot, Sept. 26, 1852, *ibid.*).
9. Webster to Fillmore, July 13, 1852, DWW, XVIII, 535–563.
10. Webster to Fletcher Webster, July 4, 1852, *ibid.*, XVI, 658.
11. Webster to Fillmore, July 26, 1852, *ibid.*, XVIII, 544–545.
12. Harvey: *Reminiscences*, 198–200; Curtis: *Webster*, II, 651–652.
13. Webster, Speech of July 25, 1852, DWW, XIII, 539–542.
14. Harvey: *Reminiscences*, 201–203.
15. Winthrop to Kennedy, July 12, 1852, Winthrop MSS.
16. *Ibid.*
17. Ulrick B. Phillips: *The Life of Robert Toombs* (New York, 1913), 109–110; Rudolph Von Abele: *Alexander H. Stephens* (New York, 1946), 139–140.
18. William R. Nevins to Fillmore, June 30, 1852, Fillmore MSS.
19. John L. Stephens to Webster, Aug. 13, 1852, DWLC.
20. George T. Curtis to Alexander H. Stephens, Aug. 13, 1852, Stephens MSS.
21. Webster quoted in Curtis: *Webster*, II, 651–652.
22. Winthrop to Kennedy, Aug. 23, 1852, Winthrop MSS.
23. *Ibid.*
24. Seward to Schouler, Aug. 22, 1852, Schouler MSS.
25. Fletcher Webster to Webster, Aug. 25, 1852, DWLC.
26. Webster to Fletcher Webster, Aug. 26, 1852, MS. Houghton Library.
27. Everett to Abbot, Oct. 19, 1852, Everett MSS.
28. Winfield Scott to Everett, Sept. 15, 1852, *ibid.*
29. Lawrence to Amos Lawrence, Sept. 3 and 16, 1852, Amos and William R. Lawrence MSS. At the same time Lawrence complained to his brother that Webster had let State Department affairs go to the point where little if anything was being done.
30. Everett to Abbot, Oct. 14, 1852, Everett MSS.
31. *Ibid.*
32. Webster to Fillmore, Sept. 12, 1852, DWW, XVIII, 552.

33. C. C. Felton quoted in Curtis: *Webster,* II, 667–670.
34. Ticknor quoted in *ibid.,* 677–680.
35. Abbot quoted in *ibid.,* 679.
36. Webster to Fillmore, Sept. 12, 1852, DWW, XVIII, 552.
37. Abbot to Everett, Oct. 12, 1852, Everett MSS.
38. M. H. Grinnell and others to Webster, Sept. 24, 1852, DWW, XVI, 666–667, note.
39. Grinnell to Webster, Oct. 9, 1852, *ibid.*
40. Harvey: *Reminiscences,* 200.
41. Abbot to Ann Abbot, Oct. 2, 1852, Abbot MSS.
42. Harvey: *Reminiscences,* 428–438.
43. Webster to Fillmore, Sept. 28, 1852, DWW, XVIII, 554.
44. Abbot to Ann Abbot, Sept. 27, 1852, Abbot MSS.
45. Webster to Fillmore, Oct. 8, 1852, DWW, XVIII, 557.
46. Webster to Fillmore, Sept. 28, 1852, *ibid.,* 554.
47. Harvey: *Reminiscences,* 436–437.
48. Abbot to Everett, Oct. 27, 1852, Everett MSS.
49. Everett to Abbot, Oct. 14, 1852, *ibid.*
50. Everett's draft can be found in the Abbot MSS.
51. Webster to Grinnell and others, Oct. 13, 1852, DWW, XVI, 667. The letter is endorsed on the back: "Written at the especial request & in consequence of the importunity of Mr. Edward Curtis, and never sent" (*ibid.,* note).
52. Webster to Grinnell and others, Oct. 12, 1852, *ibid.,* 666–667. It is endorsed: "Mr. Webster's original letter written to the New York Gentlemen as dictated by him to Mr. Abbot. Oct. 12, '52" (*ibid.,* note).
53. Abbot to Everett, Oct. 15, 1852, Everett MSS.
54. Abbot to Everett, Oct. 17, 1852, *ibid.*
55. Abbot to Everett, Oct. 18, 1852, *ibid.*
56. Abbot to Everett, Oct. 27, 1852, *ibid.*
57. *Ibid.*
58. Webster to Fillmore, Oct. 17, 1852, DWW, XVIII, 559.
59. Ticknor to Abbot, Oct. 16, 1852, Abbot MSS.
60. Curtis: *Webster,* II, 689.
61. *Ibid.,* 693.
62. Abbot, notes of a conversation, MS., n.d., Abbot MSS.
63. Curtis: *Webster,* II, 694.
64. Abbot to Fillmore, Oct. 23, 1852, DWW, XVIII, 560.
65. George T. Curtis to Archelaus Wilson, Oct. 21, 1852, Abbot MSS.
66. Webster State Executive Committee, "Announcement," Oct. 22, 1852, *ibid.* On Nov. 3, 1852, the members of the Committee resolved to constitute themselves "an American Union Party" and sustain "any National Administration, of whatever name, which is practically conducted according to the maxims of policy laid down by WASHINGTON and WEBSTER" (Webster State Executive Committee, "Resolves," Nov. 3, 1852, *ibid.*).
67. Winthrop to Clifford, Oct. 25, 1852, Winthrop MSS.

# Bibliography

# Index

# Bibliography

*I. Note*

Carefully assembled soon after his death by four literary executors —
Edward Everett, George Ticknor, C. C. Felton, and George T. Curtis
— Webster's papers were subsequently divided and scattered in smaller
collections. At present the largest single group of manuscripts is located
in the New Hampshire Historical Society. The Library of Congress contains another, as does Dartmouth College. The Massachusetts Historical
Society and Houghton Library, Harvard University, both have small but
rich Webster collections.

Until very recently the most readily available source for those interested
in Webster was the National Edition of his *Writings and Speeches*, 18
vols. (Boston, 1903). Edited by James W. McIntyre, the National Edition
contains all of Webster's major addresses, many of his legal and diplomatic papers, and a fair sampling of correspondence, though it is notably
lacking in letters to Webster.

Within the last few years the defects of the National Edition have been
remedied by a splendid long-range project at Dartmouth College. As evidence of the continuing interest in Webster, the College, in association
with University Microfilms, has undertaken to assemble and reproduce
the entire body of his papers. Organized under the direction of Edward
Connery Lathem, Librarian of the College, and currently carried on under
the very able editorship of Professor Charles M. Wiltse, the project is
sponsored in part by the National Historical Publications Commission. To
date it has produced *The Microfilm Edition of the Papers of Daniel Webster* (Ann Arbor, 1971) and a printed *Guide and Index to the Microfilm*
(Ann Arbor, 1971). All told *The Microfilm Edition* reproduces over 16,000
items on forty-one reels of film, including correspondence, both to and
from Webster, business papers, congressional papers, and State Department papers. Further microfilming as well as a selective letterpress edition
are planned for the future.

As my own research was completed before the publication of *The Micro-*

*film Edition* references throughout this study are to the standard, previously available sources on Webster, including the National Edition. For unpublished items I relied chiefly on the originals already at Dartmouth when the microfilm project was undertaken, on the materials at Houghton Library and the Massachusetts Historical Society, and on the large collection at the Library of Congress. The great bulk of the Webster papers in the New Hampshire Society can be found in the National Edition, the principal exception being letters to Webster. Typescript copies of most of these are available at the Library of Congress and whenever possible I used them.

In addition to Webster's own papers, the George J. Abbot collection at Yale University proved to be an unusually good source of material. Abbot was a clerk in the State Department from 1850 to 1852 and served as Webster's secretary during that time. Though his association with Webster was brief, he nonetheless managed to save much of interest and value.

Other collections particularly useful for various phases of this study were the papers of the following individuals, all at the Massachusetts Historical Society: Edward Everett, Harrison Gray Otis, Robert C. Winthrop, Leverett Saltonstall, Nathan Appleton, Amos A. Lawrence, and Thomas W. Ward. The papers of John Tyler and John J. Crittenden in the Library of Congress were also quite helpful, as were those of Millard Fillmore at the Buffalo Historical Society. The Henry Clay papers, the Library of Congress, contain surprisingly little fresh information about Webster.

A complete list of all manuscript collections consulted appears below.

Of the several major biographies of Webster the most venerable is George T. Curtis's *Life of Daniel Webster,* 2 vols. (New York, 1872). Curtis was one of Webster's literary executors and a lifelong admirer. His proximity to his subject — both emotionally and in time — dimmed his perception at many points, but his volumes are still the most complete study of Webster's life available and contain quantities of invaluable information.

Henry Cabot Lodge's *Daniel Webster* (Boston, 1883) is an interesting attempt at a balanced interpretation of Webster's career written thirty years after his death. Lodge had great admiration for Webster as an orator, a jurist, a diplomat, and, up to 1850, a politician and statesman. He considered the Seventh of March Speech "a tragic mistake," however, and develops the thesis at length in the book.

Claude M. Fuess, *Daniel Webster,* 2 vols. (Boston, 1930) is in many respects an excellent narrative biography. Balanced and eminently readable, it presents a view of the man that is at once engaging and convincing. The book's principal defect is that it was based almost entirely on published sources.

Richard N. Current's *Daniel Webster and the Rise of National Conservatism* (Boston, 1955) is, as the title indicates, primarily a study of Webster's conservatism and offers several interesting insights on that subject.

More recently, Maurice G. Baxter in *Daniel Webster and the Supreme Court* (Amherst, 1966) has treated Webster's career as an advocate before the nation's highest court, and Norman D. Brown in *Daniel Webster and the Politics of Availability* (Athens, Ga., 1969) offers a first-rate analysis of Webster's presidential ambitions and role in national politics during the 1830s.

In addition to these, there are many other books of lesser note about Webster. Some of them, along with other published sources consulted, are cited below.

For years the convolutions of early Jacksonian politics and the events immediately preceding the Civil War have commanded a substantial measure of historical interest and attention. Yet, oddly, the period in between has suffered relative neglect. There is no adequate general history of the United States during the 1840s, and one finds less good, monographic literature dealing with the decade than with either the one before or the one following it. There are notable exceptions, however.

The whole subject of expansionism and Manifest Destiny is admirably treated from a variety of perspectives in several different studies, including Justin H. Smith, *The Annexation of Texas* (New York, 1941) and *War with Mexico* (New York, 1919); Albert K. Weinberg, *Manifest Destiny: A Study of Nationalist Expansionism in American History* (Baltimore, 1935); Frederick Merk, *Manifest Destiny and Mission in American History: A Reinterpretation* (New York, 1963); Otis A. Singletary, *The Mexican War* (Chicago, 1960); and William Goetzmann, *When the Eagle Screamed: The Romantic Horizon in American Diplomacy, 1800–1860* (New York, 1966).

A great deal has been written about American nationalism both in general and during the pre-Civil War period, but nothing to my mind as thoughtful or provocative as David M. Potter's brilliant analysis, "The Historian's Use of Nationalism and Vice Versa," *The American Historical Review,* LXVII (July 1962), 924–50.

There is still no fully detailed history of the Compromise of 1850, but in *Prologue to Conflict; The Crisis and Compromise of 1850* (Lexington, Ky., 1963) Holman Hamilton provides a series of unusually penetrating, insightful discussions of the events of that troubled year.

Massachusetts politics during the 1840s have been treated at length in a number of studies. Two that I found especially useful were Arthur B. Darling, *Political Changes in Massachusetts, 1824–1848* (New Haven, 1925), and Kinley J. Brauer, *Cotton versus Conscience: Massachusetts Whig Politics and Southwestern Expansion, 1843–1848* (Lexington, Ky., 1967).

For a broader understanding of the period and Webster's role in it the biographies of other men are often the best available source. Among the biographies of Webster's contemporaries the following proved particularly helpful: George Rawlings Poage, *Henry Clay and the Whig Party* (Chapel Hill, N.C., 1936); Charles M. Wiltse, *John C. Calhoun: Sectionalist, 1840–1850* (Indianapolis, 1951); Albert D. Kirwan, *John J. Crit-*

*tenden: The Struggle for the Union* (Lexington, Ky., 1962); Robert J. Rayback, *Millard Fillmore: Biography of a President* (Buffalo, 1959); Glyndon G. Van Deusen, *Thurlow Weed: Wizard of the Lobby* (Boston, 1947), and *William Henry Seward* (New York, 1967); David Donald, *Charles Sumner and the Coming of the Civil War* (New York, 1960); Martin Duberman, *Charles Francis Adams, 1807–1886* (Cambridge, 1961); Charles Sellers, *James K. Polk: Continentalist, 1843–1846* (Princeton, 1966); Frank Otto Gatell, *John Gorham Palfrey and the New England Conscience* (Cambridge, 1963); Samuel Flagg Bemis, *John Quincy Adams and the Union* (New York, 1956); Oliver P. Chitwood, *John Tyler, Champion of the Old South* (New York, 1939); and David Tyack, *George Ticknor and the Boston Brahmins* (Cambridge, 1967). Holman Hamilton in *Zachary Taylor: Soldier in the White House* (Indianapolis, 1951) presents a sympathetic reappraisal of Taylor's role in 1850 and brings an impressive array of evidence to bear in support of his point, but the reader will want to weigh Hamilton's conclusions carefully against the more traditional view presented in Allan Nevins' *Ordeal of the Union*, 2 vols., (New York, 1947).

## II. List of Sources Consulted

### A. MANUSCRIPT COLLECTIONS

Abbot, George J., MSS., Yale University.
Adams, Charles Francis, MSS., Massachusetts Historical Society (microfilm).
Appleton, Nathan, MSS., Massachusetts Historical Society.
Appleton, William, MSS., *ibid.*
Baldwin Family, MSS., Yale University.
Clay, Henry, MSS., Library of Congress.
Crittenden, John J., MSS., Library of Congress.
Curtis, Edward, MSS., *ibid.*
Curtis, George T., MSS., *ibid.*
Cushing, Caleb, MSS., *ibid.*
Everett, Edward, MSS., Massachusetts Historical Society.
Fillmore, Millard, MSS., Buffalo Historical Society.
Fillmore, Millard, MSS., Library of Congress.
Hoar, George F., Autograph Collection, Massachusetts Historical Society.
Knollenberg MSS., Yale University.
Lawrence, Abbott, scattered letters in Houghton Library, Harvard University.
Lawrence, Amos, MSS., Massachusetts Historical Society.
Lawrence, Amos A., MSS., *ibid.*
Mann, Horace, MSS., *ibid.*
Otis, Harrison Gray, MSS., *ibid.*
Prescott, William H., MSS., *ibid.*
Raymond, Henry J., MSS., New York Public Library.
Saltonstall, Leverett, MSS., Massachusetts Historical Society.

Sargent, John O., MSS., *ibid.*
Schouler, William, MSS., *ibid.*
Stephens, Alexander H., MSS., Library of Congress.
Sumner, Charles, MSS., Houghton Library.
Ticknor, George, MSS., Dartmouth College.
Tyler, John, MSS., Library of Congress.
Ward, Thomas W., MSS., Massachusetts Historical Society.
Webb, J. Watson, MSS., Yale University.
Webster, Daniel, MSS., Dartmouth College.
Webster, Daniel, MSS., Houghton Library.
Webster, Daniel, MSS., Library of Congress.
Webster, Daniel, MSS., Massachusetts Historical Society.
Webster, Daniel, MSS., New Hampshire Historical Society.
Winthrop, Robert C., MSS., Massachusetts Historical Society.

B. PUBLIC DOCUMENTS

*Congressional Globe*
*Massachusetts House Documents,* 1843.
*Massachusetts Senate Documents,* 1845.
*Register of Debates in the Congress of the United States.*
Richardson, James D. (ed.), *The Messages and Papers of the Presidents,* 20 vols. (New York, 1897).

C. NEWSPAPERS

Albany *Evening Journal.*
Boston *Atlas.*
Boston *Courier.*
Boston *Daily Advertiser.*
Boston *Whig.*
*The Liberator.*
New York *Courier and Enquirer.*
New York *Tribune.*
Springfield *Republican.*
Washington *National Intelligencer.*
Washington *Union.*
Washington *Republic.*

D. PUBLISHED CORRESPONDENCE, REMINISCENCES, DIARIES, ETC.

Adams, Charles Francis (ed.), *Memoirs of John Quincy Adams,* 12 vols. (Philadelphia, 1874–77).
Adams, Henry, *The Education of Henry Adams* (Boston, 1918).
Appleton, Nathan, "Abbott Lawrence," *Collections of the Massachusetts Historical Society,* IV (1858), 495–507.

Atkinson, Brooks (ed.), *Selected Writings of Ralph Waldo Emerson* (New York, 1950).

Benton, Thomas H., *Thirty Years' View,* 2 vols. (New York, 1858).

Blaine, James G., *Twenty Years of Congress,* 2 vols. (Norwich, Conn., 1884–86).

Choate, Rufus, "Rufus Choate Letters," Essex Institute *Historical Collections,* LXIX (1933), 81–87.

Coleman, Mrs. Chapman (ed.), *The Life of John J. Crittenden, With Selections from his Correspondence and Speeches,* 2 vols. (Philadelphia, 1871).

Colton, Calvin (ed.), *The Private Correspondence of Henry Clay* (New York, 1855).

——— (ed.), *The Works of Henry Clay,* 6 vols. (New York, 1857).

"Diary of Thomas Ewing, August and September, 1841," *American Historical Review,* XVIII (1912), 97–112.

Dickens, Charles, *American Notes for General Circulation and Pictures from Italy* (London, 1910).

Emerson, Ralph Waldo, *Journals of Ralph Waldo Emerson,* 10 vols. (Boston, 1912).

Fitzpatrick, J. C. (ed.), "Autobiography of Martin Van Buren," *Annual Report of the American Historical Association,* II (1918).

Forney, John W., *Anecdotes of Public Men* (New York, 1873).

Greeley, Horace, *Recollections of a Busy Life* (New York, 1868).

Hamilton, James A., *Reminiscences of James A. Hamilton* (New York, 1869).

Harvey, Peter, *Reminiscences and Anecdotes of Daniel Webster* (Boston, 1877).

Hildreth, Richard, *My Connection with the Atlas Newspaper* (Boston, 1839).

Hill, Hamilton Andrews, *Memoir of Abbott Lawrence* (Boston, 1883).

Hoar, George F., *Autobiography of Seventy Years,* 2 vols. (New York, 1903).

Jameson, J. Franklin (ed.), "Correspondence of John C. Calhoun," *American Historical Association Annual Report . . . for the Year 1899* (Washington, 1900).

Lanman, Charles, *The Private Life of Daniel Webster* (New York, 1852).

Lawrence, Amos Adams, "Letters of Amos Adams Lawrence," *Massachusetts Historical Society Proceedings,* LIII (1919), 48–57.

Lawrence, William R. (ed.), *Extracts from the Diary and Correspondence of the Late Amos Lawrence* (Boston, 1855).

Lyman, Samuel P., *The Life and Public Career of Daniel Webster* (New York, 1852).

March, Charles W., *Daniel Webster and His Contemporaries* (New York, 1859).

Martineau, Harriet, *Retrospect of Western Travel,* 2 vols. (New York, 1838).

McGrane, Reginald (ed.), *The Correspondence of Nicholas Biddle Dealing with National Affairs, 1807–1844* (Boston, 1919).

McIntyre, James W. (ed.), *The Writings and Speeches of Daniel Webster,* 18 vols. (Boston, 1903).

Nevins, Allan (ed.), *The Diary of Philip Hone, 1828–1851,* 2 vols. (New York, 1927).

—— (ed.), *The Diary of a President* (New York, 1929).

Parker, Edward G., *Reminiscences of Rufus Choate, The Great American Advocate* (New York, 1860).

Parker, Theodore, *The Slave Power* (Boston, 1907).

Perry, Benjamin F., *Reminiscences of Public Men* (Philadelphia, 1883).

Phillips, Ulrich B. (ed.), "The Correspondence of Robert Toombs, Alexander H. Stephens, and Howell Cobb," *American Historical Association Annual Report . . . for the Year 1911* (Washington, 1913).

Poore, Ben, *Perley's Reminiscences of Sixty Years in the National Metropolis,* 2 vols. (Philadelphia, 1886).

Qualfe, Milo Milton (ed.), *Polk Diary,* 4 vols. (Chicago, 1910).

Severance, Frank H. (ed.), *Millard Fillmore Papers,* 2 vols. *Publications of the Buffalo Historical Society,* X and XI (Buffalo, 1907).

Seward, Frederick W. (ed.), *William H. Seward: An Autobiography from 1801 to 1834. With a Memoir of His Life, and Selections from His Letters, 1831–1846* (New York, 1891).

Smith, Seba, *My Thirty Years Out of the Senate, By Major Jack Downing* (New York, 1859).

Story, William W. (ed.), *Life and Letters of Joseph Story,* 2 vols. (Boston, 1851).

Ticknor, George, *Remarks on the Life and Writings of Daniel Webster of Massachusetts* (Philadelphia, 1831).

Tocqueville, Alexis Charles Henri Maurice Clerel de, *Democracy in America,* 2 vols. (New York, 1945).

Tyler, Lyon Gardiner, *The Letters and Times of the Tylers,* 2 vols. (Richmond, 1884).

Van Tyne, C. H. (ed.), *The Letters of Daniel Webster* (New York, 1902).

Weed, Thurlow, *Autobiography,* 2 vols. (Boston, 1883–84).

Winthrop, Robert C., "Memoir of Hon. Nathan Appleton," *Massachusetts Historical Society Proceedings,* V (1860–62), 224–26.

Winthrop, Robert C., Jr., *A Memoir of Robert C. Winthrop* (Boston, 1897).

Wise, Henry A., *Seven Decades of the Union* (Philadelphia, 1881).

E. GENERAL HISTORICS AND SPECIAL STUDIES

Agar, Herbert, *The Price of Union* (Boston, 1950).

Arieli, Yehoshua, *Individualism and Nationalism in America Ideology* (Cambridge, 1964).

Beard, Charles A. and Mary R., *The Rise of American Civilization* (New York, 1930).

Benson, Lee, *The Concept of Jacksonian Democracy* (New York, 1961).

Billington, Ray A., *The Protestant Crusade; a Study of the Origins of American Nativism* (New York, 1938).

Boorstin, Daniel J., *The Americans: The National Experience* (New York, 1965).

Bowers, Claude G., *The Party Battles of the Jackson Period* (Boston, 1922).

Brauer, Kinley J., *Cotton versus Conscience: Massachusetts Whig Politics and Southwestern Expansion, 1843–1848* (Lexington, 1967).

Brooks, Van Wyck, *The Flowering of New England* (New York, 1936).

Burnham, Walter Dean, *Presidential Ballots, 1836–1892* (Baltimore, 1955).

Burns, Edward M., *The American Idea of Mission; Concepts of National Purpose and Destiny* (New Brunswick, N.J., 1957).

Campbell, Stanley W., *The Slave Catchers: Enforcement of the Fugitive Slave Law, 1850–1860* (Chapel Hill, 1970).

Carroll, Eber M., *Origins of the Whig Party* (Durham, N.C., 1925).

Catterall, Ralph C. H., *The Second Bank of the United States* (Chicago, 1903).

Channing, Edward, *A History of the United States*, Vol. VI, *The War for Southern Independence* (New York, 1956).

Cole, Arthur C., *The Irrepressible Conflict, 1850–1865* (New York, 1934).

———, *The Whig Party in the South* (Washington, 1913).

Craven, Avery O., *Civil War in the Making, 1815–1860* (Baton Rouge, 1959).

———, *The Coming of the Civil War* (Chicago, 1957).

———, *The Growth of Southern Nationalism, 1846–1861* (Baton Rouge, 1953).

Dalzell, Robert F., Jr., *American Participation in the Great Exhibition of 1851* (Amherst, 1960).

Dangerfield, George, *The Awakening of American Nationalism, 1815–1828* (New York, 1965).

———, *The Era of Good Feelings* (New York, 1952).

Darling, Arthur B., *Political Changes in Massachusetts, 1824–1848* (New Haven, 1925).

Davis, David Brion, *The Problem of Slavery in Western Culture* (Ithaca, 1966).

DeVoto, Bernard, *The Year of Decision: 1846* (Boston, 1942).

Dumond, Dwight Lowell, *Antislavery Origins of the Civil War in the United States* (Ann Arbor, 1939).

Eaton, Clement, *The Growth of Southern Civilization* (New York, 1961).

Elkins, Stanley M., *Slavery: A Problem in American Institutional and Intellectual Life* (Chicago, 1968).

Filler, Louis, *The Crusade Against Slavery, 1830–1860* (New York, 1960).

Fischer, David H., *The Revolution of American Conservatism* (New York, 1965).

Floan, Howard R., *The South in Northern Eyes* (Austin, 1958).

Foner, Eric, *Free Soil, Free Labor, Free Men* (New York, 1970).

Foner, Philip S., *Business and Slavery* (Chapel Hill, N.C., 1941).

Gabriel, Ralph Henry, *The Course of American Democratic Thought; an Intellectual History Since 1815* (New York, 1940).

Gatell, Frank Otto, and Paul Goodman, *Democracy and Union: The United States, 1815–1877* (New York, 1972).

Genovese, Eugene D., *The Political Economy of Slavery; Studies in the Economy and Society of the Slave South* (New York, 1965).

Goetzmann, William H., *When the Eagle Screamed: The Romantic Horizon in American Diplomacy, 1800–1860* (New York, 1966).

Griffin, Clifford S., *Their Brothers' Keepers: Moral Stewardship in the United States, 1800–1865* (New Brunswick, N.J., 1960).

Gunderson, Robert Gray, *The Log-Cabin Campaign* (Lexington, Ky., 1957).

Hamer, Philip May, *The Secession Movement in South Carolina, 1847–1852* (Allentown, Pa., 1918).

Hamilton, Holman, *Prologue to Conflict* (Lexington, Ky., 1963).

Hammond, Bray, *Banks and Politics in America from the Revolution to the Civil War* (Princeton, 1957).

Handlin, Oscar, *Boston's Immigrants: A Study in Acculturation* (Cambridge, 1959).

Handlin, Oscar and Mary, *Commonwealth, A Study of the Role of Government in the American Economy: Massachusetts, 1774–1861* (New York, 1947).

Hart, Albert Bushnell (ed.), *Commonwealth History of Massachusetts,* 5 vols. (New York, 1927–30).

Hartz, Louis, *The Liberal Tradition in America; an Interpretation of American Political Thought Since the Revolution* (New York, 1955).

Holt, Michael Fitzgibbon, *Forging a Majority: The Formation of the Republican Party in Pittsburgh, 1848–1860* (New Haven, 1969).

Howe, M. A. DeWolfe, *Boston, the Place and the People* (New York, 1903).

Jaffa, Harry V., *Crisis of the House Divided: An Interpretation of the Issues in the Lincoln-Douglas Debate* (Garden City, N.Y., 1959).

Kirkland, Edward C., *Men, Cities and Transportation: A Study in New England History* (Cambridge, 1948).

Kraditor, Aileen S., *Means and Ends in American Abolitionism: Garrison and His Critics on Strategy and Tactics, 1834–1850* (New York, 1969).

Lambert, Oscar D., *Presidential Politics in the United States, 1841–1842* (Durham, N.C., 1936).

Lewis, R. W. B., *The American Adam* (Chicago, 1955).

Livermore, Shaw, Jr., *The Twilight of Federalism: The Disintegration of the Federalist Party, 1815–1830* (Princeton, 1962).

Marx, Leo, *The Machine in the Garden; Technology and the Pastoral Ideal in America* (New York, 1964).

Matthiessen, F. O., *American Renaissance: Art and Expression in the Age of Emerson and Whitman* (New York, 1941).

McCormick, Richard P., *The Second American Party System: Party Formation in the Jacksonian Era* (Chapel Hill, 1966).

McGouldrick, Paul F., *New England Textiles in the Nineteenth Century: Profits and Investment* (Cambridge, 1968).

Merk, Frederick, *Manifest Destiny and Mission in American History: A Reinterpretation* (New York, 1963).

Meyers, Marvin, *The Jacksonian Persuasion* (Stanford, 1957).

Miller, Perry, *The Life of the Mind in America, From the Revolution to the Civil War* (New York, 1965).

―――, *The Raven and the Whale* (New York, 1956).

Milton, George Fort, *The Eve of Conflict* (Boston, 1934).

Morison, Samuel Eliot, *The Maritime History of Massachusetts, 1783–1860* (Boston, 1921).

Mueller, Henry R., *The Whig Party in Pennsylvania* (New York, 1922).

Nagel, Paul C., *One Nation Indivisible: The Union in American Thought, 1776–1861* (New York, 1964).

Nevins, Allan, *Ordeal of the Union,* 2 vols. (New York, 1947).

Nichols, Roy F., *The Democratic Machine, 1850–54* (New York, 1923).

―――, *The Disruption of American Democracy* (New York, 1948).

―――, *The Stakes of Power, 1845–1877* (New York, 1961).

North, Douglass C., *The Economic Growth of the United States, 1790–1860* (Englewood Cliffs, N.J., 1961).

Nye, Russel B., *The Cultural Life of the New Nation, 1776–1830* (New York, 1960).

―――, *Fettered Freedom: Civil Liberties and the Slavery Controversy* (East Lansing, Mich., 1949).

Osterweis, Rollin G., *Romanticism and Nationalism in the Old South* (New Haven, 1949).

Parrington, Vernon L., *Main Currents in American Thought,* I, *The Romantic Revolution in America* (New York, 1930).

Pessen, Edward, *Jacksonian America: Society, Personality, and Politics* (Homewood, Ill., 1969).

―――, *Most Uncommon Jacksonians: The Radical Leaders of the Early Labor Movement* (Albany, 1967).

Qualfe, Milo Milton, *The Doctrine of Non-Intervention with Slavery in the Territories* (Chicago, 1910).

Rhodes, James Ford, *History of the United States From the Compromise of 1850 to the Final Restoration of Home Rule at the South in 1877,* 7 vols. (New York, 1910).

Richards, Leonard L., *"Gentlemen of Property and Standing": Anti-Abolition Riots in Jacksonian America* (New York, 1970).

Santayana, George, *Character and Opinion in the United States* (Garden City, N.J., 1956).

Schlesinger, Arthur M., Jr., *The Age of Jackson* (Boston, 1945).

Shryock, Richard Harrison, *Georgia and the Union in 1850* (Durham, N.C., 1926).

Singletary, Otis A., *The Mexican War* (Chicago, 1960).

Smith, Elbert B., *The Death of Slavery: The United States 1837–65* (Chicago, 1969).

Smith, Henry Nash, *Virgin Land; The American West as Symbol and Myth* (Cambridge, 1950).

Smith, Justin H., *The Annexation of Texas* (New York, 1941).

―――, *War with Mexico,* 2 vols. (New York, 1919).

Smith, Theodore C., *The Liberty and Free Soil Parties in the Northwest* (Cambridge, 1897).

Smith, Timothy L., *Revivalism and Social Reform in the Mid-Nineteenth Century* (New York, 1957).

Somkin, Fred, *Unquiet Eagle; Memory and Desire in the Idea of American Freedom, 1815–1860* (Ithaca, 1967).

Stampp, Kenneth M., *The Peculiar Institution* (New York, 1956).

Stanwood, Edward, *A History of the Presidency from 1788 to 1897* (Boston, 1928).

Staudenraus, Philip J., *The African Colonization Movement, 1816–1865* (New York, 1961).

Stephens, Alexander H., *A Constitutional View of the Late War Between the States,* 2 vols. (Philadelphia, 1868–70).

Synder, Charles McCool, *The Jacksonian Heritage: Pennsylvania Politics, 1833–1848* (Harrisburg, 1958).

Taussig, Frank W., *The History of the Present Tariff, 1860–1883* (New York, 1885).

Taylor, George Rogers, *The Transportation Revolution* (New York, 1951).

Taylor, William R., *Cavalier and Yankee: The Old South and American National Character* (New York, 1961).

Turner, Frederick J., *The United States, 1830–1850* (New York, 1935).

Tyler, Alice F., *Freedom's Ferment: Phases of American Social History to 1860* (Minneapolis, 1944).

Van Deusen, Glyndon G., *The Jacksonian Era, 1828–1848* (New York, 1959).

Von Holst, Herman Edward, *Constitutional and Political History of the United States,* 8 vols. (Chicago, 1876–92).

Ware, Caroline F., *The Early New England Cotton Manufacture; A Study in Industrial Beginnings* (Boston, 1931).

Weinberg, Albert K., *Manifest Destiny: a Study of Nationalist Expansionism in American History* (Baltimore, 1935).

Williams, Elgin, *The Animating Pursuits of Speculation* (New York, 1949).

Wilson, Henry, *Rise and Fall of the Slave Power in America,* 3 vols. (Boston, 1872–77).

F. BIOGRAPHICAL WORKS

Bartlett, Irving H., *Wendell Phillips, Brahmin Radical* (Boston, 1961).

Baxter, Maurice G., *Daniel Webster and The Supreme Court* (Amherst, 1966).

Bemis, Samuel Flagg, *John Quincy Adams and the Union* (New York, 1956).

Benson, Allan L., *Daniel Webster* (New York, 1929).

Bergen, Frank, *Webster's Work For the Union* (New Haven, 1918).

Beveridge, Albert S., *Abraham Lincoln, 1809–1858,* 4 vols. (Boston, 1928).

*Biographical Directory of the American Congress, 1774–1961* (Washington, 1961).

Brown, Norman D., *Daniel Webster and the Politics of Availability* (Athens, 1969).

Capers, Gerald M., *John C. Calhoun, Opportunist: A Reappraisal* (Gainsville, 1960).

———, *Stephen A. Douglas: Defender of the Union* (Boston, 1959).

Chambers, William N., *Old Bullion Benton: Senator from the New West* (Boston, 1956).

Chitwood, Oliver P., *John Tyler, Champion of the Old South* (New York, 1939).

Cleaves, Freeman, *Old Tippecanoe: William Henry Harrison and His Time* (New York, 1939).

Coit, Margaret, *John C. Calhoun* (Boston, 1950).

Commager, Henry Steele, *Theodore Parker* (Boston, 1936).

Current, Richard N., *Daniel Webster and the Rise of National Conservatism* (Boston, 1955).

————, *Old Thad Stevens: A Story of Ambition* (Madison, Wis., 1942).

Curtis, George T., *Life of Daniel Webster*, 2 vols. (New York, 1872).

Curtis, James C., *The Fox at Bay: Martin Van Buren and the Presidency, 1837–1841* (Lexington, Ky., 1970).

Donald, David, *Charles Sumner and the Coming of the Civil War* (New York, 1960).

————, *Lincoln Reconsidered* (New York, 1955).

Duberman, Martin B., *Charles Francis Adams, 1807–1886* (Cambridge, 1961).

Duniway, Clyde Augustus, "Daniel Webster," *The American Secretaries of State and their Diplomacy*, Samuel Flagg Bemis (ed.), V (New York, 1928), 3–66.

Dyer, Brainerd, *Zachary Taylor* (Baton Rouge, 1946).

Eaton, Clement, *Henry Clay and the Art of American Politics* (Boston, 1957).

Edgell, David P., *William Ellery Channing; an Intellectual Portrait* (Boston, 1955).

Emerson, Donald E., *Richard Hildreth* (Baltimore, 1946).

Fehrenbacher, Don E., *Prelude to Greatness: Lincoln in the 1850's* (Stanford, 1962).

Fisher, Sydney George, *The True Daniel Webster* (Philadelphia, 1911).

Fiske, John, "Daniel Webster and the Sentiment of Union," *Essays Historical and Literary*, 2 vols. (New York, 1902).

Friend, Llerena, *Sam Houston: The Great Designer* (Austin, 1954).

Frothingham, P. R., *Edward Everett, Orator and Statesman* (Boston, 1925).

Fuess, Claude M., *Daniel Webster*, 2 vols. (Boston, 1930).

————, *The Life of Caleb Cushing*, 2 vols. (New York, 1923).

————, *Rufus Choate* (New York, 1928).

Gatell, Frank Otto, *John Gorham Palfrey and the New England Conscience* (Cambridge, 1963).

Going, Charles Buxton, *David Wilmot, Free Soiler* (New York, 1924).

Govan, Thomas P., *Nicholas Biddle, Nationalist and Public Banker, 1786–1844* (Chicago, 1959).

Hamilton, Holman, *Zachary Taylor: Soldier in the White House* (Indianapolis, 1951).

Hofstadter, Richard, *The American Political Tradition and the Men Who Made It* (New York, 1948).

Johnson, Allen, et al. (eds.), *Dictionary of American Biography*, 22 vols. (New York, 1928–58).

Johnson, Gerald W., *America's Silver Age: The Statecraft of Clay-Webster-Calhoun* (New York, 1939).

Kennedy, John F., *Profiles in Courage* (New York, 1955).

Kirwan, Albert D., *John J. Crittenden: The Struggle for the Union* (Lexington, Ky., 1962).

Klein, Philip S., *President James Buchanan: A Biography* (University Park, Pa., 1962).

Lewis, Walker (ed.), *Speak for Yourself, Daniel: A Life of Webster in His Own Words* (Boston, 1969).

Lodge, Henry Cabot, *Daniel Webster*, American Statesman Series Edition (Boston, 1899).

MacLeish, Archibald, *Scratch* (Boston, 1971).

Mayo, Bernard, *Henry Clay: Spokesman of the New West* (Boston, 1937).

McCall, Samuel W., *Daniel Webster* (Boston, 1902).

McCormac, Eugene Irving, *James K. Polk* (Berkeley, 1922).

McCoy, Charles A., *Polk and the Presidency* (Austin, 1960).

McMaster, John Bach, *Daniel Webster* (New York, 1902).

Messerli, Jonathan, *Horace Mann, a Biography* (New York, 1972).

Morgan, Robert J., *A Whig Embattled: The Presidency under John Tyler* (Lincoln, Neb., 1954).

Morison, Samuel Eliot, *The Life and Letters of Harrison Gray Otis, Federalist, 1765–1848*, 2 vols. (Boston, 1913).

Nichols, Roy F., *Franklin Pierce: Young Hickory of the Granite Hills* (Philadelphia, 1958).

Nye, Russel B., *William Lloyd Garrison and the Humanitarian Reformers* (Boston, 1955).

Ogg, Frederic Austin, *Daniel Webster* (Philadelphia, 1914).

Parks, John H., *John Bell of Tennessee* (Baton Rouge, 1950).

Parton, James, "Daniel Webster," *North American Review*, CIV (1867), 65–121.

Phillips, Ulrich B., *The Life of Robert Toombs* (New York, 1913).

Poage, George Rawlings, *Henry Clay and the Whig Party* (Chapel Hill, N.C., 1936).

Rayback, Robert J., *Millard Fillmore: Biography of a President* (Buffalo, 1959).

Reed, Elizabeth A., *Daniel Webster* (Milwaukee, 1899).

Remini, Robert V., *Andrew Jackson* (New York, 1969).

———, *Andrew Jackson and the Bank War* (New York, 1967).

———, *Martin Van Buren and the Making of the Democratic Party* (New York, 1959).

Schurz, Carl, *Life of Henry Clay*, 2 vols. (New York, 1889).

Seager, Robert, *And Tyler Too: A Biography of John and Julia Gardiner Tyler* (New York, 1963).

Sellers, Charles, *James K. Polk: Continentalist, 1843–1846* (Princeton, 1966).

Shapiro, Samuel, *Richard Henry Dana Jr., 1815–1882* (East Lansing, Mich., 1961).

Shenton, James P., *Robert John Walker: A Politician from Jackson to Lincoln* (New York, 1961).

Strode, Hudson, *Jefferson Davis: American Patriot, 1801–1861* (New York, 1955).

Tefft, Rev. B. F., *Life of Daniel Webster* (Philadelphia, 1854).

Thomas, Benjamin P., *Abraham Lincoln: A Biography* (New York, 1953).

Thomas, John L., *The Liberator: William Lloyd Garrison* (Boston, 1963).

Tyack, David, *George Ticknor and the Boston Brahmins* (Cambridge, 1967).

Van Deusen, Glyndon G., *Horace Greeley: Nineteenth Century Crusader* (Philadelphia, 1953).

———, *The Life of Henry Clay* (Boston, 1937).

———, *Thurlow Weed: Wizard of the Lobby* (Boston, 1947).

———, *William Henry Seward* (New York, 1967).

Von Abele, Rudolph, *Alexander H. Stephens: A Biography* (New York, 1946).

Ward, John W., *Andrew Jackson: Symbol for an Age* (New York, 1955).

Weisenburger, Francis P., *The Life of John McLean: A Politician on the United States Supreme Court* (Columbus, 1937).

Whicher, Stephen E., *Freedom and Fate: An Inner Life of Ralph Waldo Emerson* (Philadelphia, 1969).

Wilkinson, William Cleaver, *Daniel Webster: A Vindication With Other Historical Essays* (New York, 1911).

Wiltse, Charles M., *John C. Calhoun: Sectionalist, 1840–1850* (Indianapolis, 1951).

Woodford, Frank B., *Lewis Cass: The Last Jeffersonian* (New Brunswick, N.J., 1950).

G. JOURNAL ARTICLES AND UNPUBLISHED DISSERTATIONS AND ESSAYS

Anderson, Godfrey R., "The Slavery Issue as a Factor in Massachusetts Politics from the Compromise of 1850 to the Outbreak of the Civil War," doctoral dissertation, University of Chicago, 1944.

Appleton, William S., "The Whigs of Massachusetts," *Massachusetts Historical Society Proceedings,* XI (1897), 278–82.

Bean, William Gleason, "Party Transformations in Massachusetts with Special Reference to the Antecedents of Republicanism, 1848–1860," doctoral dissertation, Harvard University, 1922.

Brown, Richard H., "The Missouri Crisis, Slavery, and the Politics of Jacksonianism," *The South Atlantic Quarterly,* LXV (1966), 55–72.

Carman, Harry J., and Richard H. Luthin, "The Seward-Fillmore Feud and the Crisis of 1850," *New York History,* XXIV (1943), 163–84.

Davis, David Brion, "Some Themes of Counter-Subversion: An Analysis of Anti-Masonic, Anti-Catholic, and Anti-Mormon Literature," *The Mississippi Valley Historical Review,* XLVII (1960), 205–24.

Dickerson, W. M., "Union, Secession, Abolition, as Illustrated in the

Careers of Webster, Calhoun, Sumner," *Magazine of American History,* XVIII (1890), 206–16.

Fisher, George P., "Webster and Calhoun in the Compromise of 1850," *Scribner's Magazine,* XXXVII (1905), 578–86.

Foner, Eric, "The Wilmot Proviso Revisited," *Journal of American History,* LVI (1969), 262–79.

Foster, Herbert D., "Webster's Seventh of March Speech and the Secession Movement, 1850," *American Historical Review,* XXVII (1922), 255–64.

Fuess, Claude M., "Senator Webster Goes South: A Study in Hospitality," *Massachusetts Historical Society Proceedings,* LXII (1929), 161–71.

Gatell, Frank Otto, "Conscience and Judgement: The Bolt of the Massachusetts Conscience Whigs," *The Historian,* XXI (1958), 18–45.

———, "Money and Party in Jacksonian America," *Political Science Quarterly,* LXXXII (1967), 235–52.

———, "Palfrey's Vote, the Conscience Whigs, and the Election of Speaker Winthrop," *New England Quarterly,* XXXI (1958), 218–31.

Hamilton, Holman, "The Cave of the Winds and the Compromise of 1850," *Journal of Southern History,* XXIII (1957), 331–53.

———, "Democratic Senate Leadership and the Compromise of 1850," *Mississippi Valley Historical Review,* XLI (1954), 403–18.

———, "Texas Bonds and Northern Profits," *Mississippi Valley Historical Review,* XLIII (1957), 579–95.

Harmon, George D., "Douglas and the Compromise of 1850," *Journal of Illinois State Historical Society,* XXI (1929), 453–99.

Hodder, Frank H., "The Authorship of the Compromise of 1850," *Mississippi Valley Historical Review,* XXII (1936), 525–36.

Kaplanoff, Mark D., "From Colony to State: New Hampshire, 1800–1815," unpublished Yale College Scholar of House Essay, 1970.

Marshall, Lynn L., "The Strange Stillbirth of the Whig Party," *American Historical Review,* LXXII (1967), 445–68.

McCormick, Richard P., "New Perspectives on Jacksonian Politics," *American Historical Review,* LXV (1960), 288–301.

Nathans, Sydney, "Daniel Webster, Massachusetts Man," *New England Quarterly,* XXXIX (1966), 161–81.

Parish, Peter J., "Daniel Webster, New England, and the West," *Journal of American History,* LIV (1967), 524–49.

Potter, David M., "The Historian's Use of Nationalism and Vice Versa," *The American Historical Review,* LXVII (1962), 924–50.

Russel, Robert R., "What Was the Compromise of 1850?", *Journal of Southern History,* XXII (1956), 292–309.

Schouler, James, "The Whig Party in Massachusetts," *Massachusetts Historical Society Proceedings,* L (1916–17), 39–53.

Schwartz, Harold, "Fugitive Slave Days in Boston," *New England Quarterly,* XXVII (1954), 191–212.

Sellers, Charles G., Jr., "Who Were the Southern Whigs?", *American Historical Review,* LIX (1954), 335–46.

Stenberg, Richard R., "The Motivation of the Wilmot Proviso," *Mississippi Valley Historical Review*, XVIII (1932), 535–41.

Thomas, John L., "Romantic Reform in America, 1815–1865," *American Quarterly*, XVII (1965), 656–81.

Van Deusen, Glyndon G., "Some Aspects of Whig Thought and Theory in the Jacksonian Period," *American Historical Review*, LXIII (1958), 305–22.

Van Tassel, David, "Gentlemen of Property and Standing: Compromise Sentiment in Boston in 1850," *New England Quarterly*, XXIII (1950), 307–19.

# Index